MW01155570

THE

FOOTBALL ENCYCLOPEDIA

KINGFISHER
LONDON & NEW YORK

First published in 2024 in the United States
by Kingfisher, 120 Broadway, New York, NY 10271
This updated edition published in 2024 by Kingfisher
Kingfisher is an imprint of Macmillan Children's Books, London

Distributed in the U.S. and Canada by Macmillan,
120 Broadway, New York, NY 10271

EU representative: 1st Floor, The Liffey Trust Centre,
117-126 Sheriff Street Upper, Dublin 1 D01 YC43

Authors: Alicia Williamson and Liam Jenkins
Design: Darren Jordan, RockJaw Creative
Packaged by Dynamo Limited

ISBN 978-0-7534-8119-6

Library of Congress Cataloging-in-Publication
data has been applied for.

Kingfisher books are available for special promotions and
premiums. For details contact: Special Markets Department,
Macmillan, 120 Broadway, New York, NY 10271.

For more information, please visit www.kingfisherbooks.com

Printed in China
9 8 7 6 5 4 3 2 1
1TR/0924/WKT/RV/128MA

Note to readers: The website addresses listed in this book are correct at the time of publishing. However, due to the ever-changing nature of the internet, website addresses and content can change. Websites can contain links that are unsuitable for children. The publisher cannot be held responsible for changes in website addresses or content, or for information obtained through third-party websites. We strongly advise that internet searches should be supervised by an adult.

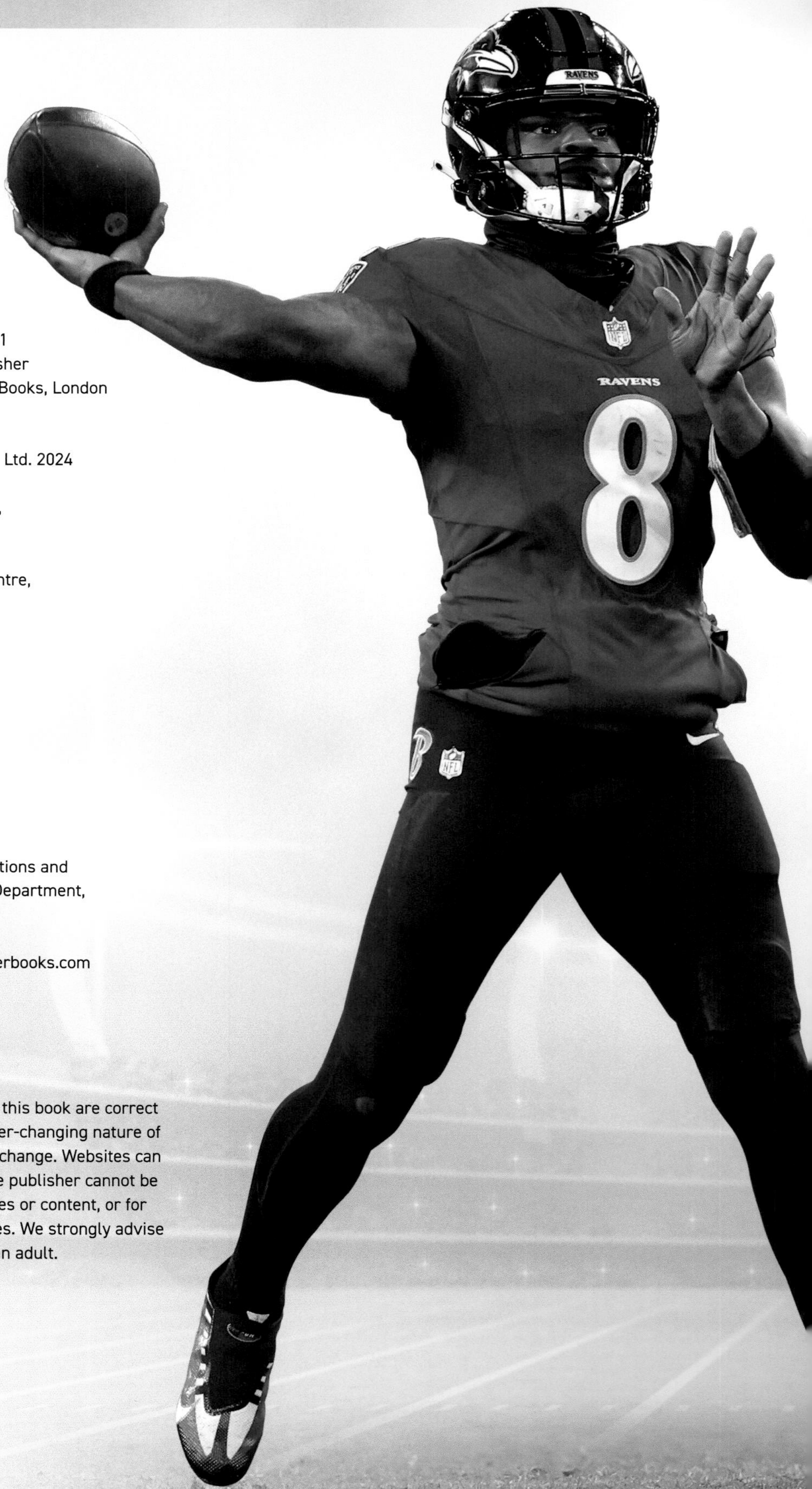

CONTENTS

NOTE TO READERS: The facts and statistics in this edition are accurate as of the 2023–2024 football season

WELCOME TO THE GRIDIRON

In the US, fall means football season. It's hands-down the country's most popular sport, and with its riveting combo of strategy, skill, strength, and speed, football frenzy is beginning to catch on around the world. Millions of fans show up and tune in to watch their teams try to outmaneuver and outpace the competition—all under extreme pressure. Players face off 11v11 on the field, ready to make and take hits with every down, battling for every yard lost or gained. It's an epic spectacle that can create and vanquish heroes, forge and topple dynasties, spur fierce rivalries, and inspire people to come together.

A HIGH-IMPACT SPORT

Tackle football is a high-impact sport, which means it can be pretty rough on the body and injuries are not uncommon. To protect players, football seasons have to be kept short, meaning that each and every game is high-stakes and high-drama—the ultimate in sports spectactorship. Major League Baseball players have a staggering 162 games in a season. NBA teams have 82. The NFL has the shortest season in pro team sports, with just 17 games over 18 weeks, so every game counts and is unmissable for fans. Tackle football requires significant, expensive equipment, but touch and flag versions can be played anywhere there's enough space for a makeshift field. Watching and playing football are baked into many communities as annual traditions, from attending a homecoming game at your alma mater to having a backyard scrimmage with your friends and family over Thanksgiving. It's a game that has a big impact on American sports, culture, and business.

◀ NFL Defensive Player of the Year T.J. Watt tackles quarterback Tyler Huntley for a "sack." Top teams average over 60 tackles a game.

▲ Star wide receiver Stefon Diggs makes an acrobatic catch under pressure as cornerback Jonathan Jones stands ready to push him out of bounds.

▲ University of Missouri fans cheer on their team alongside the Tigers mascot. Mizzou is one of 128 top-tier NCAA Division I teams that compete to be crowned national champions each year.

BY THE NUMBERS

In classic tackle football, 22 players—11 on offense and 11 on defense—square off against each other on the field at any one time. Pro football teams can carry up to 53 active players on their roster to fill their offensive, defensive, and special teams positions and provide alternates. A full college or NFL game is 60 minutes long, with four 15-minute quarters and a halftime break after the second quarter. The 60 minutes only accounts for how long the game clock runs, but it stops so often between plays to allow the sides to reset (and squeeze in commercial breaks) that the average pro game generally lasts over three hours.

The National Football Foundation estimates that over one million kids in the US play high school football, while more than 81,000 college students play on teams at 773 colleges and universities. The 32 NFL teams have 2,016 active players on their rosters. Flag football is the fastest growing area of the sport, with more than 2 million kids under the age of 17 participating, including almost half a million girls.

▲ Competitors in the NFL FLAG program. Flag football is a non-contact version of the sport. With only five players on a side, it requires speed and creativity.

HISTORY OF THE GAME

A distinctly American sport, football has been played in the US since the 1870s. While it started as a college game, amateur leagues quickly took off around the country. Football went pro in the early 20th century, and its following has kept growing ever since.

◀ Modern football bears little resemblance to soccer aside from having a ball and 11 players per side on the field at a time. The overlaps with rugby are more noticeable, especially with tackling, running the ball, and scoring.

▶ Camp served on the Intercollegiate Football Rules Committee for 48 years.

EARLY INFLUENCES

Football began as a mix of soccer and rugby. Both games originated in Europe as versions of "football." Soccer-style was called "association football," while the other was known as "rugby football." The American version kept the name football as a nod to its origins, even though kicking is only a small part of the modern game. Its official name is "gridiron football" because of the field it was first played on had a gridlike checkerboard pattern marked out on it. Early gridiron football was developed and played in colleges in New England. The first official game was played between Princeton and Rutgers in New Jersey in 1869.

THE "FATHER OF AMERICAN FOOTBALL"

Walter Camp is a key figure in the foundation of gridiron football. He played the early game as a student at Yale, where he was a halfback and team captain. After graduating, he took up coaching the team, retiring with a 67–2 record. As a member of the rules board of the Intercollegiate Football Association founded in 1876 by four Ivy League universities, Camp proposed many of the rules that helped transform England's Rugby Football Union code into the basis of an entirely new game. His innovations changed the number of players on the field from 15 to 11, leaving room for more dynamic offensive plays. He also established the system of downs, line of scrimmage, and quarterback role.

THE FIRST "PRO"

William "Pudge" Heffelfinger was secretly the first paid player in football back when the sport was supposed by played only by unpaid amateurs. A burly, six-foot-three linesman out of Yale, Heffelfinger was working as a poorly paid railroad employee when he became embroiled in a fierce local rivalry. The Pittsburgh Athletic Club and the Allegheny Athletic Association were prepping for a showdown on November 12, 1892, and both thought recruiting Pudge might just be the key to victory. When Pittsburgh offered him $250 to join their squad, Allegheny stepped in to double the offer. Pudge went to the highest bidder, who got bragging rights when he won the game for Allegheny by scoring a touchdown off a fumble recovery. Their sneaky $500 payout to him was revealed much later in a club expense sheet that was uncovered by the Pro Football Hall of Fame.

▶ During one season at Yale, the three-time All-American Heffelfinger helped his team not only go unbeaten but also completely shut out their opponents' offenses. Yale put 698 points on the board that year while not allowing the opposing teams to score a single point.

GOING PRO

In the 1890s, local athletic associations that hosted many types of sports began organizing football teams, but they weren't allowed to pay players. In 1897, the Latrobe Athletic Association became the first team to pay all its players to play. More professional teams emerged around the Northeast and Midwest, but they weren't very organized. In 1920, a meeting of ten teams in Canton, Ohio, established the organization that would become the National Football League (NFL). The Akron Pros won the first championship that year. The NFL restructured to move its teams to major cities in the 1930s, but its popularity still lagged well behind the college game. Many even thought it was crass to play for anything but the love of the game. Most of the top college players actively decided against going pro. It wasn't until the rise of television in the 1960s that pro football began overtaking college programs with televised spectacles and stepped-up competition.

◀ The Cardinals are the oldest continuous outfit in pro football, founded as a neighborhood team in Chicago in 1899.

THEN AND NOW

The first gridiron football games were played with rugby-style rules by helmet-less players on fields without hashmarks or end zones. Today, the sport has evolved into a completely unique, highly specialized game with a dizzying array of rules, officials, and associated technologies. The modern game may be more complex, but it's still a thrill for spectators.

▲ Early pro Harold "Red" Grange plays for the Bears in 1925. He was one of the most successful halfbacks in the early NFL.

PRO PLAYERS

Before football was big business, players were everyday athletes who played the game recreationally. Subs were restricted, so all players had to pitch in on offense, defense, and special teams—linemen played every snap and a quarterback might double as a kicker and safety. For most early pros, football was not their main gig. They held down day jobs that allowed them to play, which meant training was pretty minimal for most people on the field. Plenty of Heisman Trophy winners opted to get "real jobs" instead of continuing in the sport. There weren't hard rules around recruitment and contracts, so players trying to eke out a living ping-ponged around to whichever team put the most money on the table—not much by today's standards. Now, making an NFL team is extremely competitive and players have become ultra-specialized experts in their positions with superhuman physiques. Only 1.6 percent of college players will make it onto a pro roster. If they do, they have the opportunity to make millions of dollars in a season while trainers, coaches, dieticians, physical therapists, psychologists, statisticians, and other team staff help sculpt them into high-performance pros.

◀ Defensive end Myles Garrett gets ready to rush the passer. His specialized training, advanced equipment, and superhuman physique is a far cry from those of early players like "Red" (top right).

PLAYER PROTECTION

The early days of football were very dangerous. Players did not have helmets or pads for protection. Injuries were common, and several competitors died from spinal or traumatic brain injuries sustained in games or practice. In 1905, President Theodore Roosevelt called for reform in the sport after a particularly brutal season, and the organization that would become the NCAA (National Collegiate Athletic Association) was founded the following year to establish rules that would ensure safer, fairer play for all students. Helmets, which at this time were made of leather, were still optional. They would not become mandatory until 1939 in college and the 1940s in the NFL, when the first plastic helmets began to be introduced. Over time, rules on receiving, tackling, and kickoffs have been changed to try to minimize player injuries while new tech has made helmets lighter and more effective.

SCORING

According to the first standardized football rules, touchdowns (TDs) were worth four points. This went up to five in 1898 and six in 1912. Field goals (FGs) went the other way, starting at five points and eventually going down to three—just half a touchdown. These changes corresponded to updated rules that juiced up the offensive side of the game and made the touchdown the centerpiece of the game. While initially football followed rugby in only allowing backward passing, in 1906, the forward pass was introduced and revolutionized the game. Forward passes were more likely to get blocked, defended, or intercepted, but they also led to some spectacular gains and higher-scoring games. Suddenly, football became as much about speed and agility as it was about sheer strength. The most recent addition to scoring scales is the two-point conversion as an option for a try after a touchdown. Colleges adopted it in 1958, where they are now mandatory once a game reaches double overtime, but two-point conversions weren't brought into the NFL until 1994.

◀ The Browns' QB and kicker Tom "Two Point" Tupa became the first player in NFL history to score a two-point conversion after faking an extra point in a 1994 season opener against the Bengals.

TECHNOLOGY

Tech has become integral to most parts of the modern game, transforming coaching, officiating, and fan experience. Large coaching staffs and officiating teams communicate with wireless technology, playbooks have shifted from paper to digital tablets, and most quarterbacks wear earpieces to enable play-calling. While home televisions boosted the popularity of pro football in the 1960s, it also helped change things inside the stadium. Instant Replay is now used by officials, video footage has become key to how coaches and players prepare for games, and stadium mega-screens enhance spectators' views of the on-field action.

▼ Ref Pete Morelli consults with Instant-Replay technology on the sidelines to check he got the right call.

THE FIELD

Early football was called gridiron football because the field was marked out in a grid of five-yard squares. The field of play was an awkward 110 yards long, making the center the 55-yard line. There were no end zones, so any ball carried or caught beyond the goal line counted as a touchdown. The standard 100-yard field was introduced in 1912, along with 10-yard-long end zones on each side. Up until 1933, the ball was played from wherever it was downed, which could get pretty awkward if it was close to out of bounds. From the 1930s, the ball was placed at the nearest hashmark instead to start the next play. The goalposts were once an "H" shape and placed right at the goal line, which meant players had two large metal poles to contend with when trying to make a touchdown. In 1967, the goalposts changed to their current "slingshot" design with only one metal pole at the bottom, and seven years later they were moved to their current location at the back of the end zone to encourage more exciting TDs and fewer chip-in FGs.

▼ Field goals accounted for around a quarter of all scoring in the NFL in 1973, prompting owners to move the goal posts back to make the kicking game less attractive to offenses.

MAKING AN IMPACT

Football has long been a US institution, but its reach goes well beyond borders and its impact goes well beyond the field. In recent years, the NFL has begun investing in making football a global sport, with players and fans from all around the world.

AMERICA'S FAVORITE SPORT

Football officially passed baseball as people's preferred sport to watch in the US in 1972. A 2024 Gallup News Poll shows it still firmly holds that title, with 41 percent of US adults identifying it as their favorite sport. Baseball is a distant second at 10 percent. Super Bowls are regularly among the most-watched TV events, and even the regular season gets bigger viewership numbers than any other form of programming. Nearly 140 million Americans engaged with the NFL over the course of 2023 alone, 58 percent of those on a weekly basis. An impressive 29.2 million fans in the US also played fantasy football during the 2023–2024 season. The NFL has designed the game with TV audiences in mind—every game in the short season feels like a special occasion and an opportunity to socialize with friends and family. Now that its dominance in the US is complete, the NFL is looking to attract an international following.

▲ The NFL has always had foreign players in its ranks, including some Hall-of-Famers. In 2017, it launched the International Player Pathway to actively recruit overseas talent. One of its major successes is the Nigeria-born defensive end Efe Obada, who was scouted during a tryout in London in 2017.

◀ While some criticized Kaepernick's kneeling as disrespectful, he undoubtedly got people talking about an important social issue.

A PLATFORM FOR CHANGE

The star-power of many NFL players means that they are often in a position to promote causes and help tackle issues they care about. Many have started foundations, donated time and money to nonprofits, and served as spokespeople for campaigns related to problems like childhood obesity and poverty, gun violence, and medical research. The NFL gives out a Walter Payton Man of the Year Award annually to recognize players who are game-changers off the field through their service to the community.

Some pros have also used their visibility to protest social injustice. Hall-of-Fame running back Jim Brown became a prominent civil rights activist in the 1950s and 60s. More recently, quarterback Colin Kaepernick backed the Black Lives Matter movement by taking a knee during the US national anthem before a game. The controversial move kickstarted an international conversation, with many other athletes following suit. Many others in pro sports adopted his gesture to raise awareness about racism—including in England, where pro soccer players all take a knee before matches.

GOING GLOBAL

Gridiron football has not spread around the world in the same way soccer has, but the US is not the only place it's played. Canada and Mexico both have pro leagues, and 41 countries in Europe have teams, too. The International Federation of American Football (IFAF) is active in 70 countries globally, and they've hosted women's and men's flag football championships every two years since 2002. They led the charge to get flag football included in the World Games, starting with the competition held in Birmingham, Alabama, in 2022, and in the Summer Olympics starting with the 2028 Games in Los Angeles. The NFL is doing its part to expand the global reach and popularity of the game with programs, camps, and recruitment efforts around the world. NFL FLAG was established in 1994 to get more kids playing football not only in the US, where there are over half a million participants, but also internationally, with programs in Canada, Mexico, the UK, Germany, France, China, and more. They're also busy courting new audiences, even hosting NFL regular season games in stadiums outside the US.

▲ Quarterback Russell Wilson poses with an NFL FLAG football team from Panama, who were at the Pro Bowl to compete in the 17U Girls Division Championship Game.

MÉXICO
FedEx
BANORTE
MEXICO
#NFLMEXICO
CHARGERS
BUD LIGHT
CHARGERS
CHARGERS
CHICANO POWER
WORLDWIDE

SNAPSHOT

NFL ACTION ABROAD

The first NFL game played outside the US boasted the highest attendance of any regular-season game in league history with a crowd of 103,467 fans. It was held on October 2, 2005, in Mexico City at Azteca Stadium and featured two teams from states that share a border with Mexico—the Arizona Cardinals and the San Francisco 49ers. Two years later, the NFL officially launched its International Series of games played abroad to spread gridiron football beyond North America. Since then, the NFL has scheduled regular-season games in England, Mexico, Germany, Brazil, and Spain. Nearly 40 have taken place "across the pond" in London, UK, at Wembley and Twickenham Stadiums.

The International Series is part of the NFL's efforts to grow a global fanbase for what has long been seen as a strictly American sport. There are signs it's working—they've scored millions of new followers in Europe (18 million in Germany alone), South America (nearly 20 million in Brazil), and Asia (around 7 million just in South Korea).

◀ Chargers fans attend an NFL Monday Night Football game held at Mexico City's Azteca Stadium on November 19, 2019. Since the franchise was once located in San Diego, very close to California's boundary with Mexico, the Bolts have an especially strong following south of the border where the sport is known as "fútbol americano." These diehard fans were disappointed on this occasion as Chargers' quarterback Philip Rivers was intercepted four times by AFC West division rivals, the Chiefs, in a 17–24 loss. The audience for the NFL in Mexico has grown to 48 million in recent years—pretty impressive for a country with a population of 120 million where soccer is by far the most popular sport!

FOOTBALL 101

Football might look like a complicated game on the surface, but once you get the basics down, you'll be feeling like Andy Reid in no time!

THE SETUP

A college or pro game lasts 60 minutes and is broken into four quarters of 15 minutes.

Each team has two 11-person groups—the offense and defense—as well as a "special teams" unit. The goal is to score as many points as possible, which can be done in multiple ways: touchdowns, extra points, two-point conversions, field goals, and safeties.

A standard gridiron football field is 100 yards long with an "end zone" on each end. Each team is assigned an end zone that they need to get the ball into in order to score a touchdown.

HOW TO PLAY

The game will start with one team kicking the ball to the other, giving them possession. From there, the team with the ball will bring out their offense, while the other team rolls out their defense. For the offense, the aim of the game is to get the ball into the opponent's end zone for a touchdown. They have four tries to move the ball 10 yards downfield (that is, closer to their opponent's end zone) and can gain yards by either running or passing the ball. If they get past that 10-yard mark, they get four more attempts to get another 10 yards. The job of the defense is to stop them and win the ball back for their team. At the end of the game, the winner is the team who has scored the most points!

THE LOWDOWN ON DOWNS

Each attempt to gain yardage is called a "down." The officials keep track of how many downs (1st through 4th) a team has had and how many yards they have to go to get a new set of downs. For instance, if a team is on "2nd & 7," that means it's the offense's second attempt, and they must advance seven more yards to stay on the field. If the offense then completes a pass of 12 yards, they would move 12 yards down the field and—having gained more than the necessary 10 yards—begin a fresh set of attempts ("1st & 10") at wherever the ball-carrier was tackled. If the defense is able to stop the offense from gaining 10 yards on their first three downs, the offense has a tactical choice to make on their fourth down. They can decide either to take one more shot at reaching the 10-yard mark or to punt the ball away to the other team. If they use their final attempt and fail, their opponents will get the ball from where the offense left off, which could be disastrous! If the offense is close enough to the end zone for their kicker to send a ball through the uprights, they will likely opt to try a field goal. If they miss the kick, their opponents will get the ball from the spot where the kick was taken.

▼ Football scoreboards display the downs as well as the game clock and score. This big screen in the Wolverines' "Big House" shows which team has possession and that they are on their 2nd down with 11 yards to go, starting from their own 48-yard line.

◀ Heisman winner Bryce Young of Alabama's Crimson Tide throws a perfect spiral pass.

KEY SKILLS

PASSING: This is when a player (often a quarterback) throws the ball to a teammate. The pointed shape of the ball means that throwing it accurately requires a particular technique, called a "spiral pass." Doing it well requires your whole body.

CATCHING: In order to record a catch, players must catch a pass in bounds, secure the ball with their arms or and hands, and make a move while remaining in control of the ball.

RUSHING: When the offense chooses to "run" the ball, it is handed off to a "running back" who tries to gain "rushing yards" by running hard and looking for gaps in the defense.

BLOCKING: To give the offensive backfield time to make a play, players on the line of scrimmage must block defenders from reaching the ball. Blockers can push but not pull or hold.

TACKLING: The most common way a defense can "stop" the offense is by making a tackle where a defender brings the player carrying the ball to the ground. They can only make contact below the shoulders and above the knees. If anything above the ankle on the leg or above the wrist on the arm of the ball-carrier hits the ground, it counts as a tackle.

FORCING TURNOVERS: The defense get possession of the ball by forcing a "turnover," either by "intercepting" a pass intended for a receiver or by knocking a live ball out of an opponent's hands for a "fumble" and scooping it up.

SNAPPING: A play begins when the ball is "snapped" back to the quarterback. The center places the ball on the ground in front of them, squats down to hold it, then throws the ball behind them through their legs for the quarterback to catch.

KICKING: Placekickers are responsible for kicking the ball to the other team off a tee at the beginning of each half and at the end of a scoring possession. They are also the super-humans tasked with converting field goals and extra points.

PUNTING: This is a special type of kick based on the rugby drop-kick and is only used after a failed set of downs. The punter takes a snap directly and hoofs the ball hard and high, aiming to pin the other team as far back as possible.

FACT FILE

The spiral passing technique is the quickest and most accurate way to throw a football. A pro quarterback can throw a ball at around 60 mph, with 600 rotations per minute (10 per second!) on the spiral.

FACT FILE

A "pick six" is when a defender intercepts a pass intended for one of the other team's receivers and carries the ball all the way to the opposite end zone. This ultimate defensive play counts as a touchdown!

GETTING TO KNOW THE GEAR

Football is a very physical sport, filled with heavy hits, punishing blocks, spiraling spin moves, and game-changing tackles. Player safety is always the highest priority, and the equipment used to play the game has a crucial role in ensuring injuries are kept to a minimum.

THE JERSEY

Players are all identified by wearing team jerseys on the field, with their chosen number on the front and back along with their name. Players are now allowed to pick any number from 0–99, depending on their position. For instance, quarterbacks must still choose between 0–19 to help mark them out on the field. NFL teams are allowed three different colored jerseys per season: one for home games, one for road games, and an alternative to be used in certain primetime matchups or when the opposing uniforms may clash or be too similar. Since the league's 75th anniversary in 1994, the NFL has also invited franchises to showcase "throwback" jerseys inspired by vintage team uniforms.

▲ The NFL exclusively use footballs made by the company Wilson for their game balls—the specific model is called "the Duke," after the nickname of former Giants owner Tim Mara, who passed away in 2005.

▼ It's a tradition for players to exchange signed jerseys with one another after games as a show of respect. Here, Travis Kelce swaps with Sauce Gardner after a Chiefs–Jets game.

THE BALL

A football is oval-shaped with pointed ends. It's usually made from brown leather and has white laces on the top, which act as a grip for the quarterback. An official full-size ball is 11–11.25 in long and 21–21.25 in around the middle. It weighs 14–15 oz (under a pound) and is inflated to 12.5–13.5 psi. NFL teams are allowed to bring 12 balls to each game to use when they are on offense.

FACT FILE

Did you know that the ball is sometimes referred to as "the pigskin"? That's because the very first footballs were made out of inflated pigs' bladders! Today, the inners are made from rubber.

CLEATS

Football cleats are the item some players get most excited about. It's a chance for them to express themselves through eye-catching colors and sleek designs. Of course, they're practical, too, with cone-shaped studs made of metal, plastic, or rubber on the bottom to grip the turf in all weathers and help players explode into motion and sprint much faster. They come in different heights for different positions—lineman wear high-tops to provide maximum support and traction while wide receivers wear low-cut cleats to keep them light and mobile.

◀ Studs vary in length from a half inch to an inch, depending on playing conditions. The worse the weather, the longer the studs you need.

HELMETS

The helmet is the most important piece of protective gear a football player can wear. Designed to prevent nasty head injuries like concussions, the helmet is built out of a strong plastic designed to take heavy impacts, while the interior is lined with foam to keep things comfy and absorb those harder hits. Today, after studies of former NFL players have shown that multiple concussions lead to long-term brain damage, there is constant research into new materials and measures that can keep head injuries to a minimum.

▶ Modern helmets feature a wireless communication device so that coaches can deliver play calls.

▶ Some players like to wear visors, which add extra facial protection and help prevent glare.

▶ A faceguard that's usually made out of titanium metal is also a prominent feature. It absorbs hits to the face, either from other players or from hitting the dirt.

PADS

Protective equipment doesn't stop with a helmet. Football players commonly wear shoulder, hip, knee, and thigh pads made of strong, thin plastic and shock-absorbing foam, too. The most notable padding is what's known as a "shell." They're worn by players under their jerseys to help prevent upper body injuries. From the 1950s—90s, the upper-body pads were HUGE. While this may have added an intimidation factor for some, they also impeded players' range of movement. Today, they're much sleeker while still offering protection.

THE GRIDIRON

The standard tackle football field is sometimes referred to as the "gridiron" due to its gridlike structure. Some are made from grass grown specially on sod farms and some use artificial turf (in the NFL, the split is 50–50), but they all have the same features and dimensions. Teams have groundskeepers to maintain the turf and re-paint the markings each week.

FIELD OF PLAY

This is the area of the field between the end zones—a 100-yard stretch of turf that's 53 and a third yards wide.

END ZONE

This is the area a ball-carrier needs to get into in order to score a touchdown. The end zone is 10 yards long, and there is one situated at both ends of the field of play, seperated from it by the **goal line**.

SIDELINES

The two lines running up the side of the field are called sidelines. If a player carrying the ball steps over one of these lines, they are deemed **out-of-bounds** and the play clock stops.

GOALPOSTS

At the back-middle of each end zone is a set of goalposts. Kickers need to kick the ball over their 10-foot-high **crossbar** and between their 35-foot-tall **uprights**, which are 18.5 feet apart, to convert a field goal or extra point.

YARD MARKINGS

The numbers running up each side of the field tell you how far away the opposing end zone is. The field is split into two sections of 50 yards, with one counting up and the other counting down. If you had a play from "your own 40," you'd be 60 yards away. But a play from the "opposing 40" means you'd only be 40 yards from your opponents' end zone. There are also horizontal lines that are 5-yard markers. So, the one between the 20 and 30 would be 25 yards.

HASHMARKS

Little hashes marking individual yards appear in two rows running down the length of the field. These actually serve an important purpose besides identifying yardage. They also determine where the ball is placed for a new play. If a player is tackled in between the two rows of hashmarks, the ball will be placed wherever the ball was marked down. However, if the ball is marked down between the hashmarks and sideline, the ball will be placed just inside the nearest hashmark to start the next play. This means that where teams line up can shift from side to side on the field, which forces some adjustments to strategy.

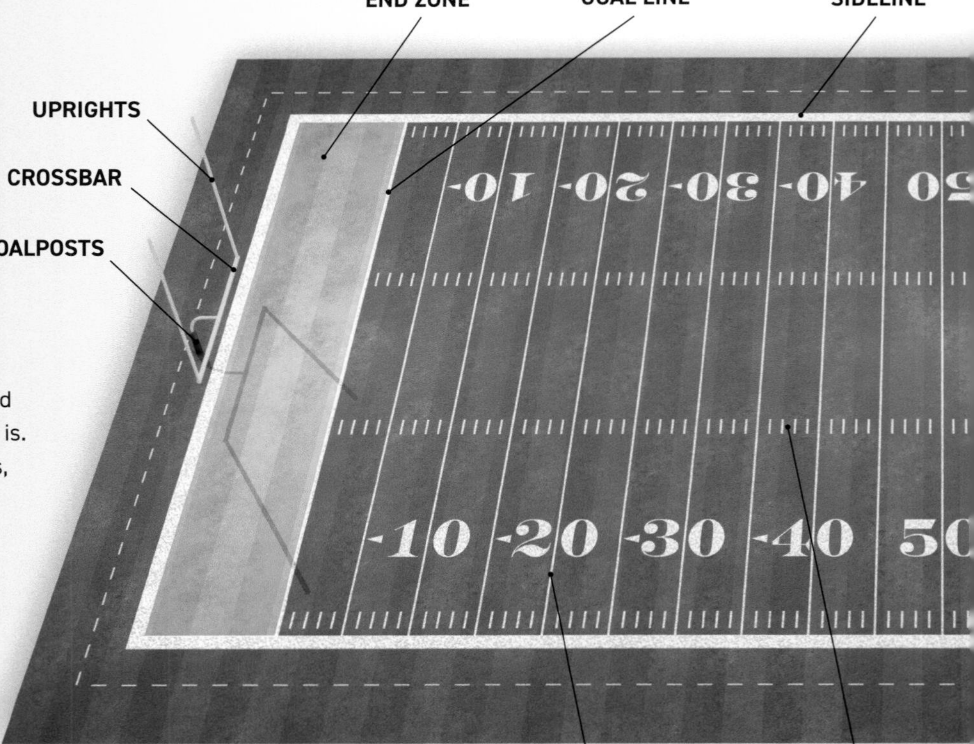

THE CHAIN CREW

There are a pair of officials known as the "chain crew" that follow the teams up and down the field to keep track of downs, mark the current position of the ball, and show where the offense needs to get to in order to bring up another first down. They do this by lining up brightly colored rods in line with the ball and the target. It's much easier for players to see than trying to guess, and they don't get to see the handy digital TV markers that we do at home!

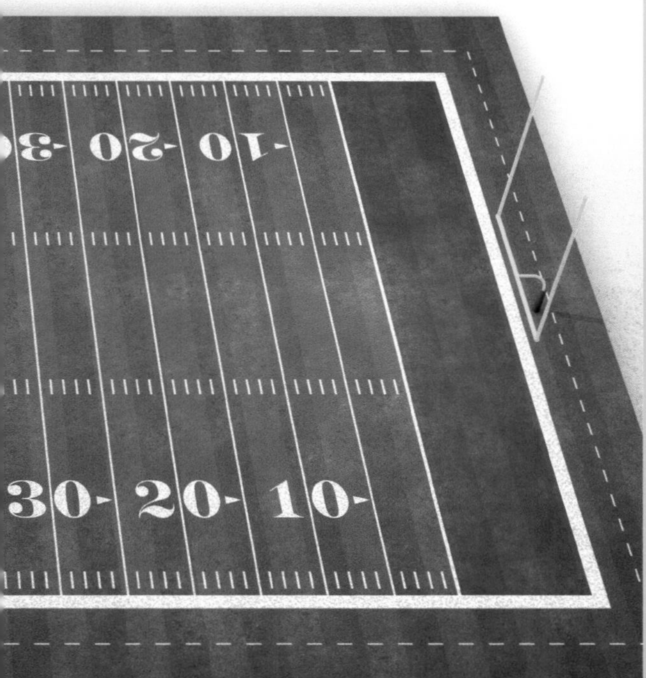

LINE OF SCRIMMAGE

Before a new play starts, the offense sets up along an invisible line just behind where the ball was last spotted. Defenders aren't allowed to cross this "line of scrimmage" before the ball is snapped.

THE BACKFIELD

The backfield is the area of play behind where each team lines up. Whereas lineman stick to the line of scrimmage, offensive backs (like quarterbacks and halfbacks) typically line up in the "backfield" while cornerbacks and safeties lurk in the "defensive backfield."

THE POCKET

When the quarterback snaps the ball, his offensive line will drop back around him in order to stop defensive players reaching him and keep a clean "pocket" of space for him to work from. This is sometimes also referred to as the "tackle box."

SCORING

The touchdown may be the most famous way to put points on the board, but football games are often won by the slimmest of margins, so every point counts. Here are all the ways teams can rack them up—from masterful offensive drives and solid special teams plays to dominant defensive performances.

◀ Seattle Seahawks running back Marshawn Lynch reaches forward to put the ball over the goal line for a TD in a game against the 49ers.

TOUCHDOWN (TD)

Worth a whopping six points, a touchdown is scored when a player has possession of the ball within the opposition's end zone, by running it in, catching it, or recovering it. The ball must completely pass over the goal line for it to count. Touchdowns are usually the result of offensive drives down the field, but the defense can also score them if they force a turnover and run back the live ball to the other team's end zone.

TRY

After scoring a touchdown, teams have a choice to try for either one or two additional points. Most often, a coach will opt to go for a single extra point because it's almost a guaranteed score. To earn an extra point, the placekicker must kick the ball through the uprights from a play starting at the 15-yard line. If a team needs two points for some strategic reason, a coach can try the trickier two-point conversion instead. In this case, the offense is given the ball at the two-yard line and has one play to get it into the end zone by passing or running.

FACT FILE

Going for a two-point conversion is a high risk-high reward situation—it's riskier to attempt it, but your team gets a bigger reward if successful. Over 90 percent of extra points attempted are made whereas fewer than half of two-point conversions succeed.

FACT FILE

The longest field goal in NFL history was a 66-yarder kicked by Justin Tucker of the Baltimore Ravens in 2021. The ball blasted off Tucker's foot in the very last second of regulation to give him the game-winning score and an NFL record!

FIELD GOAL (FG)

Field goals are worth three points. To score one, the offense must kick the ball from behind the line of scrimmage, and it must pass completely over the crossbar and between the uprights without touching the ground or another offensive player. The further an offense is from the end zone, the harder it is to bash in the ball and the more likely it is to be blocked by the defense because of the low angle of the kick. A team will only attempt one if it's within their placekicker's range. The actual distance of a kick is around 17 yards more than where the offense is on the field. Most pros can boot a field goal in from 50 yards and some from 60 yards.

▶ Placekicker Rob Bironas holds the record for most field goals scored in a single game. He put in eight for 24 points on October 21, 2007, during the Tennessee Titan's 38–36 win over the Texans.

POINT-SCORING RECORDS

ALL-TIME TOP POINTS SCORER:
Adam Vinatieri, placekicker—2,673 (1996–2019)

MOST TOUCHDOWN PASSES:
Tom Brady, quarterback—649 (2000–2022)

MOST TOUCHDOWN RECEPTIONS:
Jerry Rice, wide receiver—197 (1985–2004)

MOST RUSHING TOUCHDOWNS:
Emmitt Smith, running back—164 (1990–2004)

MOST POINTS SCORED IN ONE GAME:
Washington—72 (vs New York Giants, November 27, 1966)

FASTEST TOUCHDOWN SCORED:
Randal Williams, wide receiver—3 seconds (October 12, 2003)

SAFETY

When the offense has been pushed so far back that they have to take a snap or drop back into their own end zone, they must be extra careful. If the ball goes dead while in their possession there–for instance, because the player with the ball is tackled behind their own goal line–then the other team is awarded two points. The team on defense can also score a safety if the offense commits a foul (such as holding or intentional grounding) in their own end zone. Getting points in this defensive way is extra-punishing because the ball also goes to the offense of the team that just scored, giving them another immediate scoring opportunity.

▲ Kansas City's linebacker Justin Houston sacks Denver's QB Trevor Siemian in his own end zone to score a safety. Houston is the joint record holder for most safeties forced with four.

RULES AND FOULS

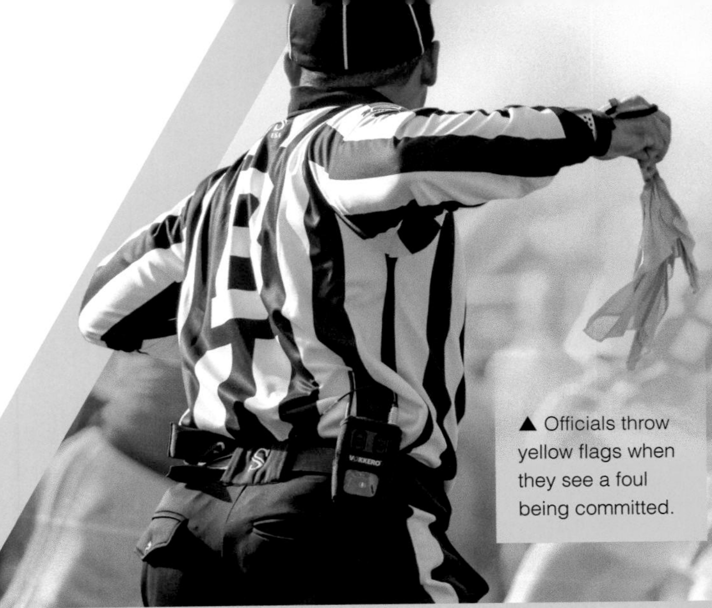

▲ Officials throw yellow flags when they see a foul being committed.

Football has a long and complicated rulebook. Even veteran players and the most passionate fans will sometimes be left scratching their heads after a call on the field, but, most of the time, you can get by just by knowing the basics. Here's a breakdown of the game's key rules and penalties.

THE PLAY CLOCK

Before each play, there is a 40-second timer that you'll usually see next to the "down and distance marker." This is the amount of time that the offense has to snap the ball and start the next play. If the play-clock "expires" (hits zero), the offense will receive a 5-yard penalty and be forced to repeat the down from five yards further back.

OFFSIDES

Just like soccer, football has offsides. However, in this case, the penalty is handed out whenever a defensive player either lines up ahead of the ball or crosses the line of scrimmage before the ball is snapped. If that defensive player makes contact with an offensive player before the ball is snapped, it's called **encroachment**. Any of these offenses are met with a 5-yard penalty for the defense, so the offense would get a free 5-yard gain. Similarly, if an offensive player jumps before the ball is snapped, this is called a **false start** and will be met with a 5-yard penalty against them.

▶ Fans make noise before a snap to try and delay the offense by limiting their communication. The louder the stadium, the more likely the visitors are to get pushed back by false start penalties.

HOLDING

Holding occurs when a player illegally "holds" their opponent to stop them from getting to the ball. Think of it as more than a block and less than a tackle. The penalty for this is a 10-yard penalty for the offense. If the defense is called for holding, the offense gets a 5-yard gain and a fresh set of downs.

PASSING RULES

Football formations come in many different shapes and sizes. You might see three receivers lined up as far away from the ball as possible or a pair of running backs with no receiver in sight. Offenses like to jiggle their formations from play to play to keep opponents on their toes, but there are some guidelines they have to follow . . .

WHO IS AN ELIGIBLE RECEIVER?

Not all players are "eligible" to catch a pass. Typically, only the receivers, tight ends, running backs, and quarterbacks are allowed to catch, while the offensive line is not. However, if a player starts at either end of the line of scrimmage or one yard behind it when the ball is snapped, they can be deemed eligible. So sometimes you might see a sneaky offensive lineman bruising their way into the end zone! If an ineligible player catches a pass, the play is negated and the offense is given a 5-yard penalty.

THE FIVE MOST DEVASTATING PENALTIES IN FOOTBALL

1. PASS INTERFERENCE

The pass interference (PI) call has been one of the most controversial of the last decade with several huge games and moments defined by the throw—or non-throw—of the flag. A PI call is made when a defending player prevents a receiver from making a catch. Tackles can only be made when the ball is caught, so substantial contact prior to the catch (anything from a shove to a jersey tug just as the ball is thrown) risks a PI call. PI is an incredibly costly penalty in that the ball is placed at the spot of the foul, and it's an automatic first down. If a receiver runs 25 yards and gets tugged before leaping for a catch, that kind of PI call can completely transform a game. Offensive pass interference can also be called, which is when a receiver makes illegal contact with a defender in order to gain an advantage when making a catch. The penalty for this is usually 10 yards and the loss of a down. So, a 3rd & 3 could become 4th & 13!

2. ROUGHING THE PASSER

Another scary penalty, this is called when the quarterback has thrown the ball, but a pass-rusher hits the quarterback anyway (pictured left). Because it puts a key player in danger, this move will result in a 10- or 15-yard penalty and a first down.

3. ROUGHING THE KICKER

When a defender hits a kicker or punter after the ball has been kicked, the defense is penalized with an automatic 15-yard gain for the offense, who then gets a fresh set of downs.

4. UNNECESSARY ROUGHNESS

If a player hits a defenseless ball-carrier, or one already going to the ground, or makes a nasty, "unnecessary" hit above the shoulders, this can result in a costly penalty that'll give the offense 15 yards and a fresh set of downs. The flag is also thrown if a defender tries to fly in for a challenge while a ball-carrier is heading out of bounds or is already over the sideline.

5. UNSPORTSMANLIKE CONDUCT:

Imagine this. It's 3rd & 3 with the game on the line, and, as a safety, you make a huge tackle that seals the game. You burst into celebration and taunt the opposing player. A flag gets thrown. It's an automatic 15-yard penalty, and now the offense has a HUGE chance to steal the game back. That's unsportsmanlike conduct, and it can be absolutely gut-wrenching for the team of a player who gets a little too cocky too quickly and appears to disrespect their opponents in a moment of passion.

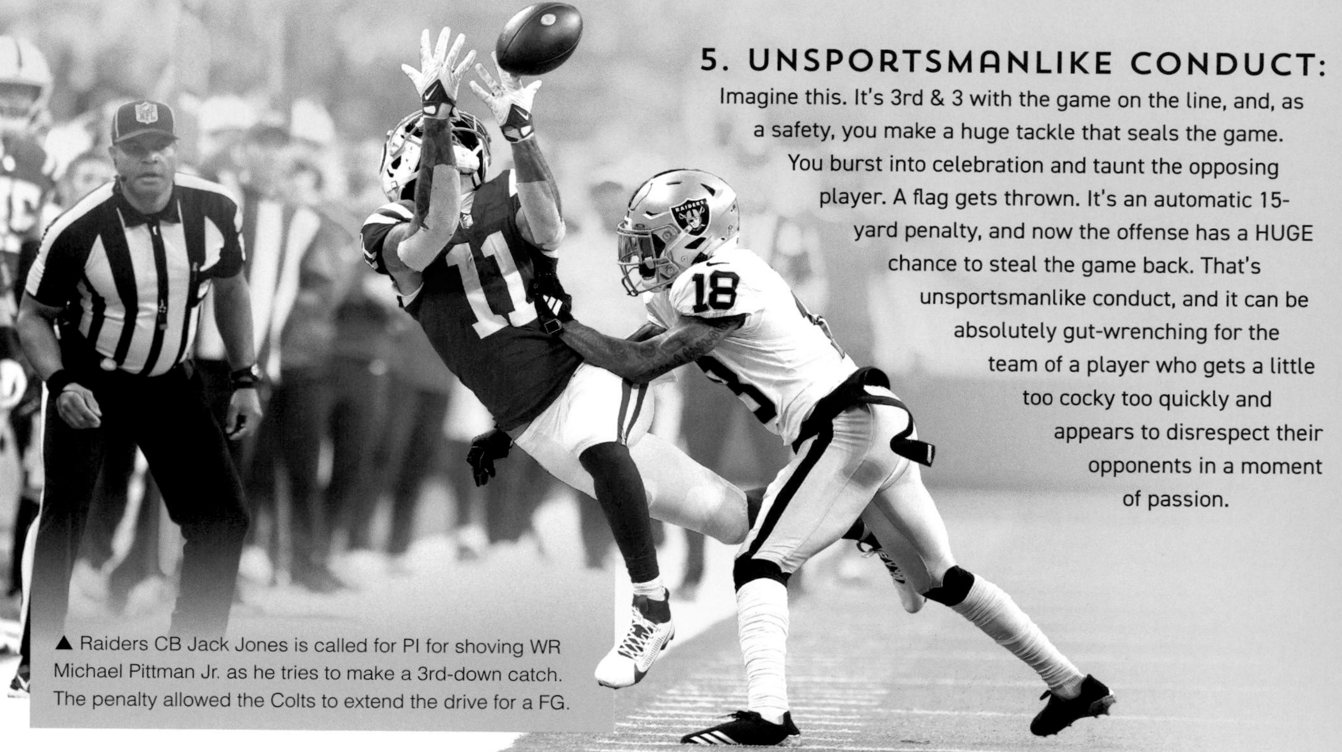

▲ Raiders CB Jack Jones is called for PI for shoving WR Michael Pittman Jr. as he tries to make a 3rd-down catch. The penalty allowed the Colts to extend the drive for a FG.

THE OFFICIALS

With so many rules to keep track of, football needs a strong, specialized team of officials to enforce them. Sometimes referred to as the "zebras" because of their black-and-white uniforms, football officials have the difficult job of making split-second decisions that can define a game. Luckily, there's plenty of them, and they all work together to get the call right while creating a safe and fair environment for all.

▲ The seven game officials and replay crew line up before kickoff.

▲ Art McNally became the first official to be enshrined in the Pro Football Hall of Fame in 2022. During his 23 years as the NFL's director of officiating, he transformed the profession by introducing detailed weekly performance reviews to help raise the game of officials.

TODAY'S OFFICIATING TEAM

Officiating has come a long way over the years. What was once just a few guys doing their best to make sense of such a complex game has now become an army of zebras who go through just as much training as the players on the field to ensure they're ready for any situation on game day. As technology has advanced, the use of new camera angles and Instant Replay have become imperative to keeping the game fair and assisting officials with high-stakes calls. They wear wireless mics to talk to each other and announce on-field decisions to spectators. Beyond a perfect understanding of the rules, today's officials are also expected to be fit enough to keep up with the players.

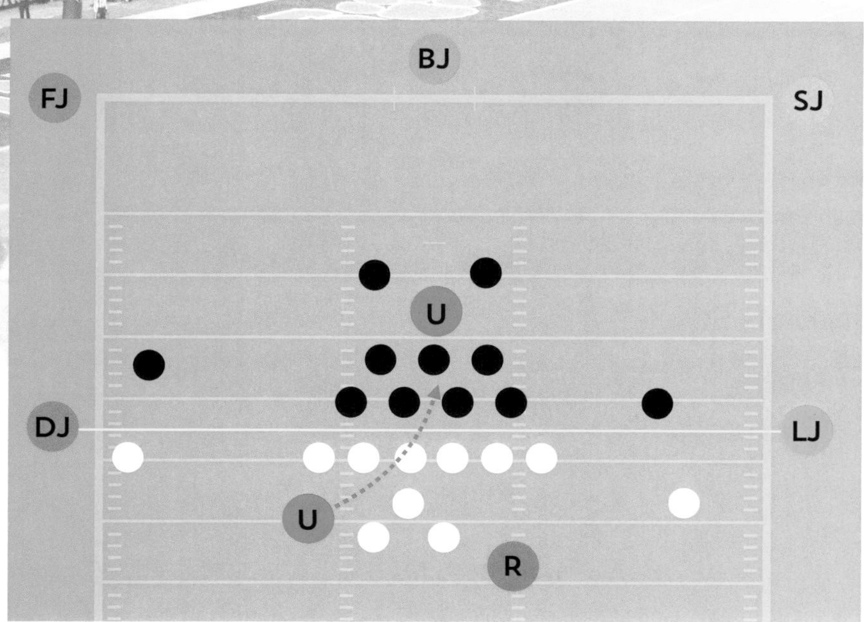

FACT FILE

While Instant Replay was first used in 1963 for a televised Army–Navy game, it wasn't officially adopted until 1999 in the NFL and 2006 in the NCAA.

REFEREE

The person at the center of it all, the head ref is responsible for making the final call on any flags thrown, as well as for keeping their eyes on the offensive backfield for any penalties committed during a play.

UMPIRE

The umpire lines up in the defensive backfield to keep an eye on any sneaky or illegal blocks and acts as a second pair of eyes for the referee. They also help with making pass interference calls, judging whether or not a pass is complete, and determining where a ball-carrier stepped out of bounds or was tackled. They also count the number of offensive players on the field before the snap.

DOWN AND LINE JUDGES

The down judge complements the umpire by standing on the sideline opposite the line of scrimmage to watch for any offsides and penalties in the neutral zone or backfield. They also coordinate with the umpire on any plays developing toward their sideline. Standing opposite, the line judge also aids with these tasks, as well as watches plays in the shorter areas of the field on their side.

FIELD JUDGE

The field judge is responsible for helping monitor plays in the defensive backfield and aiding with PI's, tackles, and fouls impacting the ball-carrier. They also count the defensive players on the field before the snap.

SIDE AND BACK JUDGES

The final two officials split duties in the defensive backfield. The back judge keeps an eye on tight ends and running backs. Meanwhile, the side judge watches receivers lined up on their side of the field, tracking routes deeper into the secondary and aiding the field judge and umpire with their decisions.

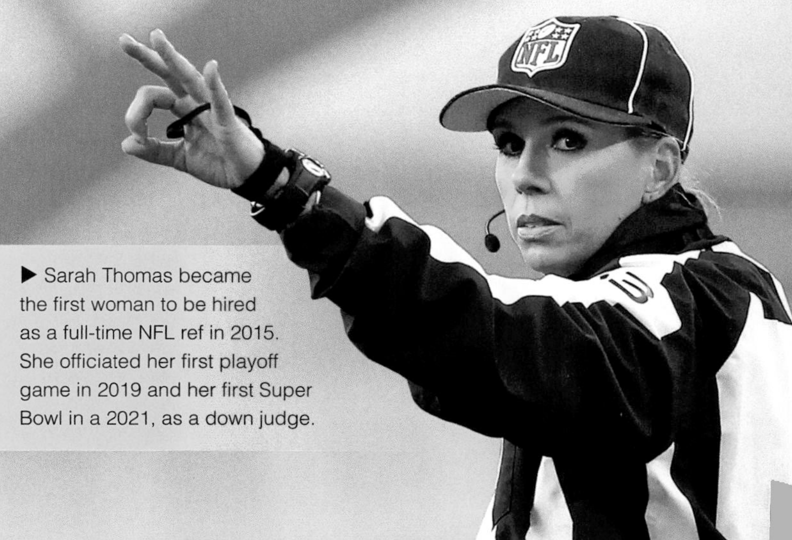

▶ Sarah Thomas became the first woman to be hired as a full-time NFL ref in 2015. She officiated her first playoff game in 2019 and her first Super Bowl in a 2021, as a down judge.

OFFENSIVE POSITIONS

Now that we've learned the basics about how to play football, it's time to get familiar with the different positions in the game. Each of the 11 players on either side of the ball has their own unique role to help their team win. The offensive side has possession of the ball and tries to make plays to move the ball down the field toward the other team's end zone to score points.

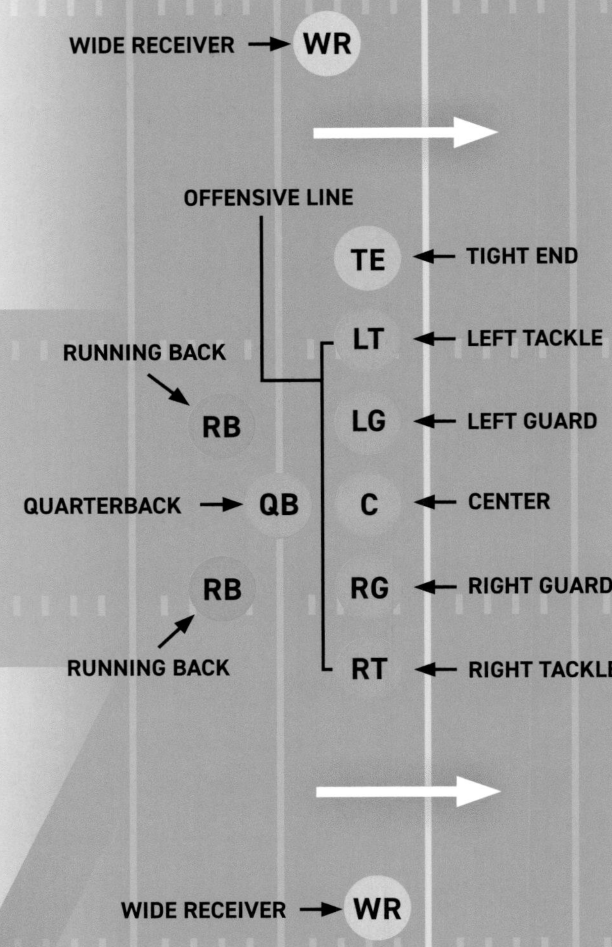

QUARTERBACK (QB)

The most important position on any team, the quarterback is the player responsible for passing the ball and managing the offensive game. The center snaps the ball to the QB on every play, and, from there, it's down to them to either hand the ball off to a running back or find an open receiver. For a quarterback to excel, they need to be very quick at processing situations. While arm strength and athleticism obviously matter, the ability to figure out what's happening in front of them, to feel pressure and improvize, or to use their eyes to freeze defenders and create holes for their players are vital. Chiefs QB Patrick Mahomes is the perfect blend of the mental and physical traits that define top QBs, with incredible arm-talent plus the off-the-charts football IQ to elude defenders, find the best "read" for a pass, and turn dead plays into touchdowns.

◀ Mahomes scrambles to make a play under pressure.

▶ Halfbacks (HB) are the primary rushers, but bulkier blocking fullbacks (FB) like Kyle Juszczyk (pictured) also carry the ball.

RUNNING BACK (RB)

Lining up in the **backfield** either beside or behind the QB, a running back's job is to secure the ball and simply run with it as hard as they can. Running backs come in all shapes and sizes, and their effectiveness ususally comes down to how well they fit the offensive scheme their team runs. Derrick Henry, for instance, is a bowling ball of a runner who embraces physicality and bursting through narrow holes in the offensive line, whereas someone like Christian McCaffrey is far more elusive and renowned for his electric playmaking as a dual-threat back (someone who can catch as well as run), making his biggest plays outside of the offensive line.

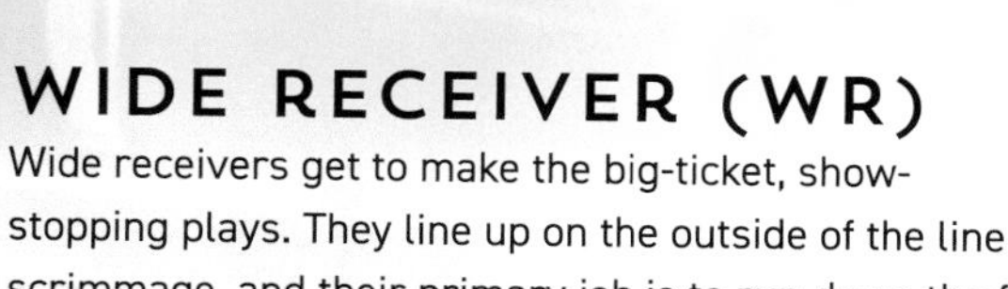

WIDE RECEIVER (WR)

Wide receivers get to make the big-ticket, show-stopping plays. They line up on the outside of the line of scrimmage, and their primary job is to run down the field and catch the football on passing plays. To do that, they need speed and techniques like fakes and footwork to "create separation" from defenders.

Like running backs, WRs come in all shapes and sizes. Some like A.J. Brown (pictured) embrace a physically dominant style of play, boxing out defenders as if he was catching a rebound in basketball, while guys like Justin Jefferson are so silky with their route-running, it makes them nearly impossible to defend.

▶ Brown beats two DBs to make a catch.

OFFENSIVE LINE

An offensive line is made up of five players.

Two **TACKLES (RT and LT)** line up on either side (sometimes known as "book ends"). These are the biggest and strongest of the group, and their job is to try and seal the edge from pesky edge rushers and keep the quarterback safe while forcing open holes on run plays.

GUARDS (RG and LG) are often a little smaller than tackles and a little more agile, lining up on either side of the center. They have a similar responsibility but handle the meaty defensive tackles storming at them as well as opening the primary rushing lanes for running backs.

CENTERS (C) have the most difficult role on the offensive front. They have to snap the ball and then immediately explode back into their stance to block defensive tackles or push to the next level to aid in run-blocking.

TIGHT END (TE)

Lining up between the offensive line and wide receivers, the TE has two primary roles: first, to contribute in run-blocking plays and help the offensive line, and second, to double-up as an extra pair of hands for the QB to target.

The very best in the game can do both excellently, and there is no finer example than Travis Kelce, who is simply magical as a receiver yet physical enough to make a real difference when blocking. His presence has single-handedly changed games, and he's become the heartbeat of the Chiefs' offense over the last decade.

▲ Kelce throws a key block to spring his RB.

DEFENSIVE POSITIONS

You wouldn't think it'd be very hard to move the football all of 30 feet when you have four tries to do it. But when you have a well-organized, hard-tackling defense lined up against you, it really is. Defensive players work together to stop the other team from scoring and regain possession of the ball for their team. They do so by rushing the passer, shutting down running lanes, defending and blocking passes, forcing fumbles, making interceptions, and tackling the ball-carrier.

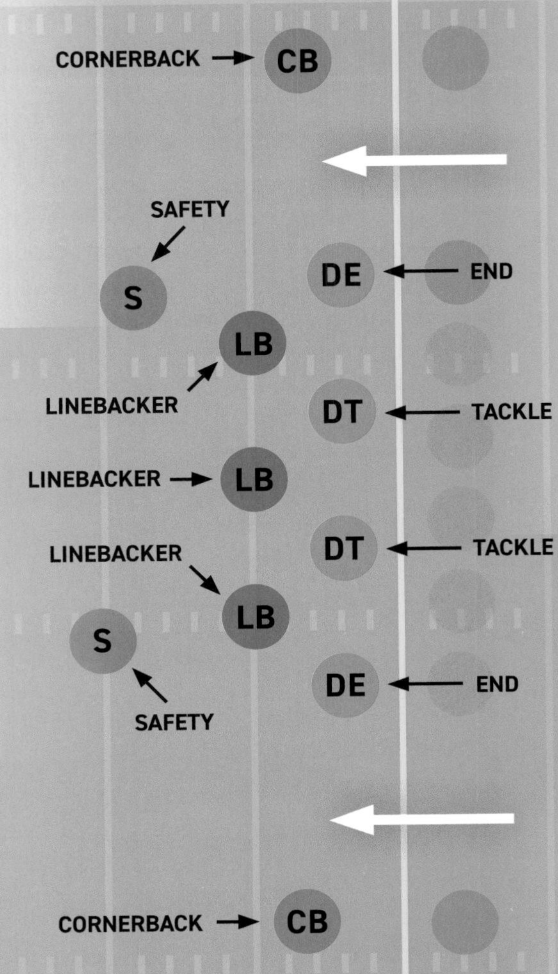

DEFENSIVE LINE:

Lining up opposite the offensive front, a defensive line typically features up to four pass-rushers, with a mix of **defensive tackles (DT)** and **defensive ends (DE)**. The ends are quicker and have an array of stunning moves in their arsenal to blow past offensive tackles. This helps them rush the quarterback and seal the edge on run plays.

Tackles are the big boys. Their job consists of closing the holes that the offensive line tries to open for the run game and mauling their way to the quarterback. The best in this position are able to strike a balance between wreaking havoc in the offensive backfield and anchoring their position to close down any gaps a running back may sneak through.

◀ The Notre Dame D-line in action as the ball is snapped in a game against Clemson.

LINEBACKER (LB):

Linebackers sit in the middle of the defense. They're usually the top tacklers on a team and often responsible for the defensive play-calling. They split duties after the snap. Sometimes they "blitz" and rush the passer, giving the defensive line some extra support, and at other times they sit back, hoping to cut off RBs and receivers as they run across the middle. Much like the QB position, instincts and processing are everything. Being able to consistently be in the right place at the right time is far more valuable than someone who bites on every adjustment a QB makes or move a receiver tries to fool him with.

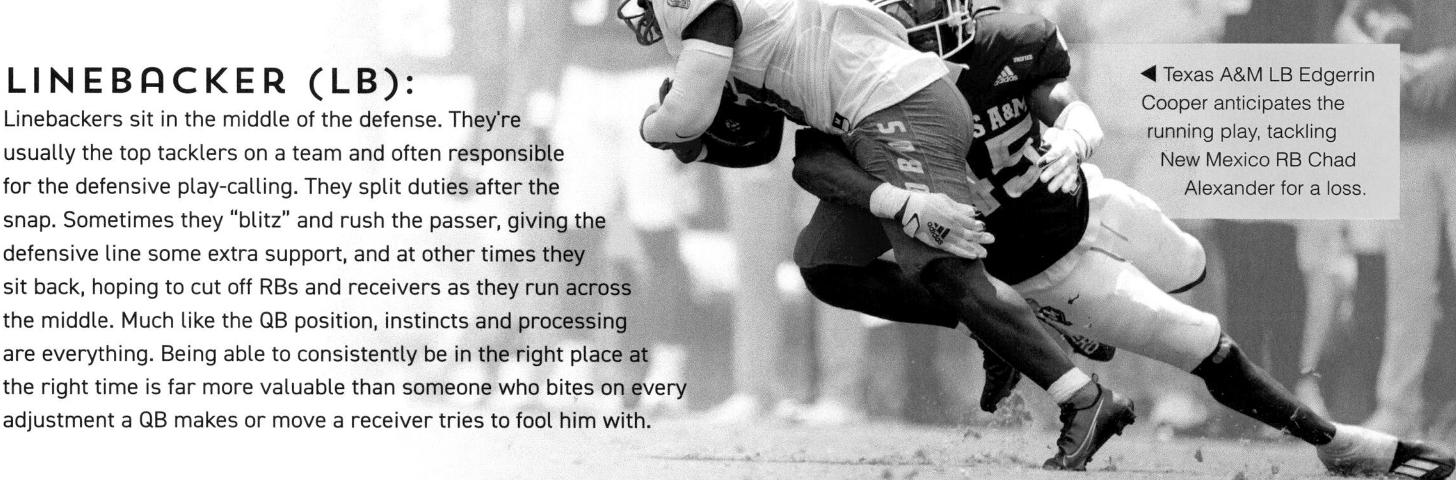

◀ Texas A&M LB Edgerrin Cooper anticipates the running play, tackling New Mexico RB Chad Alexander for a loss.

THE SECONDARY OR DEFENSIVE BACKS:

These defenders, cornerbacks and safeties, generally sit farthest from where the ball is snapped.

FACT FILE

A safety can be designated as a strong safety (SS) or free safety (FS). The SS is generally bigger and stronger, assigned to cover the "strong" side of the offense where the TE lines up. The speedy FS tends to hang the farthest back, watching the play develop and free to respond accordingly.

CORNERBACK (CB):

Some consider this the hardest position to play in football. The main job of a corner is to line up opposite receivers and stop them from catching the ball. That's easier said than done when zebras are watching your every move and even a minor tug of a jersey can wipe out a stop. On top of that, CBs need to be strong enough as tacklers to bring down ball-carriers and quick enough to keep up with the fastest players in the game! It's not a job for the faint of heart, but cornerbacks provide some of the biggest plays in the game as a result.

◀ CB Darious Williams jumps up in coverage to defend a pass targeting wideout Wan'Dale Robinson.

SAFETY (S):

The last line of defense, the job of a safety is to hang back and prevent deep passes or big plays from getting past them. Sometimes they'll play closer to the ball in a bid to help the linebackers, and at other times they'll work in tandem with corners to "bracket" elite receivers, hoping the quarterback will look elsewhere. The best safeties in the game are highly versatile, a perfect blend of a cornerback and linebacker. Someone like Tyrann Mathieu, for instance, has lined up just about everywhere in his career, making him a matchup nightmare for opposing offensive coordinators.

▼ Matheiu makes a tackle.

SPECIAL TEAMS POSITIONS

Special teams is the final phase of football and just as important as the offense and defense. The unit (with the exception of the kicker, punter, and long snapper) is built up of players already on the roster. They handle kickoffs, punts, field goals, and extra points. Because coaches don't want to risk superstars on high-speed kick returns, a lot of players make their first impact on special teams before earning their stripes on offense or defense.

◀ Placekicker Younghoe Koo keeps his cool to knock in a game-winning field goal on the last play of the game.

PUNTER

If your team goes 3 and out, the punter will be the player responsible for "flipping the field." Their aim is to punt the ball as deep into enemy territory as they can without it crossing the goal line. If the ball goes into the end zone, it results in an automatic touchback, meaning the offense gets to start at their own 20-yard line. Pinning the opposing offense inside their own 10-yard line can provide a real spark of life for a team who've just lost momentum, so finding a punter you can trust to make long, accurate punts with serious hangtime can be worth its weight in gold.

KICKER

The placekicker is responsible for kicking field goals and extra-point attempts. They often do the booting for kickoffs, too. Tasked with reliably getting the ball through the uprights no matter the situation, there might be no higher-pressure role in football. They have to execute every single time they take a snap. Games can often come down to one kick—are you clutch enough to take the game-winning field goal as the clock runs out?

▶ Seahawks' Michael Dickson makes a blustery punt down the field.

◀ RB Nyheim Hines weaved down the field, skirting tackles to score a record two kick-return TDs in one game against the Pats in 2023.

RETURNERS

The job of a returner is to catch the kick or punt and try to gain as much field position as possible. Often running backs or zippy wideouts, the returner needs to have outstanding patience and catlike agility to shake off an army of storming defenders all focusing on them and them alone. Few things in football are as exciting as a kick- or punt-return touchdown!

GUNNERS AND JAMMERS

Think of these like receivers and corners for special teams. The gunner lines up where a wideout would, and their main aim is to burst down the sideline and tackle the returner. Often some of the quickest players on the field, they have to try and trap the returner so they can't bring the ball back the other way. The jammer's mission is simply to stop the gunner and needs a similar level of athleticism as a result.

◀ Long snapper Josh Harris lines up at center for a punt play.

LONG SNAPPER

Believe it or not, this is one of the hardest jobs to get in football. Why? Because there's only one per team! Whereas every other position has potential for a backup or off-season battle, a long snapper's only job is to snap the ball to the kickers and punters. These snaps are much farther than what we see from the center, making it a really specialized role that's hard to perfect.

A **holder** is also on the field and responsible for holding the ball steady while the kicker makes his attempt. Mind those fingers!

BLOCKERS

Just like in regular plays, there is also an offensive and defensive line. Comprised of starting tackles and guards on offense and pass-rushers on defense, the objectives are similar. The defense is trying to jump up and get their hands on the kick as it leaves the turf or break through the line to throw their body in the way of the kick, while the offensive blockers' job is to stop them and protect the kicker or punter at all costs.

You'll sometimes see quicker players like LBs try to storm over the top of the line as the ball is snapped. It's a high-risk move since it could result in a costly penalty if mistimed even slightly, but, done well, it could force a crucial turnover.

◀ Rams LB Bobby Wagner blocks a Bucs field goal attempt.

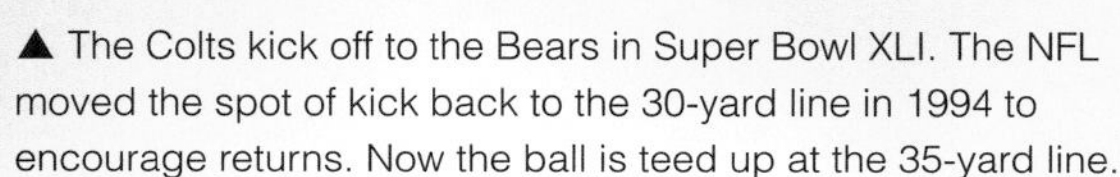

▲ The Colts kick off to the Bears in Super Bowl XLI. The NFL moved the spot of kick back to the 30-yard line in 1994 to encourage returns. Now the ball is teed up at the 35-yard line.

▶ Hall-of-famer Devin Hester skirts tackles (even from kicker Adam Vinatieri) to become the first player in history to return the opening kickoff of a Super Bowl for a touchdown.

SNAPSHOT

THE KICKOFF

Rules aren't set in stone. They are constantly being redesigned to enhance competition and safety. The kickoff is a perfect example. Every half of football starts with one. They also happen after every scoring drive. With around 10 per game, it's an important play that can either result in a return (where a returner catches or scoops up the ball and moves it as far as they can up the field while the rest of their team blocks for them) or a touchback (where play is stopped and the ball is automatically placed on a particular yard marker). Returns are risky plays that are thrilling to watch, but, because in the classic version (pictured above) two teams sprinted toward each other from opposite ends of the field, they've resulted in a lot of injuries from high-speed collisions over the years. While previous NFL regs encouraged returns, since 2011 concern over concussions has led to so many rule changes that only 21.5% of kickoffs were returned at all in 2023. In 2024, the the league announced an entirely new, safer approach to revive the excitement of the kickoff. The two special teams squads will line up five yards away from one another on the receiving teams' end of the field and aren't allowed to move until a returner catches the ball or it hits the ground. With no fair catches allowed, returns are set to make a serious comeback.

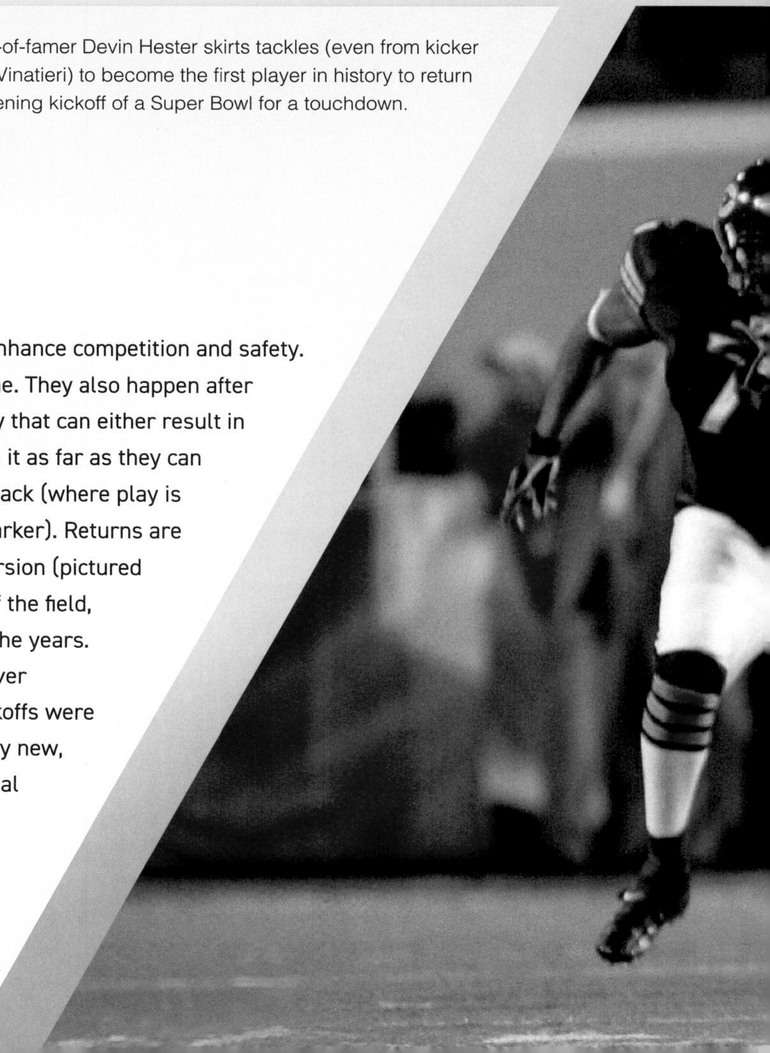

QUARTERBACKS

PATRICK MAHOMES

BORN 1995 • PRO: 2017–PRESENT

PASSING YARDS: 28,424 • TD PASSES: 219

From his earliest days in Texas playing catch with his MLB pitcher dad in the backyard, people could tell Mahomes had an arm. He's paired that natural talent with an unstoppable winning mentality to keep impressing on bigger and bigger stages. "I wish I could make it easier," he's said, "but I feel like I play better when we are down," and this seems to be his superpower. He completes deep balls at impossible angles on third downs even though the defense know a pass is coming. He regularly wipes out double-digit deficits to steal victories. His first season as the starter at Kansas City, he passed for more than 5,000 yards and 50 touchdowns. He proceeded to lead the Chiefs to six consecutive AFC Championships and three Super Bowl wins in six years, bagging two NFL MVPs and three Super Bowl MVPs in the process. At this rate, he's bound for a career to put him in contention for the GOAT.

▲ Mahomes revs up his team in a huddle. The ten-year deal worth $503 million he signed in 2020 was the biggest contract in NFL history.

◀ Unitas led the league in passing yards and touchdowns four times and was picked for first-team All-Pro honors five times.

BRETT FAVRE

BORN 1969 • PRO: 1991–2010

PASSING YARDS: 71,838 • TD PASSES: 508

When this Southern Mississippi alum came off the backup bench to become Green Bay's starter in 1992, he reinvigorated the iconic team. From 1995 to 1997, Favre was voted NFL MVP a record three times in a row as he led the league in passing touchdowns and brought his team to two Super Bowls. He came away with the title in Super Bowl XXXI, ending a 30-year championship drought in Green Bay. Over the course of his career, this "iron man" and expert reader of the field would play 299 consecutive games over 20 years, becoming the first QB in history to record a win against all 32 NFL teams. When he opted to put off retirement to play for the Vikings, he ended up having a monster 4,202-yard season.

JOHNNY UNITAS

1933–2022 • PRO: 1956–1973

PASSING YARDS: 40,239 • TD PASSES: 290

Drafted in ninth round by the Steelers and let go before the season even began, this undersized prospect out of Louisville didn't get off to the best start in the NFL, but he'd go on to become the model for the modern play-caller. Unitas was working construction and playing semi-pro football on the weekends when he tagged along with a local teammate to a tryout in Baltimore. The Colts signed him, and, though his first pro pass resulted in a pick-six, they'd soon be glad they gave him a chance. By the end of his career, he'd pulled in three championships, three league MVPs, and 10 Pro Bowl selections. His standout performance in the 1958 NFL Championship—often referred to as the "Greatest Game Ever Played"—resulted in the first overtime in NFL history, followed by a majestic 80-yard game-winning drive. His televised genius drew in many new football fans. He retired as the best QB to have played the game and was voted into the Pro Football Hall of Fame in Canton in 1979.

▼ This 11-time Pro Bowler and six-time All-Pro joined the ranks in Canton in 2016.

JOE MONTANA

BORN 1956 • PRO: 1979–1994

PASSING YARDS: 40,551 • TD PASSES: 273

The captain of the new "West Coast offense" that dominated the NFC West and the whole league during the 1980s, Montana led the San Francisco 49ers to four NFL championship titles (1982, 1985, 1989, 1990), racking up three Super Bowl MVPs along the way. Montana was a master of reading the field and making defenses pay as soon as they thought he wasn't going to chuck a long ball down the field. He saw so much success because he knew how to keep his cool and find a way to win. In fact, he started his junior season at Notre Dame as the third-string QB and only became the starter when he came off the bench to deliver an epic comeback victory. Over the course of his pro career, the two-time NFL MVP led his team to 31 fourth-quarter comeback wins—including one in Super Bowl XXIII. He entered the Pro Football Hall of Fame in 2000.

▶ Joe Montana and Patrick Mahomes share the joint record for most touchdown passes thrown in a single NFL postseason—11.

NFL PASSING RECORDS

MOST CAREER PASSING YARDS
Tom Brady, 89,214 (2000–2022)

MOST PASSING YARDS IN A SINGLE SEASON
Peyton Manning, 5,477 (2013)

MOST PASSING YARDS IN A GAME
Norm Van Brocklin, 554 (September 28, 1951)

MOST PASSING TOUCHDOWNS
Tom Brady, 649 (2000–2022)

MOST CAREER YARDS PER GAME
Drew Brees, 280 (2001–2020)

HIGHEST CAREER QB RATING
Drew Brees, 98.7 (2001–2020)

HIGHEST SINGLE-SEASON QB RATING
Aaron Rodgers, 122.5 (2011)

TOM BRADY

BORN 1977 • PRO: 2000–2022

PASSING YARDS: 89,214 • TD PASSES: 649

With a glittering 23-year career, full of records and championships, Brady is generally acknowledged to be the NFL's GOAT—not bad for a sixth-round pick who had to battle his way up from the seventh-string QB at Michigan to become a starter. It turns out he was the best draft deal of all time, bringing the Patriots their first Super Bowl win in just his second season when he came off the bench to replace an injured Drew Bledsoe as starter in Week 3. A smart and durable competitor, Brady would take New England to nine more championships, winning six. With a seemingly unmatchable 88 postseason passing TDs to his name, this five-time Super Bowl MVP and 15-time Pro Bowler is a playoffs legend. The next guy on the list (Joe Montana) has around half that total (45). When he transferred to the Bucs for his last three seasons, Brady did it all again, bringing NFL championship glory to Tampa Bay and securing his seventh title—that's more than any franchise in history!

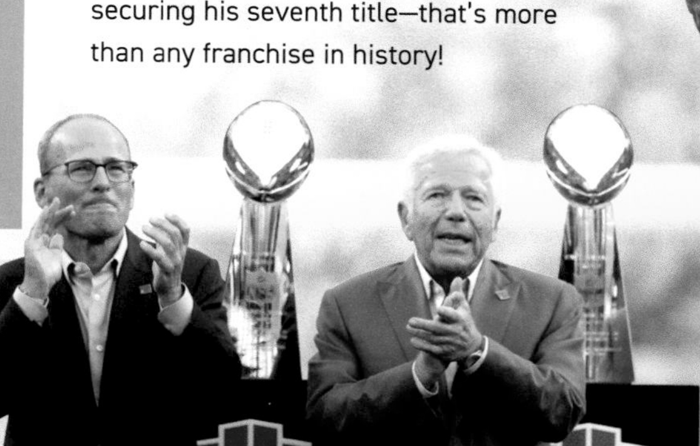

▶The Pats' #12 stands surrounded by the astonishing six Lombardi Trophies he brought to the franchise in a 2023 ceremony held at Gillette Stadium to celebrate his retirement.

PEYTON MANNING

BORN 1976 • PRO: 1998–2015
PASSING YARDS: 71,940
TD PASSES: 539

Manning, who spent more than 20 hours a week studying tape, called himself a "student of the game" and, when it came to football, he was always top of the class. He came from an NFL family—his dad Archie played QB for the Saints and his younger brother Eli won two Super Bowls with the Giants. Sixty colleges vied for him out of high school. He chose Tennessee, where he became the Volunteers' all-time leading passer. He went #1 overall to the Colts in the 1998 draft, putting in a debut season to remember as he set five rookie passing records. His numbers only went up from there. He threw for more than 4,000 yards in 14 seasons and was named first-team All-Pro seven times. When he came back from a neck injury to play four seasons in Denver, he went out on a high, throwing for a record-breaking 5,477 yards and 55 TDs one season, helping to bring an NFL title (his second) to the Mile-High City in Super Bowl 50, his very last game as a pro.

▼ Manning was named league MVP five times over 10 years—more than any other player to date.

◀ An exceptional rushing QB since high school, Jackson is the youngest-ever recipient of the Heisman Trophy, which he won his sophomore year at Louisville.

LAMAR JACKSON

BORN 1997 • PRO: 2018–PRESENT
PASSING YARDS: 15,887 • TD PASSES: 125

This Heisman winner out of Louisville has not disappointed in the big leagues. In his first season with the Ravens, at a day shy of 22, he became the youngest quarterback to start a playoff game. He sky-rocketed to the top of the league the following year, starting with the very first game, in which he threw for 324 yards and five touchdowns to become the youngest QB in NFL history to earn the highest possible 158.3 passer rating. He proceeded to obliterate teams the whole season as the Ravens went 14–2 and outscored the opposition by 249 points. Jackson came away as the unanimous 2019 NFL MVP. The most dangerous dual-threat in the game with over 5,000 rushing yards and 29 rushing TDs, Jackson is now one of the highest paid players ever after a blockbuster $260 million, five-year contract with a $72.5 million signing bonus agreed in 2023—the year he notched his second MVP.

FACT FILE

Hall of Famer Sammy Baugh helped usher in the era of the forward pass. The Redskins' seven-time All-NFL QB was such an impressive all-arounder that in 1943 he led the league in passing, punting, and interceptions.

DREW BREES

BORN 1979 • PRO: 2001–2020
PASSING YARDS: 80,358 • TD PASSES: 571

Brees led his high school team to a state championship in Texas, but his comparatively small size made many programs underestimate his potential. He shined at Purdue and was drafted by the Chargers in 2001. Though he had one standout season with the Bolts, it wasn't until he teamed up with head coach Sean Payton at the Saints that he developed into one of the finest quarterbacks in league history. Brees would go on to top the NFL in passing yards for seven seasons, clock a record five seasons with 5,000+ passing yards, go 52 straight games with a touchdown pass, and throw for a record seven TDs in one game. Known for his consistently high completion percentage (he once recorded a game with a near-perfect 98.7%), Brees had a 70.62% completion rate in 2009, the year he'd take the New Orleans all the way to the Super Bowl, winning the franchise's first championship.

▶ Brees surpassed Peyton Manning's all-time touchdown passes record (539) during a stellar 2019 game against the Colts that saw him go 29-for-30 with four touchdowns. He's currently second after Tom Brady.

▲ Marino was an excellent pocket passer with an amazingly quick release. He managed to get sacked less than any other quarterback in league history.

DAN MARINO

BORN 1961 • PRO: 1983—1999 • PASSING YARDS: 61,361 • TD PASSES: 420

The winningest quarterback never to win a Super Bowl, Marino spent his entire pro career with the Miami Dolphins after shining as a four-year starter at Pitt. While he may not have gotten to hoist the Lombardi Trophy, Marino's career was still filled with honors—from NFL MVP in 1984 to the Walter Payton Man of the Year Award in 1998. During his MVP year, he became the first quarterback to pass for more than 5,000 yards in a single season and set an AFC Championship record by passing for 421 yards and four touchdowns in the Dolphins' rout of the Steelers. It was one of 10 times that Marino would lead Miami into the postseason during his 17 years with the franchise. He was the NFL's undisputed passing leader upon retirement. Though most of his records have been overtaken now, he still holds quite a few, including the one for the most seasons leading the league in completions (six). In 2019, he was named to the prestigious roster of the NFL 100 All-Time Team, and he was enshrined in the Pro Football Hall of Fame in 2005.

AARON RODGERS

BORN 1983 • PRO: 2005—PRESENT • PASSING YARDS: 59,055 • TD PASSES: 475

Rodgers' accuracy and decision-making are second-to-none. He recorded the highest overall passer rating of any quarterback in history for a single season (122.5 in 2011) and also by far tops the charts in terms of his ratio of touchdowns to interceptions: 475–105. Rodgers won the starting QB spot at Cal after transferring there from a local community college. He was picked by the Packers in the first round but didn't get the starting job at Green Bay until four years later when his mentor Brett Favre was traded to the Jets. Rodgers ensured the Pack were regular playoff contenders, captaining them to a Super Bowl victory in 2010 by throwing for 304 yards with three TDs and zero picks. He was named MVP of that game and of the league four times, including back-to-back selections in 2020 and 2021. He transferred to the Jets in 2023, tearing his Achilles just four snaps into the season, but, at age 40, he's ready to make a comeback.

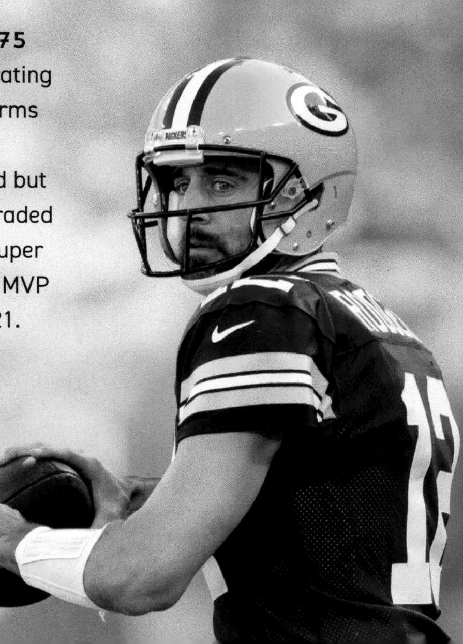

▶ In a 42–24 win against the Raiders on October 20, 2019, Rodgers completed more than 80 percent of his passes for an average of 13.8 yards per attempt to come away with a 158.3 passer rating—the highest you can get in the NFL.

WIDE RECEIVERS

DON HUTSON

1913–1997 • PRO: 1935–1945

RECEPTIONS: 488 • TDs: 99

▶ Hutson made going deep an NFL staple. His 488 career catches was 200 more than any of his peers.

In one fabled game in 1945, this Alabama alum caught four touchdowns—and kicked five extra points—in a single quarter. Though Green Bay's Hutson was gifted as a placekicker and safety, he made his biggest mark at the wide-receiver position, pioneering many of the routes that wideouts still use to beat the secondary in the modern game. The inventor of the Z-out was the first receiver to draw double and triple coverage, but that didn't stop him from retiring with 18 NFL records. His 99 TD receptions was not surpassed for 44 years, and he's still eleventh in all-time receiving TDs in spite of playing 84 fewer games than the person at tenth. The two-time MVP was elected into the very first class of the Pro Football Hall of Fame in 1963. The Packers named their indoor training facility after Hutson in 1994—a fitting tribute to the wideout who led the league in receptions eight times while helping Green Bay to three NFL Championships.

JERRY RICE

BORN 1962 • PRO: 1985–2004 • RECEPTIONS: 1,549 • TDs: 208

With his 22,895 receiving yards, 1,549 receptions, 11 seasons averaging more than 100 receiving yards per game, and 14 seasons with more than 1,000 receiving yards, no one is even close to touching the wideout records Rice set during his legendary 20-year career in the NFL. It's likely no one will. Even though this humble son of a smalltown brick mason played his college ball at the relatively unknown Mississippi Valley State, his status as the NCAA's all-time leader in receiving TDs saw him drafted in the first round by the 49ers in 1985. By 1987, he'd set the record for most TD receptions in a season—22. His time at San Francisco secured his claim as one of the greatest NFL players to ever grace the field, as he helped them win three Super Bowls while topping the league in receiving yards and TDs four times. He was named MVP of Super Bowl XXIII after his record-breaking performance: 11 receptions for 215 yards. Rice briefly played for the Raiders, Seahawks, and Broncos before hanging up his helmet in 2005. A shoo-in for the Hall of Fame, he was inducted in 2010.

▲ Alworth ended his career with 10,266 receiving yards, averaging a staggering 18.9 yards per catch.

LANCE ALWORTH

BORN 1940 • PRO: 1962–1972

RECEPTIONS: 542 • TDs: 85

Alworth got offers to go pro in baseball straight out of high school. He decided to do football at the University of Arkansas instead, leading his team to three conference championships and topping the charts for yards off punt returns. He went pro in 1962, playing most of his career with the Chargers. Nicknamed "Bambi" for his deerlike runs and graceful leaping catches, Alworth raised the bar for flankers, going seven seasons with an average of 100+ receiving yards per game. In his second season, he was named MVP after helping his team to the AFL Championship, where he pulled in a 48-yard TD in a victory over the Patriots. Alworth, who still holds the record for most games with more than 200 receiving yards, joined the ranks in Canton in 1978.

▶ Rice playing for the San Francisco 49ers in a game against the Atlanta Falcons, 1994.

▲ Moss playing in a 2010 game against the New York Jets.

TERRELL OWENS

BORN 1973 • PRO: 1996–2010 • RECEPTIONS: 1,078 • TDs: 153

Owens, nicknamed "T.O.", has always known how to take his chances. He got his first start in high school when a teammate fell ill. Coming out of the University of Tennessee at Chattanooga where he did basketball and track in addition to football, T.O.'s talent went largely under-the-radar. Fatefully, he was drafted in the third round by his idol Jerry Rice's team, the 49ers, where he entered the gameday lineup after his hero was knocked out with an ACL injury. With nine seasons with more than 1,000 receiving yards and 15,934 overall, Owens has some of the best career stats of all time, but his antics on and off the field led to controversy and saw him frequently released from teams—including the Eagles, Cowboys, Bills, and Bengals. When the six-time Pro Bowler officially became a Hall-of-Famer in 2018, he chose to hold his own personal induction ceremony at his alma mater.

RANDY MOSS

BORN 1977 • PRO: 1998–2013
RECEPTIONS: 982 • TDs: 156

Growing up in West Virginia, Moss was an exceptional high school football player, but he lost the chance to play Division I college football following an arrest and failed drug test. The Vikings decided to give him a third chance, drafting him in the first round in 1998. The gamble paid off, and the rookie phenom immediately made good, leading Minnesota to a record-breaking 15–1 season that saw them score the most points of any team in history. In 2003, he had a career-high 111 receptions for 1,632 yards, securing his second of four first-team All-Pro selections. A 2005 trade to the Raiders dampened his output, but he made a major comeback with the Patriots, breaking Jerry Rice's single-season touchdown record with 23 end-zone catches while New England made history with a perfect 16–0 regular-season record. The six-time Pro Bowler became a commentator after retiring and was enshrined in the Hall of Fame in 2018—the same year as his rival T.O.

MOST NFL RECEIVING TOUCHDOWNS

PLAYER	GAMES	TD RECEPTIONS
Jerry Rice	303	197
Randy Moss	218	156
Terrell Owens	219	153
Cris Carter	234	130
Marvin Harrison	190	128
Larry Fitzgerald	263	121
Antonio Gates	236	116
Tony Gonzalez	270	111
Tim Brown	255	100
Steve Largent	200	100

JUSTIN JEFFERSON

BORN 1999 • PRO: 2020–PRESENT
RECEPTIONS: 392 • TDs: 31

This Louisiana native's three seasons with the LSU Tigers ended with him making a record-setting four touchdown receptions during the 2019 Peach Bowl in the lead up to a National Championship victory. He wowed straight out of the gates in the pros, clocking a massive 1,400 yards in his inaugural season with the Minnesota Vikings—a new record for a rookie wideout. Named All-Pro his first three seasons, Jefferson was awarded NFL Offensive Player of the Year in 2022 after a giant season with 128 receptions for 1,809 yards. Known for running elegant routes in fearless defiance of whatever coverage defenses throw at him, Jefferson has pulled in many a physics-defying catch. His celebration dance, the Griddy, also saw him become the first NFL character to appear in the game *Fortnite*, in 2021.

▶ Justin Jefferson celebrates a 71-yard TD reception against the Titans, with his signature dance, the Griddy.

TIGHT ENDS

ANTONIO GATES

BORN 1980 • PRO: 2003–2018

RECEPTIONS: 955 • TDs: 116

This Chargers legend made eight Pro Bowls—not bad for a kid who didn't make a single catch in college. Gates left the gridiron behind to play basketball at Kent State. The Detroit native was a top player who averaged more than 20 points a game his senior year, but NBA recruiters wouldn't bite because he didn't have a typical power-forward build. When Gates turned to the NFL instead, his promising try-out saw him snapped up by San Diego as an undrafted free agent. He ended up playing his entire 15-year career with the Chargers, where he still holds the record for the most receiving yards in franchise history at 11,841. Gates was a genius at creating separation and had a special kind of mind meld with QB Philip Rivers that made them one of the most productive duos in football.

▲ Gonzalez celebrates the only playoff win of his storied career—an NFC Divisional Game against the Seahawks in 2013.

◀ Gates' 116 receiving touchdowns are the most by any tight end in NFL history.

TONY GONZALEZ

BORN 1976 • PRO: 1997–2013

RECEPTIONS: 1,325 • TDs: 111

Gonzalez busted pretty much every record for a tight end over the course of his 17-year career, setting the gold standard for the 21st-century TE. A Southern California kid, he was named Orange County Athlete of the Year in high school for his dominant performances on the football field and basketball court. He continued playing both football and basketball at Cal before declaring for the NFL draft his junior year. The Chiefs traded up to nab the top prospect. By 2001, he'd become Pro Bowl material—a distinction he'd earn 14 times as he racked up TDs, each one punctuated with his signature "dunking" of the ball over the uprights. A week into joining the Falcons in 2009, he became the first TE to pass the 1,000-reception mark. The ten-time All-Pro remained a potent offensive weapon until retirement, getting his career-high 149 receiving yards in a game against the Pats during his final season. A 2019 inductee to the Hall of Fame, Gonzalez still holds the record among NFL tight ends for most receptions (1,325) and receiving yards (15,127).

ROB GRONKOWSKI

BORN 1989 • PRO: 2010–2021 • RECEPTIONS: 621 • TDs: 93

After setting team records in his two seasons at Arizona, Gronkowski was drafted by the New England Patriots in the second round. He started strong, scoring a touchdown in his 2010 debut against the Bengals—the first of 92 TD connections he'd make with QB Tom Brady as they shored up the Pats' dynasty with three championship titles. In his banner second season, he became the first TE to lead the league in receiving touchdowns with 17. Known as "Gronk," the Pats' good-time guy was as good at throwing a key block as he was at receiving. In 2020, Brady coaxed Gronk out of retirement to join him on yet another successful Super Bowl campaign—this time with the Tampa Bay Buccaneers. He hauled in two TDs as the Bucs steamrollered the Chiefs 31–9 to take his fourth title.

▶ Gronk has scored 15 playoff TDs, including this 22-yarder to take the lead against the Seahawks in Super Bowl XLIX.

TRAVIS KELCE

BORN 1989 • PRO: 2013–PRESENT • RECEPTIONS: 907 • TDs: 77

Kelce joined his older brother Jason—who went on to be a Pro-Bowl center for the Eagles—to play college ball for Cincinnati in their home state of Ohio. The Kansas City Chiefs' new head coach, Andy Reid, had worked with Jason in Philly and decided to draft his younger brother. Kelce's rookie season was nullified by an injury, but since then, he's barely missed a game to post one of the greatest careers NFL history, passing the 10,000-mark for receiving yards in just 140 games. He also has nine Pro Bowls, seven seasons in a row with more than 1,000 yards (an NFL record for a tight end), and three Super Bowls wins. In Super Bowl LVIII, Kelce and Patrick Mahomes officially passed the Pats'Gronk and Brady for most playoff TDs by a receiver/QB partnership. An amazingly durable playmaker with a larger-than-life personality, not to mention a hit podcast, Kelce's celebrity reached "New Heights" in 2023 when he started dating pop royalty Taylor Swift.

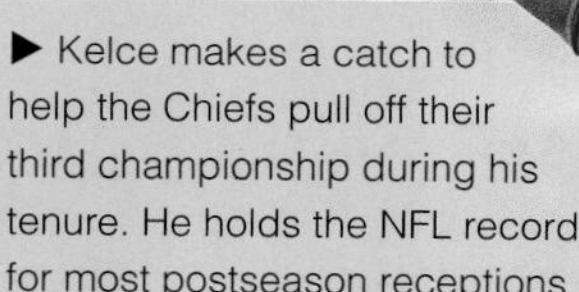

▶ Kelce makes a catch to help the Chiefs pull off their third championship during his tenure. He holds the NFL record for most postseason receptions.

▲ Witten receives the 2012 Walter Payton Man of the Year Award for community impact from the daughter of its legendary namesake.

JASON WITTEN

BORN 1982 • PRO: 2003–2020
RECEPTIONS: 1,228 • TDs: 74

Playing both TE and LB, Witten was one of the top high school players in Tennessee. He joined the Tennessee Volunteers to play D, but the coach wanted him on the other side of the ball. The reluctant receiver would go on to become one of the NFL's greatest as a hulking, hard-working iron man who hardly ever missed a game. The 11-time Pro Bowler spent most of his illustrious career with the Dallas Cowboys, where he still holds a host of franchise records, including most receiving yards (12,977) and most games played (255). Witten is also known for his philanthropy. His work with programs that tackle childhood obesity and domestic violence, as well as fund community building projects, saw him honored with the prestigious Walter Payton NFL Man of the Year Award in 2012. After his 2021 retirement, he took up coaching his son's high school team.

SHANNON SHARPE

BORN 1968 • PRO: 1990–2003 • RECEPTIONS: 815 • TDs: 62

A poor kid from smalltown Georgia, Sharpe had trouble getting noticed by NFL scouts in spite of being an offensive powerhouse for Division II Savannah State University. Most teams thought he was too small to play TE, but when the Broncos took a chance on him in the seventh round he turned out to be one of the franchise's all-time greats. The versatile receiver claimed two championship titles with Denver and another during a stint with the Baltimore Ravens. Sharpe still holds the record for the most receiving yards in a game by a tight end—the 214 (plus two TDs) he put up in a 37–34 showdown against the Chiefs in 2002. The five-time All-Pro retired in 2003 as the top tight end in the game and the very first in NFL history to surpass 10,000 receiving yards. Soon after, he became a popular commentator and in 2011, a Hall-of-Famer.

▼ On the way to winning Super Bowl XXXV, Sharpe bagged the longest offensive play in Ravens' history at the AFC Championship, turning a dire 3rd & 18 into a 96-yard TD.

RUNNING BACKS

EMMITT SMITH

BORN 1969 • PRO: 1990–2004 • RUSHING YARDS: 18,355 • TDs: 175

At 5-foot-9, Smith didn't have your typical football stature, but that didn't stop him from becoming a superstar in one of the sport's hardest-wearing positions. Even as a high school player, Smith was picked as one of the country's top prospects. Drafted out of University of Florida, he left with 58 school records. NFL teams worried he didn't have the strength or speed to survive in the league. Instead, he became its all-time leading rusher, known for eking out extra yards when the defense had counted him down. Smith played most of his career with the Cowboys where he was a key weapon for the dominant offense that won three Super Bowls in four years from 1992–1995. In Dallas, he went 11 straight seasons with 1,000+ rushing yards (his highest was 1,773), plus caught 486 passes for 11 touchdowns. Smith showed off his athletic grace to new audiences when he won Dancing with the Stars in 2006. He was inducted into the Hall of Fame in 2010.

▶ In 1993, Smith was named NFL MVP as the league's top rusher and the Super Bowl MVP after winning his second title with Dallas.

CHRISTIAN MCCAFFREY

BORN 1996 • PRO: 2017–PRESENT
RUSHING YARDS: 6,185 • TDs: 81

In 2015, this Stanford All-American passed Barry Sanders' NCAA record by notching 3,864 all-purpose yards in a single season from runs, receptions, and returns. The following year, McCaffrey was drafted by the Panthers, where he continued to excel as the ultimate "flex" player, equally ready for a handoff or a pass. In 2019, he recorded 1,000+ yards both on the ground and in the air for a league-leading 2,392 yards of offense that saw him named first team All-Pro in two positions. Carolina made him the highest paid back in history in 2020 with a four-year contract worth $64 million before trading him to the 49ers. McCaffrey was the NFL Offensive Player of the Year in 2023 with 21 TDs. He also made his first Super Bowl appearance in an overtime loss to the Chiefs.

▲ McCaffrey was named MVP of the 2016 Rose Bowl after racking up a record 368 all-purpose yards during the game.

BARRY SANDERS

BORN 1968 • PRO: 1989–1998
RUSHING YARDS: 15,269 • TDs: 109

This Kansas kid won the Heisman his junior year at Oklahoma State after setting the NCAA's single-season rushing record with 2,628 yards, contributing a jaw-dropping average of 295.5 yards of offense per game. Picked #3 overall in the 1989 draft by the Lions, he lit up Ford Field with his electrifying runs. In fact, during his decade in Detroit, Sanders never had a season with less than 1,000 rushing yards as he danced, spun, and changed direction mid-stride to evade tackles and find gaps. In 1997, he won the NFL MVP after becoming the third back in history to top 2,000 in a season. A "humble superstar," he wasn't one to celebrate touchdowns. He just handed the ball to the ref and got back to work. Sanders joined the Pro Football Hall of Fame in the Class of 2004.

◀ Sanders was named All-Pro and to the Pro Bowl every single year he was in the NFL and mysteriously retired while still in his prime.

FACT FILE

The 49ers' RB Joe Perry became the first African American player to be named NFL MVP in 1954 after he led the league in rushing yards for two seasons straight.

WALTER PAYTON

1953–1999 • PRO: 1975–1987

RUSHING YARDS: 16,726 • TDs: 125

▶ The NFL's prestigious Man of Year Award was named after Payton following his death from a rare liver disease at the age of 46.

Payton was nicknamed "Sweetness," but his motto on the field was "Never Die Easy." Defenders double- and triple-teamed him as he faked them out with stutter steps, pinballed off would-be tacklers, and leapt right over them into the end zone. A one-franchise player, Payton was drafted by Chicago with the fourth overall pick in 1975 and stuck with the Bears his entire career, only missing one game in 13 seasons. Payton had left Jackson State with 3,563 rushing yards and an NCAA record 464 points. He kept those numbers up in the pros, with 77 games rushing for more than 100 yards and 10 seasons rushing for more than 1,000 yards. He was named NFL MVP in 1977, when he ran for a record 1,852 yards, including 275 in a single game against division rivals, the Vikings. In 1985, the eight-time All-Pro helped his beloved Bears win their very first Super Bowl title.

▲ LT throws a "stiff arm" to ward off a would-be tackler. He was famous for his superhuman ability to evade defenders.

DERRICK HENRY

BORN 1994 • PRO: 2016–PRESENT

RUSHING YARDS: 9,502 • TDS: 93

This hulking back was dubbed "King Henry" before he even left high school. One of the top recruits in the country after a senior year in Florida with a mind-blowing 4,261 rushing yards, Henry committed to Alabama for college. During his junior year, he topped 2,000 yards and led the NCAA in points scored, winning his team the national championship title and himself the Heisman Trophy. He became a starter three years into his tenure with the Titans, leading the league in rushing yards and touchdowns in 2019 and 2020 and getting the nod as the 2020 Offensive Player of the Year. With super speed and strength, the 6-foot-3, 247-pound Henry has a genius for breaking tackles and racking up yards after contact—1,073 in 2020 alone. The four-time Pro-Bowler signed with Baltimore in 2024 to chase a Lombardi.

▶Henry rushes for a crucial 35-yard, fourth-quarter TD in the Titans' 22-21 win over the Chiefs in the 2018 AFC Wild Card Round.

LADAINIAN TOMLINSON

BORN 1979 • PRO: 2001–2011

RUSHING YARDS: 13,684 • TDs: 162

A basketball, baseball, and football player in high school, Tomlinson became "LT" the touchdown king in college at TCU where he set the NCAA record for most rushing yards in a game in 1999 with a 406-yard performance for six TDs. He was drafted by the Chargers #5 overall. Tomlinson was special as a relentless running back who could blaze down the open field, but he was also incredibly versatile. He had eight consecutive seasons in San Diego with more than 1,500 combined yards of offense (three topped 2,000). In one memorable win over the Raiders, LT ran, caught, and threw for a touchdown. In his finest year (2006), he won the NFL MVP by setting the single-season points record after scoring 31 rushing and receiving touchdowns. He was voted into the Pro Football Hall of Fame in 2017.

OFFENSIVE LINEMEN

▶ The ultra-tough Upshaw started 207 games in a row during the regular season, plus 24 postseason games.

GENE UPSHAW

GUARD • 1945–2008 • PRO: 1967–1981

This imposing 6-5, 255-pound lineman was snapped up by the Raiders in the first round of the first combined AFL-NFL draft of 1967. He'd played tackle, center, and end at Texas A&I, but Oakland made him a rookie starter at left guard—a position he'd play for 15 seasons. For eight of those seasons, Upshaw was named captain of the offense, enabling the bruising ground game that saw the Raiders win two Super Bowls (XI and XV) in the 1970s. Upshaw especially loved to "sweep" linebackers for outside running plays. The 7-time Pro Bowler also made his mark off the field as a rep for, then president of the players' union, the NFLPA. In 1983, he became the union's first African American executive director, helping to usher in the era of "free agency" in the NFL where players can sign with any team they want after their rookie contract expires. He was enshrined in Canton in 1987.

▲ Hannah's no.73 was retired by the Patriots in 1990, and he was named to the NFL's 100th Anniversary All-Time Team in 2019.

TRENT WILLIAMS

TACKLE • BORN 1988 • PRO: 2010–PRESENT

A massive talent who's been to the Pro Bowl nearly every single year he's played in the NFL, Williams got his start as guard at Longview High School in Texas. He was recruited by Oklahoma, forming a key part of a Sooners offense that only allowed 11 sacks all season in 2008 while scoring a record 702 points. Washington picked him fourth overall in the 2010 draft. His teammates picked him as captain the following year. In 2019, Williams missed a season due to a life-threatening cancerous growth on his head. He asked to be traded after the health scare, starting with the 49ers in 2020, who made him the highest-paid lineman in football with a contract extension worth $136.06 million in 2021. He's proved worth the price tag, being named first-team All-Pro for three seasons straight and allowing ZERO sacks in a 2023 season that saw San Francisco go all the way to the Super Bowl.

JOHN HANNAH

GUARD • BORN 1951 • PRO: 1973–1985

Raised in a football family, Hannah's dad and two brothers were all lineman for Alabama. He was also a wrestler and shot putter, but he went pro in football, taken with the fourth overall pick by New England in the 1973 draft. He played all 13 seasons of his career with the Pats, becoming the franchise's first ever player inducted into the Pro Football Hall of Fame in 1991. Hannah was named All-Pro ten times, including seven first-team nods. Sports Illustrated even dubbed him "the best offensive lineman of all time" in 1981. An elite run blocker, he was the chief difference-maker on a 1978 offense that set the then-record for rushing yards in a season (3,165) despite having no 1000+-yard running backs in its ranks. Hannah retired in 1985, immediately after helping the Pats secure their very first AFC Championship title and trip to the Super Bowl (a loss to the Bears).

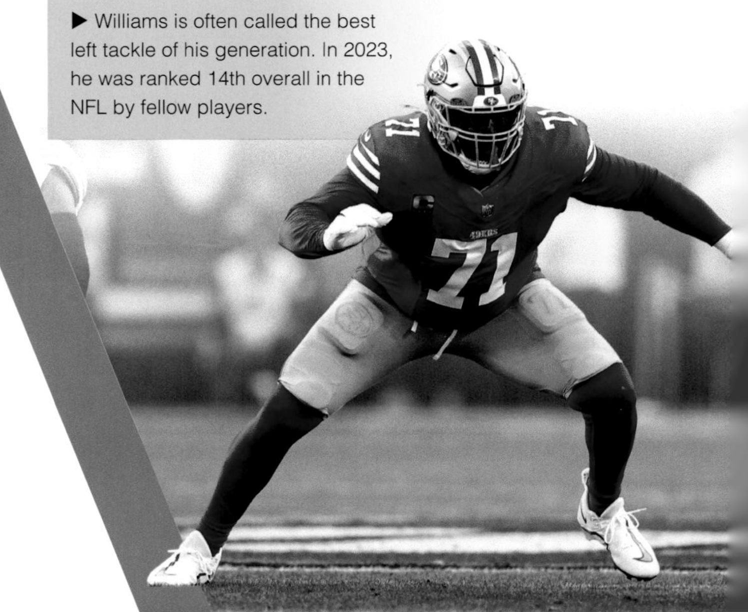

▶ Williams is often called the best left tackle of his generation. In 2023, he was ranked 14th overall in the NFL by fellow players.

JASON KELCE

CENTER • BORN 1987 • PRO: 2011–2023

Kelce was not even recruited to play football by any colleges, but he went on to become one of the greatest centers in the sport. He was a linebacker and running back in high school in Ohio, but the Cincinnati walk-on found his best position on the O-line for the Bearcats, helping them win two Big East Conference Championships. Though he was the fastest lineman in his year of the draft, Kelce wasn't scooped up until the sixth round. Still, he won the starting job at center during his rookie preseason with the Eagles and kept it for 13 years. Named first-team All-Pro six times, the stalwart snapper helped Philly win their very first Super Bowl (LII). Five years later, he lost the title game 38–35 to his brother Travis's team the Chiefs in a matchup dubbed the "Kelce Bowl." Today, the popular podcaster of New Heights fame is also an ESPN commentator.

▲ This legendary Bengals blocker is considered by many analysts to be the greatest offensive tackle in history.

▼ Kelce holds the franchise record for consecutive starts (156) and retired on a high, with three straight All-Pro seasons in a row.

ANTONY MUÑOZ

TACKLE • BORN 1958 • PRO: 1980–1992

When Muñoz was taken with the #3 overall pick in the 1980 draft, people saw it as a huge risk. The 6-foot-6 lineman had shown serious promise at USC, ending on a high with a Rose Bowl victory where his blocking allowed for a record 276 rushing yards, but it had also been racked with season-ending injuries. As it turned out, Cincinatti made a stellar bet—Muñoz not only proved to be an ironman in the pros, missing only three games in his 12 seasons with the Bengals, he also consistently put in performances that saw him named the top lineman in the league season after season. The 11-time All-Pro and 11-time Pro-Bowler was also handy as a surprise receiver, catching four touchdown passes over the course of his career. A year before his retirement due to injuries, Muñoz was named the NFL Man of the Year. In 1998, he became the first Bengal enshrined in the Pro Football Hall of Fame.

BRUCE MATTHEWS

GUARD, CENTER, TACKLE • BORN 1961 • PRO: 1983–2001

This versatile lineman started at five different positions in the pros but always with one franchise. Matthews was drafted by the Houston Oilers out of USC where he won the Morris Trophy for the top lineman in the Pac-10. He would stay with the team for an amazing 19 seasons, moving with the franchise to Tennessee in 1997 and never missing a game due to injury. His 293 career starts for a single team is an NFL record. Besides playing wherever he was needed on the O-line, Matthews also served as the long snapper for special teams. At age 37, he went to and lost his first Super Bowl. At age 40, he finally retired, with 14 Pro Bowl selections to his name. In 2007, he became the first Tennessee Titan to join the ranks of the Pro Hall of Fame. He was named as one of the Top 100 players in the league's first 100 years for NFL's 100th Anniversary.

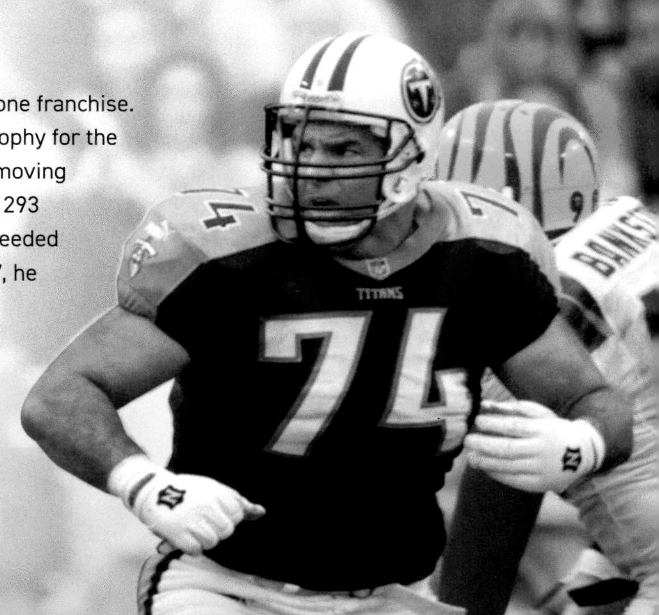

▶ Matthews was named first-team All-Pro seven times. The Titans named him to their Ring of Honor and retired the No. 74 jersey in 2002.

DEFENSIVE LINEMEN

DEACON JONES

END • 1938–2013 • PRO: 1961–1974 • SACKS: 173.5

To many, Jones was the NFL's "Secretary of Defense." Born David Jones, he gave himself the more memorable name Deacon and proceeded to have an unforgettable career. Jones earned a football scholarship to South Carolina State, then lost it after a year for attending a civil rights protest. A scout chanced to see him playing for Mississippi Vocational College, and he was picked up by the L.A. Rams in the 16th round of the draft in 1961. Speedy and strong, Jones was the All-Pro defensive end on the left who anchored one of the best D-lines in league history, the "Fearsome Foursome." He was an extaordinary pass rusher, credited with three seasons where he topped 20 sacks, not to mention, with coining the term "sack." Today, the award for the league leader in sacks is named after the Hall-of-Fame end.

▲ Jones was twice named the NFL's Defensive Player of the Year (1967, 1968). He was also a blues singer and actor.

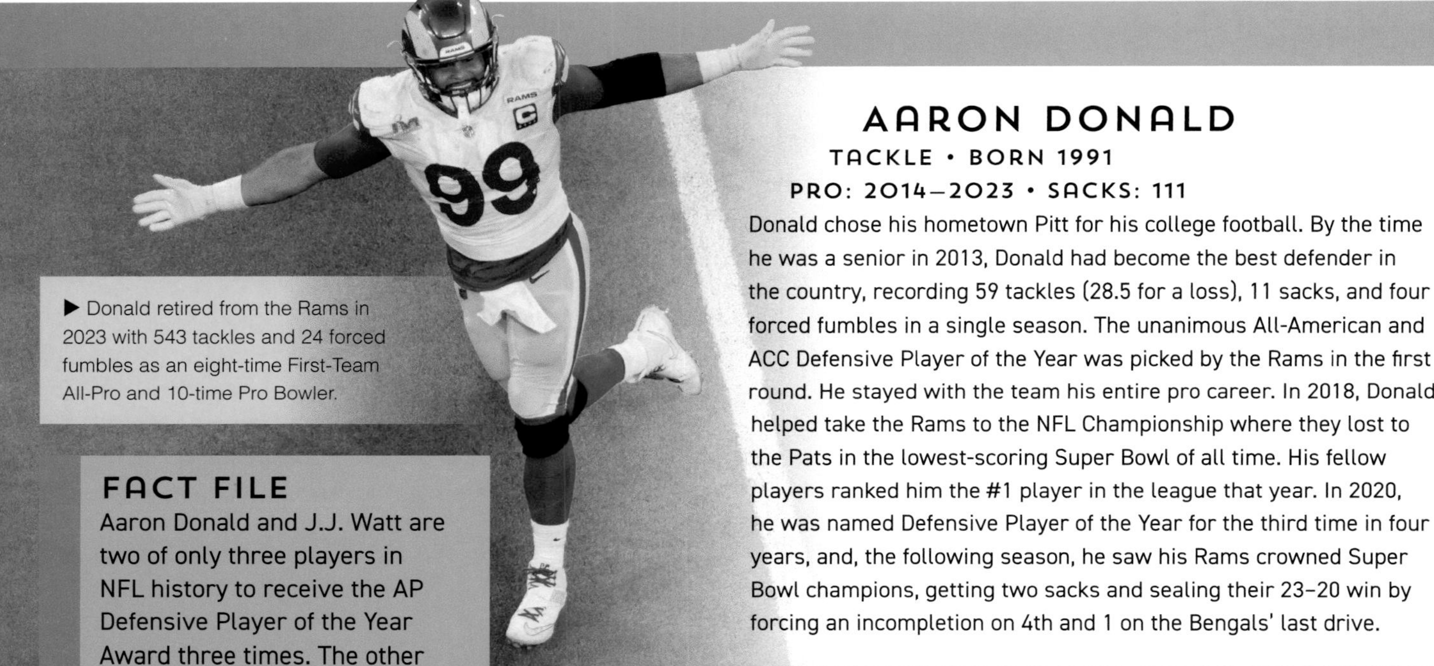

▶ Donald retired from the Rams in 2023 with 543 tackles and 24 forced fumbles as an eight-time First-Team All-Pro and 10-time Pro Bowler.

AARON DONALD

TACKLE • BORN 1991

PRO: 2014–2023 • SACKS: 111

Donald chose his hometown Pitt for his college football. By the time he was a senior in 2013, Donald had become the best defender in the country, recording 59 tackles (28.5 for a loss), 11 sacks, and four forced fumbles in a single season. The unanimous All-American and ACC Defensive Player of the Year was picked by the Rams in the first round. He stayed with the team his entire pro career. In 2018, Donald helped take the Rams to the NFL Championship where they lost to the Pats in the lowest-scoring Super Bowl of all time. His fellow players ranked him the #1 player in the league that year. In 2020, he was named Defensive Player of the Year for the third time in four years, and, the following season, he saw his Rams crowned Super Bowl champions, getting two sacks and sealing their 23–20 win by forcing an incompletion on 4th and 1 on the Bengals' last drive.

FACT FILE

Aaron Donald and J.J. Watt are two of only three players in NFL history to receive the AP Defensive Player of the Year Award three times. The other is Giants' LB Lawrence Taylor.

J.J. WATT

END • BORN 1989 • PRO: 2011–2022 • SACKS: 114.5

Watt started his college career as a tight end at Central Michigan, but when he left to become a walk-on at Wisconsin, he found his calling as an end on the defense instead. He declared for the draft after being named the Badgers' MVP his junior year and was picked in the first round by the Texans. He made five tackles and one fumble recovery in his first outing with the team, helping the franchise make its postseason debut. He got his first NFL Defensive Player of the Year award in 2012 after a stunning 20.5-sack season. The Texans made him the highest-paid non-QB in the league in 2014, and he rewarded them by being the league's top defender two years in a row—even scoring five TDs! He faced injury setbacks in 2017, but the Walter Payton Man of the Year shone off the field, raising millions of dollars in relief for victims of Hurricane Harvey in Texas.

▶ Watt sacks QB Alex Smith. He had two seasons with 20+ sacks, which is an NFL record.

REGGIE WHITE

END • 1961–2004 • PRO: 1985–2000 • SACKS: 198

White retired from the NFL as the league's all-time leader in sacks, having gone to the Pro Bowl and gotten the nod as an All-Pro in 13 of his 15 seasons. White impressed in college as an All-American out of Tennessee. After graduating, he stayed in his home state to play for the Memphis Showboats in the briefly-lived USFL before being drafted by the Eagles. Staying in Philly for eight years, he set the franchise record for most sacks in a season (21) during the 1987 strike-shortened season that had only 12 games! He signed with the Packers once he became a free agent, playing six seasons in Green Bay. His standout three-sack performance in Super Bowl XXXI, including the game-clinching tackle, capped a monster season that saw him earn his second NFL Defensive Player of the Year title. White died in 2004 at the age 43 from a heart irregularity. The Volunteers, Eagles, and Packers all paid tribute to the "Minister of Defense" by retiring his #92 jersey.

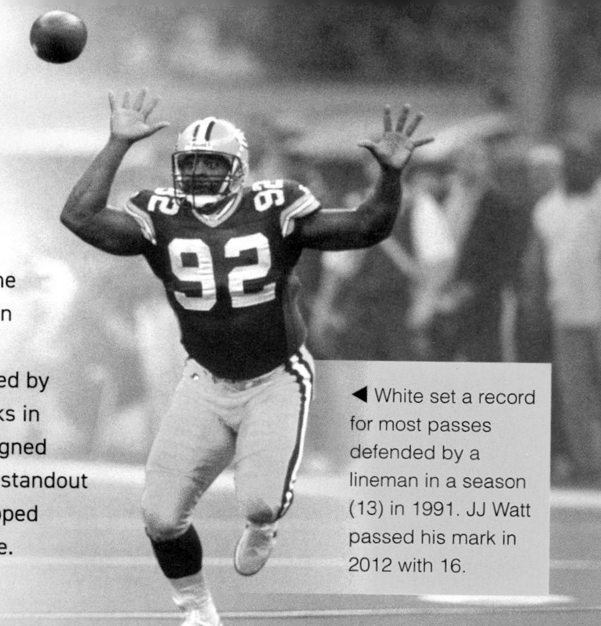

◀ White set a record for most passes defended by a lineman in a season (13) in 1991. JJ Watt passed his mark in 2012 with 16.

BRUCE SMITH

END • BORN 1963 • PRO: 1985–2003 • SACKS: 200

Smith was known as "the Sack Man" at Virginia Tech and with good reason. The elite end led the NCAA with 22 sacks his junior year and came away with the Outland Trophy for the nation's top lineman as a senior. The Bills snapped him up with the #1 overall pick in the draft. By his fifth season with the franchise, this quarterback's nightmare had already become the team's all-time sack leader with 51. He'd leave the Bills with 171, a franchise record that's not likely to be beat. He also left Buffalo with a legacy of four AFC Championship titles, 11 Pro Bowl and All-Pro selections, and two NFL Defensive Player of the Year awards. Smith signed with Washington for his last four seasons, passing Reggie White as the NFL's all-time sack leader in Week 14 of his last season, in a 20–7 win over the Giants. He retired after 19 seasons, having posted 10+ sacks in 13 of those.

▼ Smith has a staggering 1,224 career tackles and 43 forced fumbles. A shoo-in for Canton, he was admitted to the Hall of Fame in 2009.

▲ The 49ers took Bosa with the #2 overall pick in 2019. In 2023, they made him the highest-paid defender in the NFL with a $170 million contract.

NICK BOSA

END • BORN 1997

PRO: 2019–PRESENT • SACKS: 53.5

Florida-born Bosa hails from a pro football family, with a dad who played DE for the Dolphins and brother Joey who plays LB for the Chargers, not to mention an uncle, cousin, great uncle, and grandfather who were also in the NFL. No surprise then that Bosa was a five-star recruit out of high school at the storied St. Thomas Aquinas. He was nabbed by the Ohio State Buckeyes where he wowed in his sophomore year, being named to the All-Big-Ten Team, but sat out his junior season after undergoing core muscle surgery. Nevertheless, he was a top prospect when he declared for the draft in 2019. Since then, he's starred as the centerpiece of San Francisco's formidable D that has seen them crowned NFC Champs twice in five years. A three-time Pro Bowler, in 2022, he was selected as first-team All-Pro and named NFL Defensive Player of the Year after topping the league with 18.5 sacks for a loss of 138 yards.

LINEBACKERS

CHUCK BEDNARIK

1925–2015 • PRO: 1949–1962

A decorated US Army pilot in World War II, Bednarik returned home to become a legendary two-way player in the NFL. He proved himself as an All-America center at Penn before the Eagles took him #1 overall in the draft. The future Hall-of-Famer continued to be a "60-minute man" at Philly, blocking for running backs as a center then stopping them dead in their tracks as a linebacker. He was named an All-NFL LB eight times, the last coming in 1960, when he saved the NFL Championship title for the Eagles by keeping the Packers' Jim Taylor from scoring the game-winning TD.

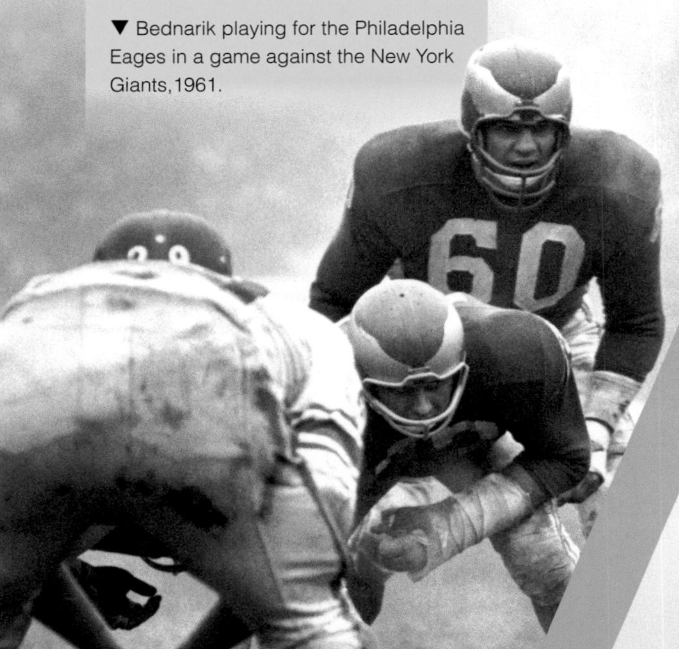

▼ Bednarik playing for the Philadelphia Eages in a game against the New York Giants, 1961.

NFL DEFENSIVE RECORDS

MOST INTERCEPTIONS
Paul Krause, safety—81 (1964–1979)

MOST FUMBLES FORCED
Robert Mathis, LB—54 (2003–2016)

MOST SACKS
Bruce Smith, end—200 (1985–2003)

MOST SOLO TACKLES
Ray Lewis, LB—1,568 (1996–2012)

MOST PASSES DEFENDED
Champ Bailey, CB—203 (1999–2013)

JUNIOR SEAU

BORN 1969 • PRO: 1990–2009
TACKLES: 1,847

Drafted with the #5 overall pick out of USC, Seau quickly became the Chargers' top tackler. Known for his passion and leadership, the nine-time All-Pro became the face of the Bolts during his 13 seasons there and was named as the team's MVP six times. He notched 16 huge tackles in the 1994 AFC Championship to help secure the Chargers' first and only conference title. The superstar LB did stints with Miami and New England, retiring after 20 years in the pros. Seau died by suicide in 2012. The tragedy raised awareness about the effects of chronic concussions in contact sports after researchers found he was likely suffering from a brain condition called CTE that is common in NFL players and can cause depression and dementia. In 2015, Seau became the first Samoan player enshrined in the Hall of Fame.

RAY LEWIS

BORN 1975 • PRO: 1996–2012 TACKLES: 2,059

The NFL record holder for most tackles (2,059) and most solo tackles (1,568), Lewis played for the Ravens his entire 17-year career in the pros. The Miami Hurricanes' leading tackler was drafted by the Ravens during their very first season in Baltimore. He would go on to define their emergence as one of the league's most competitive franchises. He was named AFC Defensive Player of the Week after clocking seven tackles in his debut game as a rookie and never slowed down from there. He topped the league in tackles three seasons, was named NFL Defensive Player of the Year twice, got 10 All-Pro nods, and went to 13 Pro Bowls. In 2000, he played a major part in earning the Ravens their first Lombardi, being named Super Bowl MVP with five tackles and four deflected passes in a total defensive shutout of the Giants. His bust was unveiled at Canton in 2018.

▶ In 2000, Lewis led a record-breaking Raven defense that only allowed 165 points and under 1,000 rushing yards all season.

DICK BUTKUS

1942–2023 • PRO: 1965–1973 • TACKLES: 1,020

The namesake of the annual awards given to the top linebackers in the NCAA and NFL, Butkus is a legend of the position. Growing up in the South Side of Chicago, Butkus played running back and linebacker. He was so dominant on D, he made 70% of the tackles for his high school team. After impressing for three years at Illinois, where Sports News named the All-American their Player of the Year in 1964, Butkus was drafted by his hometown team, the Bears. In the pros, he picked up where he had left off, making it to the Pro Bowl his rookie season, plus the next seven in a row. One of the most feared players in the league, Hall-of-Fame defender Deacon Smith described him as a "stone maniac" on the field, where he played each game as if it was his last. Unfortunately, his last came sooner than expected when a knee injury forced him to retire after nine seasons. He was inducted into the Hall of Fame in 1979.

▲ Smith was named MVP of the 2018 SEC Championship as well as of the 2018 Rose Bowl, one of best bowls in history.

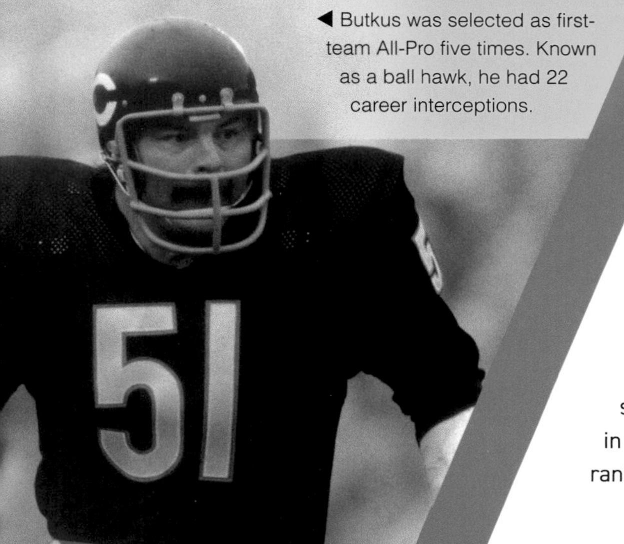

◀ Butkus was selected as first-team All-Pro five times. Known as a ball hawk, he had 22 career interceptions.

ROQUAN SMITH

BORN 1997 • PRO: 2018–PRESENT
TACKLES: 851

Smith stuck to his home state of Georgia to play college football. He became the first Bulldog to be awarded the Butkus Award for best linebacker in the NCAA after his breakout junior season where he racked up 137 tackles and was named SEC Defensive Player of the Year. After being picked by the Bears in the first round, Smith grew into a top tackler at Chicago, getting 163 tackles in 2021. He topped that stat by six in 2022 after asking to be traded to Baltimore and earning his first first-team All-Pro selection. As a Raven, Smith has won two more Butkus Awards as the top linebacker in the league as well as two Pro Bowl selections. In 2023, he became only the second Raven to record 20+ tackles in a single game—the other was Hall-of-Famer Ray Lewis. Today, he's the top-ranked and highest-paid LB in the league.

DERRICK BROOKS

BORN 1973 • PRO: 1995–2008 • TACKLES: 1,715

Brooks began playing football as a safety before his coaches at FSU switched him to outside linebacker. Though he was "undersized" for the position at 210 pounds, he more than made up for it with his speed and instincts. He came away from the Seminoles as a two-time All-American and National Champion. Taken in the first round by Tampa Bay, Brooks became the lynchpin of their famous "Tampa 2" defense. During his 14 seasons with the Bucs, he turn the longtime losers into serious playoff contenders, making the postseason in half his years there. In 2002, he also saw the Bucs win their first Super Bowl as he put in a career-best performance to be crowned the NFL Defensive Player of the Year. His 2002 stats included four interceptions returned for TDs, foreshadowing his memorable 44-yard pick six against the Raiders in Super Bowl XXXVII.

▶ Brooks led the league in solo tackles three times, finishing his Hall-of-Fame career with nine All-Pro and 11 Pro Bowl selections.

CORNERBACKS

DICK LANE

1928–2002 • PRO: 1952–1965 • INTERCEPTIONS: 68

"There is nothing I hate worse than a first down," said Dick "Night Train" Lane, a DB famous for derailing drives down the field. Lane had a tough start in Austin, Texas, where he was found discarded in a dumpster as an infant. He took many odd jobs to help support his adoptive family, playing basketball and football whenever he could. Lane was working in a Los Angeles aircraft factory after a stint in the Army when he asked for a try-out with the Rams. He blew the coaches away from his first scrimmage. Lane's 1952 rookie outing—during which he set the single-season NFL record for interceptions with 14 picks in just 12 games, including 298 return yards and two touchdowns—is generally considered to be one of the greatest regular-season performances in the history of the game. He'd go on to play 14 seasons, gaining a rep as one of the league's most intimidating tacklers.

▲ Lane spent most of his career with the Cardinals and the Lions, going to seven Pro Bowls. He had appendicitis for the one in 1962 but still managed to make an inception and block an extra point.

CHARLES WOODSON

BORN 1976 • PRO: 1998–2015

SOLO TACKLES: 981 • INTERCEPTIONS: 65

Woodson started his winning ways early. In high school, the then-running back rushed for more than 2,000 yards and was named Ohio's "Mr. Football" following a 230-point senior season. Recruited by Michigan as a CB, he got national attention as a game-changing playmaker, eventually beating out Peyton Manning to become the first and only defensive player to take The Heisman Trophy. Woodson had eight impressive seasons for the Raiders, but a 2006 move to the Packers upped his production even more. In 2009—11 seasons into his career—he won NFL Defensive Player of the Year, clocking a stunning 74 tackles, nine interceptions, four forced fumbles, two sacks, and three defensive TDs. The following year, Woodson was the Pack's defensive powerhouse and beating heart for a campaign that saw them crowned NFL champions. The nine-time Pro Bowler and eight-time All-Pro forced 33 fumbles and is tied for most defensive touchdowns (13). He entered the Hall of Fame in Canton in 2021.

▲ As a rookie, Gardner got 75 tackles and topped the league in passes defended (20).

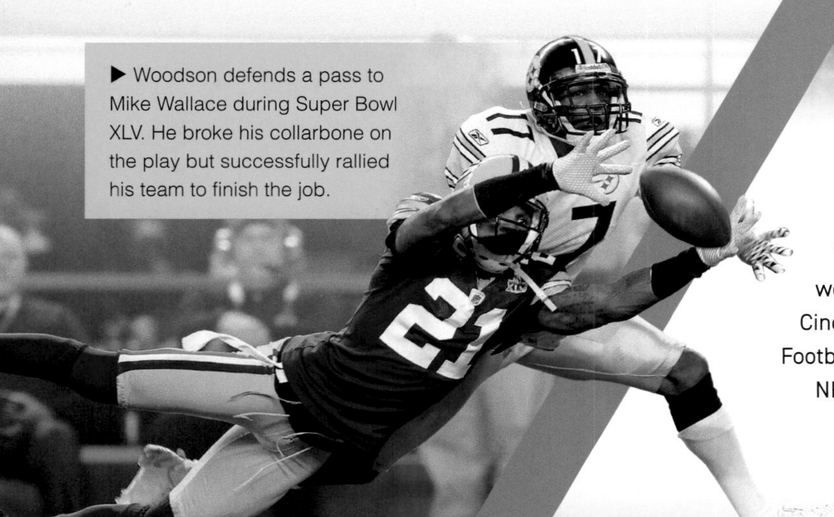

▶ Woodson defends a pass to Mike Wallace during Super Bowl XLV. He broke his collarbone on the play but successfully rallied his team to finish the job.

SAUCE GARDNER

BORN 2000 • PRO: 2022–PRESENT

SOLO TACKLES: 92 • INTERCEPTIONS: 2

Picked fourth overall in the 2022 draft by the Jets, Ahmad "Sauce" Gardner lived up to the hype. In high school, he'd wowed at both wideout and cornerback. At University of Cincinnati, he'd helped his team reach the ultra-competitive College Football Playoff. His debut season as a pro saw him named not only NFL Defensive Rookie of the Year but also first-team All-Pro as the best cornerback in the league—the first rookie CB to get the nod in four decades. Playing as No. 1, Gardner is so good at man-to-man coverage, QBs rarely target him. When they do, a tackle or deflection almost always awaits.

CHAMP BAILEY

BORN 1978 • PRO: 1999–2013

SOLO TACKLES: 812 • INTERCEPTIONS: 52

In Georgia's thrilling 35–33 victory in the 1998 Peach Bowl, Bailey starred for the Bulldogs as a wideout, kick returner, and cornerback. He was picked seventh in the draft by the Redskins where he intercepted three passes in a single game his rookie season. Even so, it wasn't until his 2004 trade to Denver that Bailey really began to shine, going four seasons in a row as first-team All-Pro. He retired as an undeniable Hall-of-Famer with a massive 908 tackles and 203 passes defended—the most in league history. He still holds the record for most Pro Bowls for a defensive back, invited in all but two years of his epic 14-year career.

▲ Sanders won his second Super Bowl with the Dallas Cowboys, where he signed a seven-year contract in 1995 that made him the NFL's highest-paid defender.

▼ Bailey deflects a pass to wideout Hines Ward in a 2006 win over the Steelers.

DEION SANDERS

BORN 1967 • PRO: 1989–2005

SOLO TACKLES: 270 • INTERCEPTIONS: 53

An outstanding all-around athlete out of Florida State, Sanders made his mark in both the NFL (where he was named first-team All-Pro six times) and in Major League Baseball. In fact, he's the only pro to hit a homer and score a TD in the same week. He would retire with 22 touchdowns—the first was scored on a punt return during his 1989 debut with the Falcons. In an exceptional 1994 season with the 49ers, the "shutdown corner" was voted Defensive Player of the Year and sealed his first Super Bowl win with a fourth-quarter interception in the end zone. Today, the retired great is getting accolades for his play-calling. Sports Illustrated named Coach Sanders Sportsman of the Year in 2023.

▲ Revis and his bronze bust were added to the Pro Football Hall of Fame in Canton, Ohio, in 2023.

DARRELLE REVIS

BORN 1985 • PRO: 2007–2017

SOLO TACKLES: 408 • INTERCEPTIONS: 29

This standout high school player picked his local D1 Pitt for college. As a Panther, Revis made one of the year's most memorable plays in 2006, with an electrifying 73-yard punt return for a touchdown in the annual Backyard Brawl against rivals WVU. The Jets traded up to get him at 14 in the draft. He had his career-best season in 2009, leading a Jets' secondary that only gave up eight TD passes the entire season. Revis helped take the team to the AFC Championship with a miraculous interception that bounced off a WR's shoe. They didn't make it to the Super Bowl that year, but he later won one during a single season with the Pats. A monster man-to-man defender, the four-time All-Pro neutralized star wideouts and made the ratings of opposing QBs plummet. Any receiver unlucky enough to be in his zone most often got stranded on "Revis Island."

SAFETIES

ED REED

BORN 1978 • PRO: 2002–2012

TACKLES: 643 • INTERCEPTIONS: 64

On a Ravens team known for steely defense, Reed was the ultimate ball hawk. His senior year at University of Miami, he had three defensive TDs and the most interceptions in the country, leading the Hurricanes to a national championship title. At Baltimore, he had eight All-Pro selections and nine Pro Bowls. He was named NFL Defensive Player of the Year in 2004 after a season with a career-high nine interceptions for 358 yards. Reed help the Ravens develop into regular playoff contenders. When they made it all the way to the Big Game his final season, he didn't squander the opportunity, finishing with five solo tackles, a deflected pass, and an interception to help seal their 34–31 win. Reed holds the NFL records for the two longest inception returns, plus the most overall return yards (1,590).

◀ In a 2008 game against the Eagles, Reed picked off a pass on second-and-goal play, breaking tackles to take it all the way back to his own end zone. At 107 yards, his classic pick-six is the longest interception return in NFL history.

▲ Krause drops back into coverage. The Vikings called him their "center fielder" since he was an All-American college baseball player and they frequently had him as their deepest defender with no one to assist.

PAUL KRAUSE

BORN 1942 • PRO: 1964–1979

INTERCEPTIONS: 81

The all-time NFL leader in interceptions, Krause picked the ball 81 times for 1,185 return yards and three touchdowns during his 16 seasons with the Redskins and Vikings. He'd been a two-way player in college. His speed, height, and receiver credentials helped him lead the league with a remarkable dozen interceptions his rookie season at Washington. Though he never matched that again, he remained a fearsome free safety, helping the Vikings reach four Super Bowls during his tenure. He passed his fellow Iowa alum Emlen Tunnell's interception record in his final season and was inducted into the Pro Football Hall of Fame in 1998.

RONNIE LOTT

BORN 1959 • PRO: 1981–1994

TACKLES: 1,146 • INTERCEPTIONS: 63

Lott was a national champion as a cornerback at USC, and he kept up his winning streak in the NFL, notching four Super Bowl victories with the 49ers. When a crushed little finger forced the hard-hitter to move to the safety position in 1985, he only got better, going first-team All-Pro for six straight seasons and twice leading the league in steals. Playing for the 49ers, Raiders, and Jets, he made more than 1,000 tackles.

▶ A versatile and disruptive defender, Lott was voted to the Pro Bowl 10 times for three different positions.

TROY POLAMALU

BORN 1981 • PRO: 2003–2014

TACKLES: 783 • INTERCEPTIONS: 32

This explosive strong safety's luscious locks brought shampoo companies knocking for endorsements while his speed, versatility, and unpredictability kept offenses guessing. Polamalu played his entire pro career with the Pittsburgh Steelers, who drafted him in the first round as an All-American out of USC. In 2008, he helped the Steelers D top the league in points and passing yards allowed during a stellar season that was capped off with his second championship title. Polamalu had a monster game in the preceding AFC Championship against division rivals the Ravens, making four tackles, defending two passes, and returning an interception for a 40-yard TD. Two years later, the eight-time Pro Bowler was named both NFL Defensive Player of the Year for his dominance on the field and Walter Payton Man of the Year for his service off of it. He was voted into Canton on his first ballot in 2020.

▶ Polamalu retired with 583 solo tackles, 107 passes defended, 14 forced fumbles, and 12 sacks.

▲ Tunnel went to nine Pro Bowls and was named to the NFL 100th Anniversary All-Time Team.

EMLEN TUNNELL

1924–1975 • PRO: 1948–1961

INTERCEPTIONS: 79

In 1948, this Coast Guard alum hitchhiked his way to a try-out at New York Polo Grounds and into football history. "Emlen the Gremlin" was the first African American player signed to the Giants and in 1967 would also be the first enshrined in the Pro Hall of Fame. He'd played halfback in college at Iowa, leading the team in offensive yards, and his rushing and receiving skills stuck with him as a defender and punt returner, gaining serious ground for his team. In his 10 seasons with the Giants, Tunnell was picked as first-team All-Pro six times and twice lead the league in punt return yards. He retired with two championships (1956 with the Giants and 1961 with the Packers) and 1,282 interception return yards.

MINKAH FITZPATRICK

BORN 1996 • PRO: 2018–PRESENT

TACKLES: 512 • INTERCEPTIONS: 19

One of the top-rated high school recruits in the nation, Fitzpatrick chose to roll with the Crimson Tide for college. He bagged two national titles with Alabama while setting records at the storied football school for the longest interception return for a TD (100 yards) and the most career pick-sixes (four). Fitzpatrick pushed to play corner, but the Dolphins drafted him as a free safety, and he's excelled in the role at Miami and Pittsburgh, scoring five pick-sixes, being named first-team All-Pro three times, and representing the AFC in four Pro Bowls. Fitzpatrick lives by the belief that "the better man you are, the better ball player you will be," and, in 2024, he was recognized for his impact on and off the field with the Bart Starr Award.

▶ At Bama, Fitzpatrick won the top honors for a college defender—the Jim Thorpe and Chuck Bednarik Awards.

KICKERS AND PUNTERS

SHANE LECHLER

BORN 1976 • PRO: 2000–2017 • PUNT AVERAGE: 47.6 YARDS

At Texas A&M, Lechler impressed as a punter, holder, and placekicker who could even throw a game-winning touchdown pass off a faked kick. The only punter drafted in his class, Lechler would go on to spend 18 seasons in the pros with the Raiders and Texans, amassing 68,676 career punting yards—the second most in NFL history—and the highest career punting average for any retired punter. At Oakland, he went on a 33-game streak with at least one punt of 50+ yards, and, in one memorable game, sent a punt flying 80 yards—well over the head of the Bears' Hall-of-Fame returner Devin Hester—to preserve the Raiders' fourth quarter lead. He was invited to the Pro Bowl seven times, was named first-team All-Pro six times, made the NFL 100th Anniversary All-Time Team, and took home the Golden Toe Award in 2009.

◀ Lechler led the NFL in punting yards four times, including his last season when the 41-year-old had 92 punts for 4,507 yards.

YALE LARY

1930–2017 • PRO: 1952–1964 • PUNT AVERAGE: 44.3 YARDS

A major weapon on a dominant Detroit Lions team that won the franchise three championship titles in the 1950s, Lary was an amazing all-around athlete. At Texas A&M, he was a football, basketball, and baseball star. Besides clocking 22,279 punting yards as a pro, Lary was a league-leading kick returner, even taking three punts back for touchdowns. He was also stellar on defense, making 50 interceptions as a safety that he returned for 787 yards. As a punter, Lary could boot the ball more than 70 yards and was renowned for his hang time. Often, the ball took so long to come down, the D had plenty of time to charge down the field and squash the other side's hopes for a return. In fact, he once had a hot streak of 32 punts in a row with zero returns. Lary was inducted into the Hall of Fame in 1979.

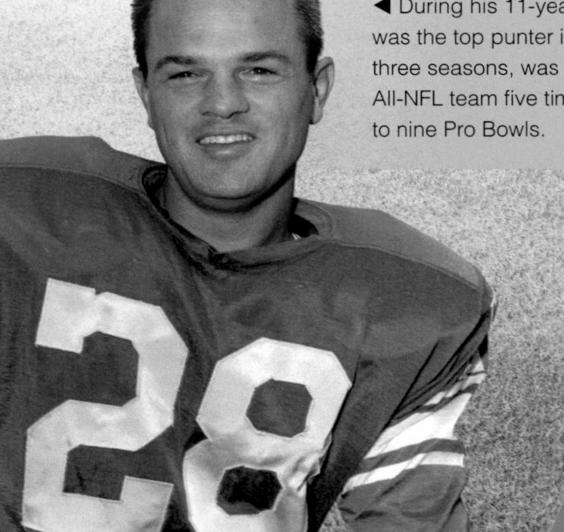

◀ During his 11-year pro career, Lary was the top punter in the league for three seasons, was named to the All-NFL team five times, and went to nine Pro Bowls.

ADAM VINATIERI

BORN 1972 • PRO: 1996–2019

FGs: 599

This undrafted free agent out of South Dakota found a home with the Patriots, playing a decade at New England before racking up 14 more seasons with the Colts. Competing for two championship-winning franchises, Vinatieri proved he had the cool to placekick many a clutch FG. Memorably, he even proved he had the cool to put in a couple of the coldest field goals—scoring off two crucial kicks made during a blizzard in an AFC divisional playoff win that led the Pats to their very first league title in Super Bowl XXXVI... where he also booted in the game-winner as the clock wound down. When he retired, a month before turning 47, he left the game with raft of records. To this day, he tops the NFL for FGs made and points scored period, with a whopping 2,673.

▶The definition of a clutch player, Vinatieri holds the record for most postseason points (238) and most seasons with 100+ points (21).

RAY GUY

1949–2022 • PRO: 1973–1986

PUNT AVERAGE: 42.4 YARDS

This guy was such an exceptional talent, he was the first punter to be taken in the first round of the NFL draft after impressing on special teams at Southern Miss. Guy stuck with the Raiders his entire career, helping to win the franchise three championships in Super Bowls XI, XV, and XVIII. His monster punts went so high, rivals suspected he'd pumped his footballs up with helium and he once famously hit the TV screen that hangs from the roof of Louisiana's Superdome. Guy retired with 44,493 punting yards under his belt. He became the first punter inducted in the Pro Football Hall of Fame in 2014 and still holds the record for most postseason punts (111).

◀ Guy was reknowned for the accuracy of his punts, regularly pinning the return team back behind their own 20-yard line.

NFL KICKING RECORDS

LONGEST FIELD GOAL
Justin Tucker, 66 yards (Sept 26, 2021)

MOST FIELD GOALS MADE
Adam Vinatieri, 599 (1996–2019)

HIGHEST FIELD-GOAL PERCENTAGE
Justin Tucker, 90.2% (2012–present)

LONGEST PUNT
Steve O'Neal, 98 yards (Sept 21, 1969)

MOST PUNTS INSIDE THE OPPONENTS' 20
Jeff Feagles, 554 (1988–2009)

HIGHEST CAREER PUNT AVERAGE
Shane Lechler, 47.6 yards (2000–2017)

◀ Morten was a two-time Golden Toe winner and seven-time All-Pro selection, but his longevity was the most impressive thing in his career. He scored in 360 consecutive games.

GARY ANDERSON

BORN 1959 • PRO: 1982–2004 • FGs: 538

Anderson grew up in South Africa, dreaming of playing pro soccer like his dad. But when he moved to the US with his family at age 18, he found that his mean rugby drop-kick made him a perfect prospect for football stardom. Never having played the game, he won a football scholarship to Syracuse where he played soccer and football before signing with Pittsburgh after graduating. He was a Steeler for 13 years and is still the team's all-time top scorer with 1,343 points. Over Anderson's 22 years in the pros, he played for five teams and went to four Pro Bowls. While with the Vikings, at the age of 39, he became the first kicker to have a perfect regular season. For all of 1998, he never missed a kick, going 35 for 35 on FGs and 59 for 59 on extra points.

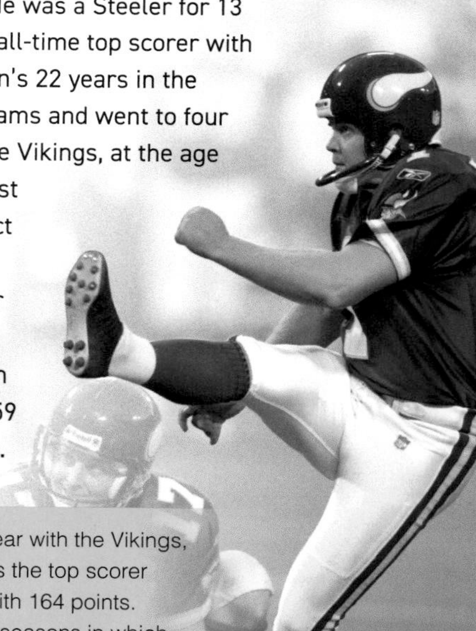

▶ In his first year with the Vikings, Anderson was the top scorer in the NFL with 164 points. He had 14 seasons in which he scored 100 or more.

MORTEN ANDERSEN

BORN 1960 • PRO: 1982–2007 • FGs: 565

One of the NFL's all-time leading scorers with 2,544 points, this placekicker graced the league for an epic 25 years, playing more regular-season games than any other pro in history (382). Andersen was born in Denmark and grew up doing gymnastics, track, and soccer. He discovered football as an exchange student in Indianapolis. It turned out he had such a formidable left leg, the "Great Dane" was recruited by Michigan State University, where he booted in the longest FG in the Big Ten—a 63-yarder. Playing the bulk of his career with the New Orleans Saints and Atlanta Falcons, Andersen scored in nearly every game he played, kicking in an insane 103 game-winning field goals. His output was so reliable, he was dubbed "Mr. Automatic." Even at age 46, he had a five-FG game against Arizona, matching his career best for the ninth time. No wonder he's one of two kickers to make the Hall of Fame.

Ray Flaherty
Coach
End
Len Ford
Defensive End
1948-49 Los Angeles Dons (AAFC) 1950-57 Cleveland Browns 1958 Green Bay Packers

SNAPSHOT

THE GREATEST EVER TO PLAY THE GAME

The Pro Football Hall of Fame was opened in 1963 in Canton, Ohio. The NFL picked the small Midwestern city of 70,000 as the site because it was where the NFL was founded in 1920. The city's team at the time, the Canton Bulldogs, were a dominant force in the early pro game, winning the first two NFL championships. The Hall of Fame was established to preserve the history of the sport and honor its most exceptional pro players. Anyone can nominate a player to be considered for inclusion in the Hall, but a committee of 50, including sports media representives from each city with an NFL franchise, decides which nominees will get in each year. Finalists must get at least 80 percent backing from the expert committee to be voted in. Players become eligible for the "ballot" five years after they retire from the NFL, and only the best of the best are voted in on their first ballot. Four to nine inductees are selected each year on the Saturday before the Super Bowl and inducted in an "enshrinement ceremony" that officially kicks off the new NFL season.

◀ Sculptors make bronze busts of every inductee, which are displayed inside the Pro Football Hall of Fame as a durable tribute to league legends. As of 2024, the Hall has enshrined 378 players, coaches, owners, and workers from the NFL's 100-year history.

▼ Giants defensive end Michael Strahan stands next to his bronze bust after it was revealed in the induction ceremony for the Pro Football Hall of Fame Class of 2014. Each inductee is gifted a gold jacket.

GET A GAMEPLAN

Winning a football game requires a lot of advanced planning and knowledge not only of the sport but of your specific opponent. The plays a team will use and the formations they'll take, the players who'll start and which roles they'll perform all require meticulous preparation so that players can execute under pressure on the day. Each coach will map out strategies for a matchup that they think will give their team the best chance of success—then game day will put them to the test.

▲ Coaches and players watch "tape" in preparation for games. They study video of their last game to see where they can make improvements and video of their next opponent to familiarize themselves with the plays and schemes.

GOING ON THE OFFENSIVE

When it comes to gaining yards, teams can do it through the air or on the ground. Hence, there are two typical types of play in football—a pass and a run. A passing play has a bigger chance of gaining more yards but also carries a greater risk of a turnover or negative play (that is, one that results in a loss of yards), while a run is often a little safer, but you likely won't gain as much yardage. The head coach will draw up a gameplan based on the strengths and weaknesses of his opponents that features a balance of both play types. For instance, if you're facing a team that has struggled to stop the run all season, then it makes sense to commit to your running backs and focus on exploiting that weakness.

▲ Tech that uses VR (virtual reality) and AI (artificial intelligence) are increasingly being used to assess players and give them more practice "reps" (repetitions of plays) without risk of injury. The latest versions allow players to play a virtual version of a matchup in advance of the actual game, improving response times.

OPTIONS, OPTIONS

There are lots of variations on the basic plays, which keep the defense guessing. A "play-action" pass starts out like a run play, but the quarterback will sometimes fake handing the ball off, drop back, and throw to a receiver. These plays are really handy to keep the opposition on their toes. If you're successful running the ball, defenders are more likely to "bite" on the fake, which creates space for receivers to catch the pass. Similarly, an "option" play gives the QB multiple options as to how move forward based on what the defense is doing.

◀ The QB fakes a handoff before dropping back for a pass.

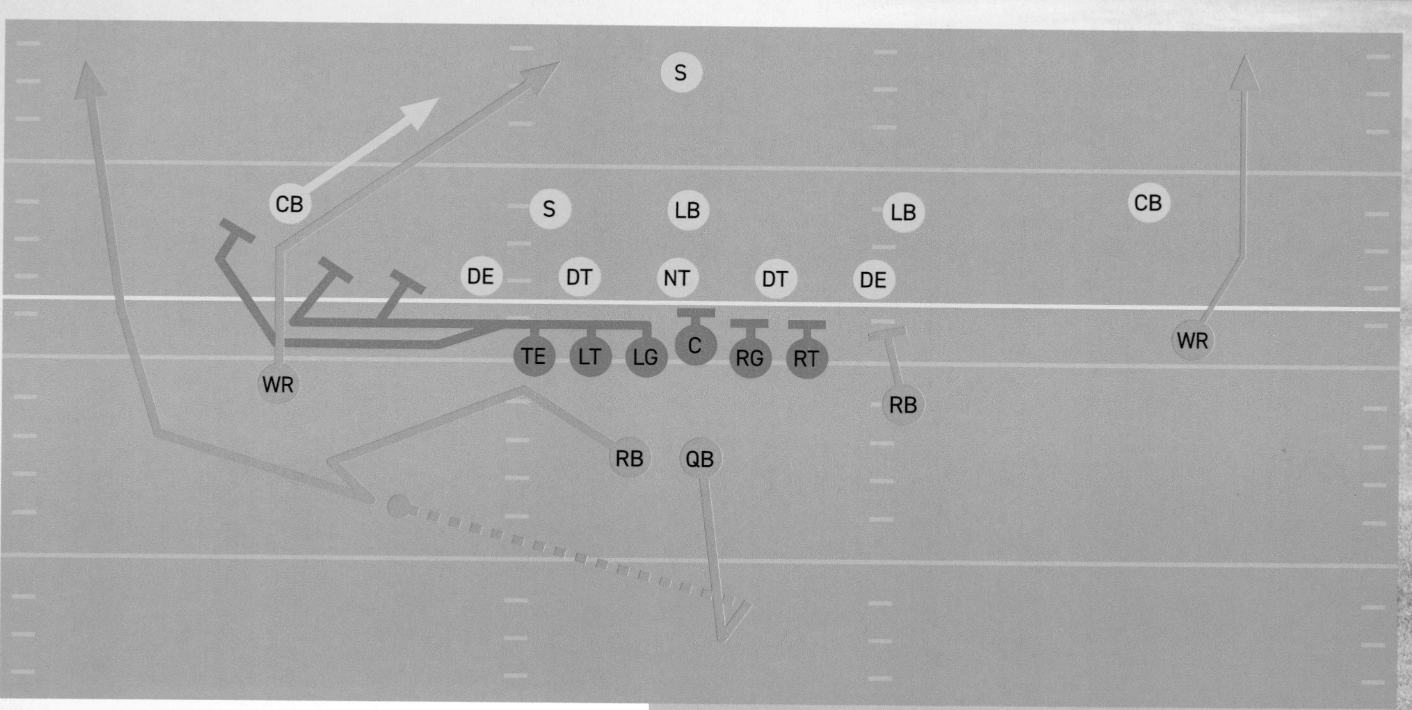

▲ Diagram for a sample screen pass play, with a running back as the receiver.

FACT FILE

The NFL has become much more pass-oriented in recent years. All 32 teams chose more than 50% passing plays during the 2023 season. The Commanders had the highest percentage—66% of their plays were through the air.

◀ Washington QB Sam Howell looks to pass.

SCREENS

In a "screen pass" play, the QB throws a lateral (that is, a pass parallel to or in a backward direction from the line of scrimmage) to a running back or receiver while the rest of the offensive line and receivers effectively act as blockers. It stretches the defense horizontally and forces players to protect the shorter areas of the field, which could later open up deep passing looks if executed correctly!

OFFENSIVE SCHEMES AND TACTICS

All coaches have "playbooks" that are basically a collection of plays to use during a game. Each coach will have a different idea of what they want their team to do given the talent they have and deploy different "schemes" to make it a reality.

SCHEMES

SPREAD

The clue is in the name for this one. The basis of a "spread" offense is to use 3+ wide receivers in order to spread the defense out and open up space for rushers or receivers.

▲ A peek at the playbook of coach Dick Vermeil, showing variations of the same play and the calls associated with them.

AIR-RAID

Popularized by offensive coordinator Kliff Kingsbury in recent years, this scheme focuses heavily on launching the ball deep down the field and passing much more frequently. It's one of the most exciting offenses to watch in action, but it needs real quarterback talent to be successful.

WEST COAST

Spearheaded by the legendary 49ers coach Bill Walsh and still popular today, the "West Coast" offense focuses on running the ball and making shorter gains through the air to wear down the defense so that they're thrown off guard when the QB suddenly pitches one deep.

▶ Running an option offense, the Navy Midshipmen line up for a play with three RBs in the backfield, all of whom could field a fake or real handoff.

OPTION

These offenses are really fun! We know what option plays are, but what about double and triple option? These plays often give the quarterback a decision to run, pass, or hand it off. Chip Kelly's Oregon team was a real pioneer of the modern-day "RPO" (run-pass option), while Army and Navy run almost nothing but these fancy option plays with up to three players running past the quarterback after the snap to create misdirection.

◀ The 49ers have taken the West Coast one step further in recent years under Kyle Shanahan by creating a ton of misdirection before the snap and relying on the speed of players like wideout Deebo Samuel (pictured) to maximize yards after the catch.

GAMEDAY TECHNIQUES

MOTION

There are two types of defensive coverage: man and zone. "Man" implies that each defender is responsible for one offensive player and will mark him accordingly. Zone gives defenders a small area of space to cover. Because these coverages are hard to read before the ball is snapped, you'll often see a receiver or RB move from one end of the line of scrimmage to the other before the snap. If a player follows them, this tells the quarterback that it's a "man coverage" play. If they go unfollowed, it's zone. Finding out that information can be critical, and you'll often see quarterbacks change the play after watching a defense react to pre-snap motion.

▲ A receiver is put in motion before the snap to sniff out the defensive coverage.

AUDIBLE

If a quarterback sees something they don't like, they'll call an "audible." This changes the play at the line of scrimmage from the one that was originally called.

► QB Peyton Manning was the king of audibles, famous for barking signals before the snap. His signature "Omaha!!" was a well-known mystery during his career.

HARD COUNT

Ever wonder what quarterbacks are saying before the snap? It's fun to impersonate by shouting "BLUEEE 49," but it also serves a purpose. The offense responds to the "cadence" of the QB, and key words are folded into these small speeches to tell the offense what to do. The ball is snapped on a certain word, which is why opposing fans make noise to try and disrupt the offense's timing and ability to hear the QB!

CLOCK MANAGEMENT

One of the biggest elements in offensive strategy is controlling the clock. If the ball-carrier is tackled but maintains possession, the clock keeps going. If they're sent out of bounds, the ball is dropped, or a pass falls incomplete, it stops. If you're leading, you often want to take as much time as you can on offensive drives. Winning offenses will run the ball heavily in the fourth quarter to drain the clock and leave their opponents with minimal time to try to score.

TIMEOUTS

One way teams control the clock is by using timeouts. Each team has three timeouts per half, which can stop the game at any point. They're sometimes used to change a play if a coach has seen a massive mismatch or even as a psychological weapon when a coach calls one right before the snap on a field goal attempt to try to "ice" the kicker into missing. However, most often they're saved as a way to control the crucial minutes at the end of each half. If your team is down 27–23 with two minutes to go, having timeouts allows you to stop the clock after a play without the ball-carrier going out of bounds, enabling running plays or passes down the middle of the field when the defense is anticipating a toss to the sideline. Defenses use timeouts for the inverse effect. If the offense is trying to drain the clock, freezing it on a crucial third down could make a huge difference if they're able to make the stop.

◄ A QB calls a timeout to stop the clock between plays, giving the offense more time to complete the drive.

DEFENSIVE PLAYS

If it's the offense's job to move the ball, it is the defense's to stop them. Much like the offense, the defense uses different formations and schemes to try and outmaneuver their opponents. The two core concepts are "man" (one-on-one coverage) and "zone" (covering a specific area of the field). Each type of defense has its own arsenal of plays that coordinators then turn into schemes.

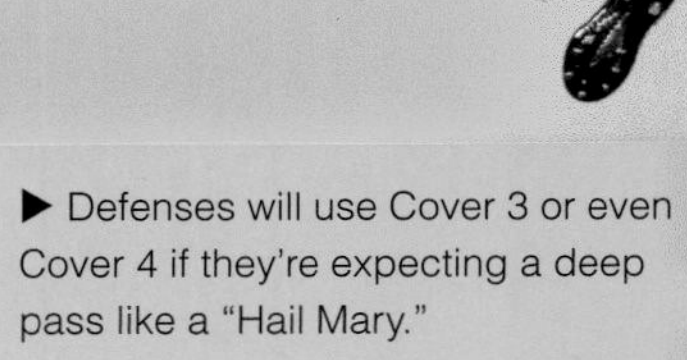

▶ Defenses will use Cover 3 or even Cover 4 if they're expecting a deep pass like a "Hail Mary."

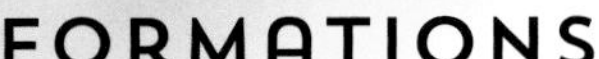

FORMATIONS

A coach's preference of formation depends on what kind of defense they want to run. If they want to pressure the quarterback and force negative plays, a 4-3 might be the call. But if they want to focus on preventing those big plays at the expense of constant pressure, a 3-4 is more suited. In the modern game, we often see hybrid defenses that switch it up to do a little bit of everything. This versatility allows the defensive coordinator to be more responsive in their play-calling and keeps the offense of their toes. The most important variables in any formation are the alignments of the defensive front and the "shell," which is how the secondary lines up.

THE FRONT

4-3

This formation consists of four defensive linemen and three linebackers. It's designed to be more aggressive because you have four players opposite the offensive line to generate pressure and three linebackers behind on clean-up duty. While 4-3 defenses are often associated with blitzing and big plays, they are often susceptible to giving up deep passes.

3-4

The 3-4 sees a "nose tackle" and two other linemen on the front with four linebackers in support. Teams who use this style of defense are often better at defending the pass due to the extra bulk and typically use better athletes to travel sideline-to-sideline in coverage, cutting off rushing lanes and deeper passes.

THE SHELL

Defensive plays are often based on how the secondary is set up since it allows the linebackers and D-line to work freely. A way to denote the coverage is to look at the number of safeties, which can vary from zero to three depending on the play.

A "COVER 2"

would imply there are two safeties in the defensive backfield. One might sit a little lower than the other, acting as a middle-man between the middle and deeper sections of the field.

A "COVER 3"

means that there are three deep defensive backs and is naturally more conservative. It is good at shutting down running lanes and often used when teams are expecting a deep pass.

"COVER 0/1"

plays also exist, but these aren't as aggressive as you might think. If you're only going to roll out one safety, the chances are that your cornerbacks are going to work over the top to funnel plays into areas of high traffic and almost act as extra safeties.

NICKEL

With the emergence of slot receivers, who line up between the wideouts and O-line, teams will often deploy an extra cornerback in place of a linebacker, known as a slot or nickel—making for five defensive backs. A "dime" defense goes a step further to add six defensive backs to disrupt obvious passing plays.

KEY DEFENSIVE TERMS

BLITZ

A type of play that sends as much pressure as possible. Often all defensive linemen and a linebacker or two—sometimes even a cornerback or safety—will storm the backfield in hopes of throwing off the play or sacking the quarterback.

TWIST/STUNT

This is when two defensive linemen switch places after the ball is snapped in order to confuse the O-line and try to open space.

INTERCEPTION/PASS BREAKUP

When a defender catches a pass intended for a receiver, it's called an interception and gives the defense possession wherever the interceptor gets tackled. A pass breakup is when the ball is swatted out of reach of the receiver so that nobody catches it, causing an "incompletion" and loss of down.

SACK / TACKLE FOR LOSS

A sack is when a quarterback with the ball is tackled behind the line of scrimmage while a tackle for loss is a tackle of any other ball-carrier behind the line of scrimmage.

FUMBLE

When an offensive player drops the ball. A "forced fumble" is when this drop is due to the impact of a defensive player. A fumbled ball is still "live," which means the defense has a chance to scoop it up and claim possession for their team.

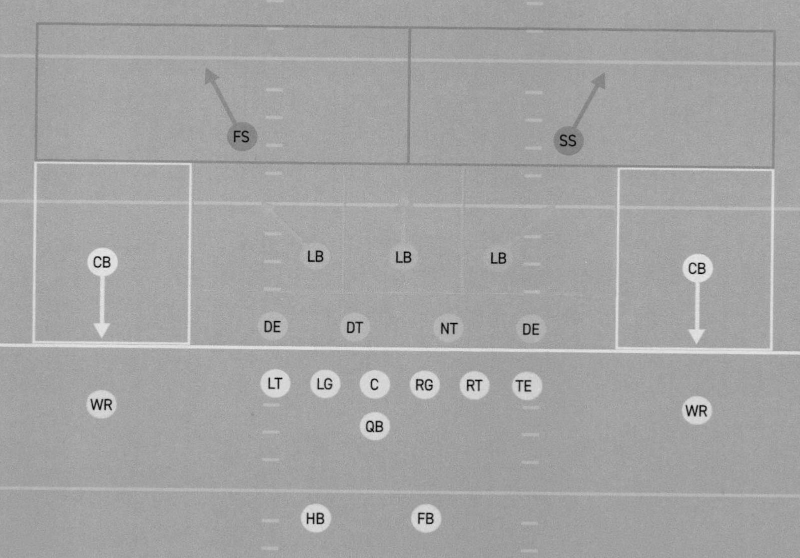

▲ An example of a 4–3 Zone Cover 2 defense, with boxes showing the zones for each player to cover while the front four pass rush.

▲ Safety Antoine Winfield Jr. makes an interception while covering a wide receiver.

▼ Defenders will try to "strip" the ball when making a tackle to create a turnover. Colts LB Robert Mathis holds the record for the most forced fumbles (52).

FAKES AND TRICK PLAYS

When the stakes are high or they have nothing to lose, you'll often see coaches take extraordinary measures to try to give their team the advantage or get them back in the game. They'll draw up fakes and tricks or "gadget plays" that attempt to catch their opponents off guard. These strategic stunts can seriously backfire, but, when they work, they can be stunningly effective and memorable. They make football thrilling to watch!

MISDIRECTION

Many offensive plays have fakes built into them, including reverse passes and motion. The 49ers do a great job of this by sometimes having two players run in opposite directions across the line of scrimmage, with the quarterback then having the option to "fake" a handoff to one and pitch to the other, creating a total mirage for the defense.

▶ The most memorable pass in Super Bowl XL wasn't made by a QB. WR Antwaan Randle El pulled off a 43-yard completion for a touchdown after QB Ben Roethlisberger tossed the ball to an RB who handed it to El on the reverse. The misdirection worked and gave the Steelers an unassailable lead.

THE FLEA FLICKER

One of the most common trick plays is called a "flea flicker." This is when the quarterback passes laterally to a receiver or running back, who then launches it downfield to another receiver. The defense typically rushes the quarterback, leaving the receiver open for a high-risk, high-reward play. It's essentially a very risky play-action look, but one that can yield huge returns if a team pulls it off!

◀ In 2001, WR David Patten became one of three players in the Super Bowl era to complete the "triple crown," scoring a rushing, a receiving, and a passing TD in one game. He scored the last on a flea flicker, catching a lateral pass from his QB before launching the ball down the field to complete a 60-yard TD.

SPECIAL TEAMS SURPRISES

Coaches weigh the score, the clock, and their team's field position when making decisions about when to punt the ball away, attempt field goals, or risk turning over the ball on downs by going for it on fourth down. Sometimes, a coach will secretly go for it by calling a fake punt or kick. Instead of booting the ball, the kicker or punter will surprise the defense by making an unexpected pass. These classic trick plays surprise a defense with a calculated risk that sees the kicker or punter try to throw the ball.

FACT FILE

Bears iconic RB Walter Payton holds the record for the most touchdown passes by a non-QB with eight, including one in a narrow 23–19 playoff victory against Washington in 1984.

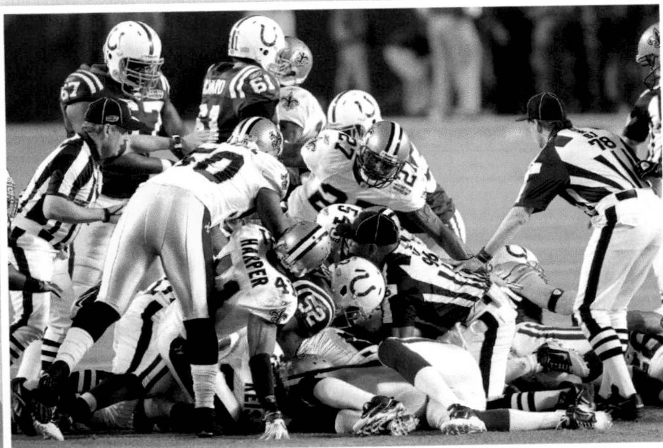

▲ Instead of kicking off to start the second half of Super Bowl XLIV, the Saints went for a surprise onside kick. The stunt paid off—not only did the Saints recover the ball, they went on to score on the ensuing drive and win the game!

▼ A QB in high school, All-Pro punter Johnny Hekker is a master of the fake punt. During his rookie season with the Rams in 2012, he pulled off two in one game against the 49ers, making a surprise pass to secure a first down and keep the drive going.

THE MUSIC CITY MIRACLE

One of the most iconic trick plays won Tennessee a 2000 wild card playoff game. With 16 seconds left on the clock, down by a single point to the Bills, the Titans went for a gadget on the kickoff return instead of trusting their fate to a "Hail Mary" pass. The kick was fielded by RB Lorenzo Neal, who handed the ball off to TE Frank Wycheck, who then made a lateral pass to WR Kevin Dyson. Dyson had never run the play before, but he ran the ball 75 yards to score the game-winning TD as the clock ran out.

◀ Dyson runs as fellow Titans line up to block for him, giving the Bills no chance.

THE COACH'S ROLE

Easily the most important position in the game, the head coach is at the heart of a team. Their decisions impact every single aspect of the game on and off the field. From helping make Draft Day decisions to picking the 53-man roster to managing players and staff, the coach lays the foundation for a franchise to build on.

▲ QB Kyler Murray gets one-on-one instruction from Cardinals head coach Jonathan Gannon during training.

FOOTBALL GENERALS

Besides their players, head coaches lead teams of coaches, often with 20+ staff members. There are offensive, defensive, and special teams coordinators and assistants; coaches for specific positions; strength and conditioning trainers; and statistical analysts who crunch the numbers to give their team the edge. It's not surprising that many top coaches have military backgrounds, since the organization of the military is similar to the structure of a football team. The head coach (HC) is like a general, their coaching staff are the officers, and their players the soldiers, preparing for a series of weekly battles. The head coach usually has control over personnel, supervises staff, oversees practice, sets the strategy and schemes, and always has the final say, but they trust many elements of training and game management to their staff.

GAME DAY

On game day, the head coach is responsible for game-planning, and most assume some kind of play-calling duty. They're the ones who call timeouts, throw challenge flags, adjust the game plan as needed, and make most of the key, split-second decisions in response to what is happening on the field throughout that 60-minute period. After the game, they face the press, then immediately analyze how their team did, reviewing the tape to see where they can make improvements for the next matchup.

▶ Long-time Saints head coach Sean Payton dials up a play from the sidelines, using a physical list of options. Coaches cover their mouths when calling plays to prevent spying, and many now use electronic playbooks. Some HCs delegate play-calling to their offensive coordinators while others prefer to do it themselves.

▶ Chargers coaching staff led by Brandon Staley look on to make sure their players are set up right for a crucial play.

COACHING ICONS

THE MASTER MOTIVATOR

Coaches set the culture for their teams. They may design stellar practice routines and game plans, but it'll all come to nothing if they cannot motivate their players to push themselves to the limit and buy into their vision. Vince Lombardi was such an incredible leader in this regard, the NFL Championship is now named after him. As he said, "Winning is not a sometime thing, it is an all the time thing." His smarts, charisma, and military background all helped him implement a strong work ethic in his team that allowed them get to the top and stay there. He preached sacrifice, grit, discipline, and togetherness so convincingly that his players were more than ready to "pay the price" for their success. The creative play-caller loved to use players outside their natural positions, which he could only pull off because his teams were so cohesive.

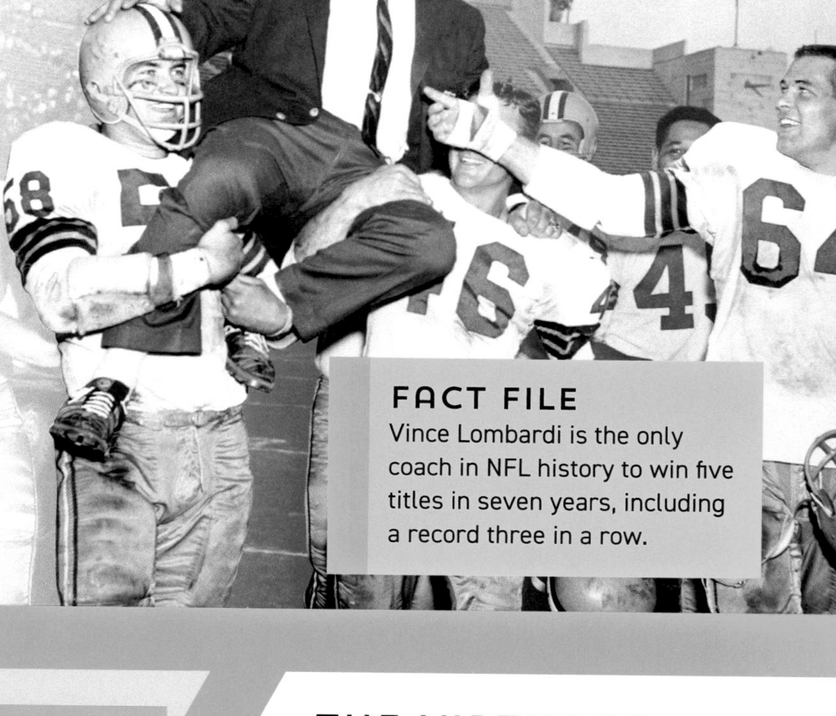

FACT FILE

Vince Lombardi is the only coach in NFL history to win five titles in seven years, including a record three in a row.

◀ Known for empathy, Noll comforts his star QB Terry Bradshaw on the bench during a game.

THE PLAYERS' COACH

Today's NFL owners value coaches who understand players and can see the game through their eyes. No one is better equipped to do that than former players. One of the greatest-ever players-turned-coach was Chuck Noll, a Cleveland Browns guard and linebacker who went on to coach the Steelers for 23 years (1969–1991). The architect of the Pittsburgh's infamous "Steel Curtain" defense, Noll brought the first titles to a franchise that had previously only made one playoff game in its 36-year history. He won four rings for them through a focus on drafting and a more personal and relatable sense of coaching.

THE VIRTUOSO TACTICIAN

Arguably the GOAT when it comes to football strategy, Bill Belichick transformed the Patriots into a dynasty and helped mold his overlooked and undersized QB Tom Brady into a title-winning machine. Granted the control of a general manager, Belichick led New England to 17 division titles and nine Super Bowls. His six NFL titles are the most of any coach in history. Belichick's teams had a buttoned-up mentality, but his military influences also made him a relentless strategist who spent hours scouting the opposition. If there was a weakness, Belichick would capitalize on it. If there was a strength, he'd reshuffle his team to take it away. He made the Pats into well-drilled shapeshifters who rarely lost their winning form.

◀ Belichick briefs his bench during a game. He left the Pats with a 333–178 overall record, notching a record 31 postseason wins.

COACHING GREATS

Meet some game-changing coaches with storied careers. These strategic geniuses and legendary leaders have given us some of the most dominant teams in the history of the game.

MIKE DITKA

BORN 1939 • RECORD: 127-101

NFL TITLES: 2

As a former all-time great on the field, Ditka's excellence off of it shocked very few. He started his playing career as a tight end with the Chicago Bears and would later spend a decade with them as a head coach after honing his craft on the Cowboys' coaching staff. Ditka won the Super Bowl in 1985, dismantling the Patriots in a blowout win with a team that's still referenced as one of the greatest in football history. A rampant rushing offense, led by the legendary Walter Payton, and a terrifying defense made them nearly impossible to beat. Ditka focused on solid blocking and tackling, figuring that if these basics were executed perfectly, the rest would follow...and it did. He made the playoffs in seven of his 10 seasons in Chicago while developing countless All-Pro level talents.

JOHN MADDEN

1936-2021 • RECORD: 112-39-7

NFL TITLES: 1

Long before he was the face of the videogame franchise EA Madden Football, he was a player and later a coach. Madden only won one Super Bowl during his lengthy run with the Raiders, but his regular-season coaching record of 103 wins and 32 losses speaks for itself, with the former lineman winning seven AFC West Championships and becoming the youngest-ever coach to notch 100 wins. Madden excelled in simplifying his philosophies for his team to understand—a trait that served him well after his coaching career when he became the voice of the NFL, too, as a famous gameday commentator.

ANDY REID

BORN 1958 • RECORD: 284-160-1

NFL TITLES: 3

Reid's legacy began with coaching the Eagles from 1999–2012, where he pioneered their West-Coast offense. He enjoyed plenty of success in Philly but was never able to win the Big Game despite so many close-calls. The ever-mustached "Big Red" landed in Kansas City in 2013, marking an upward trend for the Chiefs. When he began adding the likes of Travis Kelce and Patrick Mahomes to his roster, the rocket really started to launch. With the help of two generational talents, Reid turned the Chiefs into the first dynasty we've seen since the Patriots, winning three Super Bowls and eight consecutive AFC West championships. Reid's attention to detail, creative play-calling and teddy-bear personality have helped propel the Chiefs into the history books, and the most exciting part is, the best is likely still yet to come.

DON SHULA

BORN 1930 • RECORD: 347-173-6 • NFL TITLES: 2

The winningest head coach in NFL history, Shula spent most of his coaching career with the Dolphins. His "no-name" defense (so called because of the lack of star players on it) was one of the best the game has ever seen and perfectly summed up his coaching philosophy: he'd rather have players who bought into his system and were willing to work relentlessly every single day than proven talents. Nobody was bigger than the team, and that selflessness enabled him to move pieces around without much conflict. An unprecedented 26-year-stint in Miami saw him win two Super Bowls and record the league's only 100% perfect winning season on the books. In 33 years as a head coach, he had just TWO losing seasons—that's how good he was!

MIKE TOMLIN

BORN 1972 • RECORD: 181-110-2 • NFL TITLES: 1

According to Tomlin, "The standard is the standard." And the standard doesn't change, no matter the weather, the opponent, or the injuries on the roster. He worked his way up from a college WR coach to earn a coveted spot as the Steelers' leading man in 2007 (a franchise famous for long-term investment in coaches—they've had three in the last 55 years). Besides holding the record for the most winning seasons in a row at the start of his NFL career (17), Tomlin has brought his team to the playoffs 11 times and won a Super Bowl. While he's refreshingly flexible in his approach, you can be sure his teams will always bring the heat on defense.

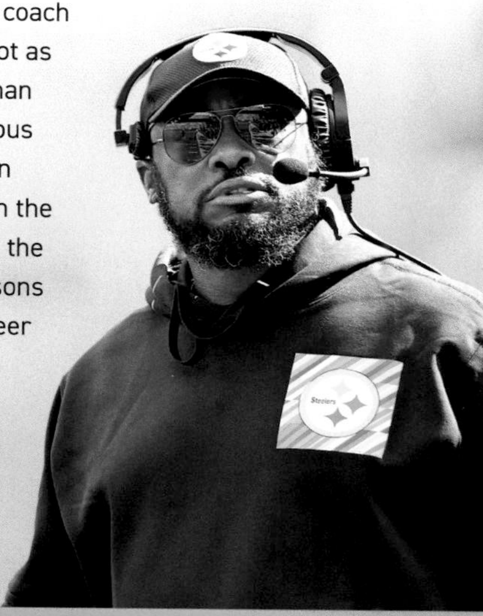

TONY DUNGY

BORN 1955 • RECORD: 148-79
NFL TITLES: 1

Another former player, Tony Dungy's coaching career somehow surpassed what he achieved on the field. His first head coaching role was with Tampa Bay in 1996, and he got right to work by installing his own version of a cover 2 defense, now commonly known as the "Tampa 2." Having played for the Steelers as a safety during their Golden era, he took a lot of those "Steel Curtain" principles and built them into his own scheme, and it worked wonders. Dungy led the Bucs to the playoffs in four of his six seasons there, but was fired in 2001 for not taking them further in the postseason. He did just that in his next job in Indianapolis, taking the Colts all the way to the promised land and beating the Chicago Bears in Super Bowl XLI to become the first ever African American head coach to win the Lombardi Trophy.

NICK SABAN

BORN 1951 • RECORD: 292-71-1 • NCAA TITLES: 7

The head coach at University of Alabama from 2007–2023, this legend of college football has won more national titles than any other coach (7) and NEVER had a losing season during his 28 years in the NCAA. Saban was a one-time Kent State defensive back working as a car salesman until he was hired as an assistant coach by his alma mater. After rising to fame at LSU with a 2004 BCS title, he spent two years in the NFL with Miami before returning to the college game. During his tenure at Bama, he coached four Heisman winners, won nine conference titles, and notched six national championships. He retired with an insane .804 winning percentage by focusing on "The Process," not the outcome.

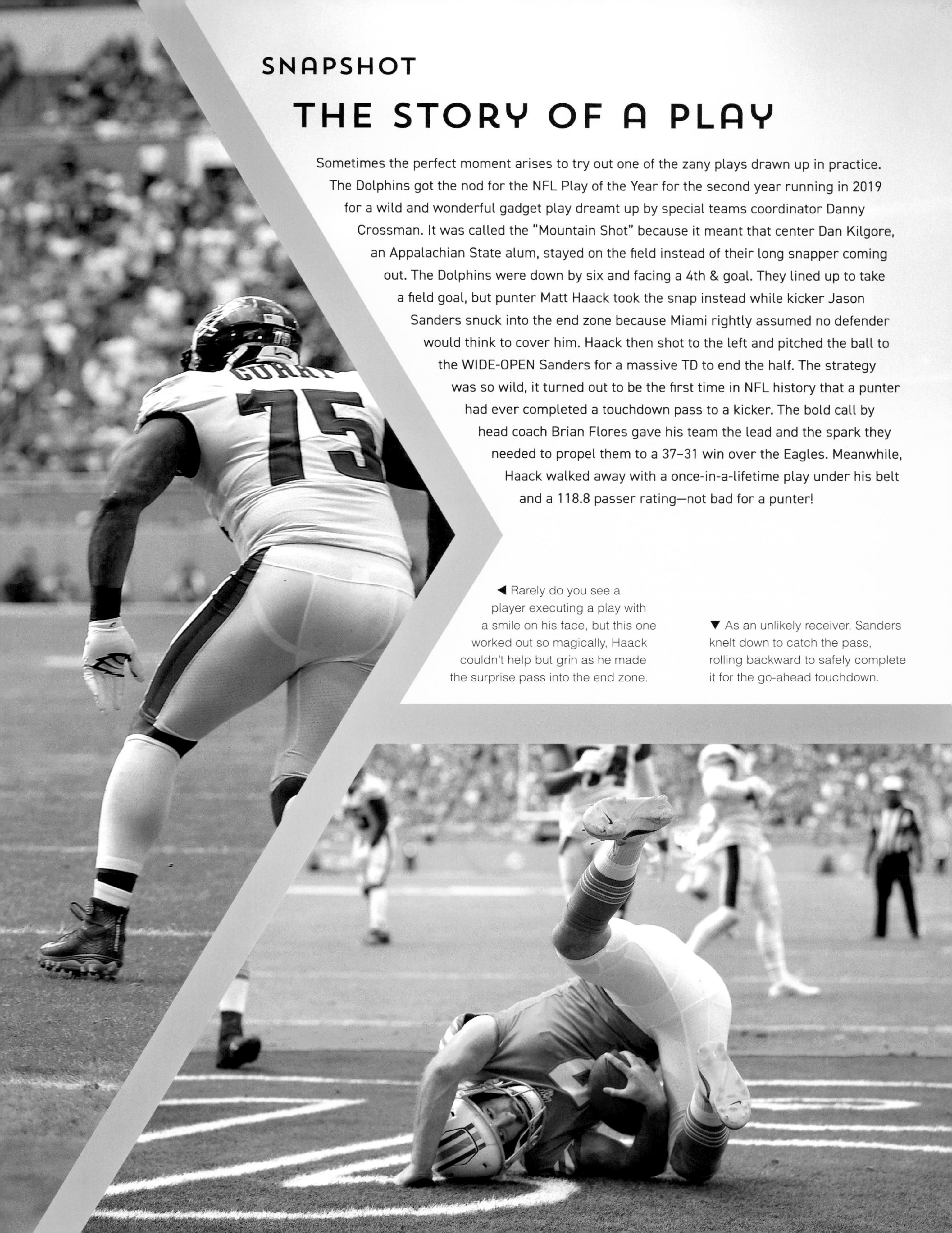

SNAPSHOT

THE STORY OF A PLAY

Sometimes the perfect moment arises to try out one of the zany plays drawn up in practice. The Dolphins got the nod for the NFL Play of the Year for the second year running in 2019 for a wild and wonderful gadget play dreamt up by special teams coordinator Danny Crossman. It was called the "Mountain Shot" because it meant that center Dan Kilgore, an Appalachian State alum, stayed on the field instead of their long snapper coming out. The Dolphins were down by six and facing a 4th & goal. They lined up to take a field goal, but punter Matt Haack took the snap instead while kicker Jason Sanders snuck into the end zone because Miami rightly assumed no defender would think to cover him. Haack then shot to the left and pitched the ball to the WIDE-OPEN Sanders for a massive TD to end the half. The strategy was so wild, it turned out to be the first time in NFL history that a punter had ever completed a touchdown pass to a kicker. The bold call by head coach Brian Flores gave his team the lead and the spark they needed to propel them to a 37–31 win over the Eagles. Meanwhile, Haack walked away with a once-in-a-lifetime play under his belt and a 118.8 passer rating—not bad for a punter!

◀ Rarely do you see a player executing a play with a smile on his face, but this one worked out so magically, Haack couldn't help but grin as he made the surprise pass into the end zone.

▼ As an unlikely receiver, Sanders knelt down to catch the pass, rolling backward to safely complete it for the go-ahead touchdown.

HIGH SCHOOL FOOTBALL

Football is played by more than a million kids in Canada and the US, and is the most popular sport for boys in 43 states. It's called "prep" football in high school because it helps prepare you to play the next level of tackle football in college—but the local competitions can be intense and even historic, bringing out communities to fill the stands.

THE SEASON

Each state has its own high school football system, and most have 8 to 10 game seasons that start around Labor Day and last through November. The teams are broken up into divisions according to the size of their schools. The teams with the best records in each division will go on to compete in a tournament at the end of the regular season to determine a state champion. The largest schools will have more than one team so that more students can play and develop their skills for a chance to play at the highest level, which is varsity. Players can work their way up from freshman football on to the sophomore and then junior varsity teams. Participating in high school football is extremely demanding–during the season, practices run for 3–4 hours most days, and teams often have to travel for weekly games.

▲ Head coach of Lake Braddock, Jim Poythress, addresses the team before a game against Centreville in 2011.

BY THE RULES

The National Federation of State High School Associations is the governing body for high school football in the US. In most states, they set the rules for the prep game, which have a few differences from college football. For instance, quarters are only 12 minutes (instead of 15), kickoffs are taken from the kicking team's 40-yard line (instead of the 35), and a tee can be used for field goals and extra points. In many states, there is also a "mercy rule" to deal with uneven matchups that stops play or has the clock run continuously if one side goes up by a large number of points in the game.

▼ Washington and McKinley High Schools of Massillon and Canton, Ohio, have one of the biggest and longest rivalries in high school football. They celebrated their 100th matchup in 1994 at Paul Brown Tiger Stadium.

ALL-AMERICA

At the end of the season, elite high school players are invited to play in a number of competing all-star exhibition games that showcase the nation's top talent for scouts and fans. The All-American Bowl has taken place every year since 2000 at the Alamodome in San Antonio, Texas. The top players from around the US are organized onto teams representing the best of the East and West. The West leads the series 13–10, but the East can claim the biggest win, a 47–3 victory in 2003. More than 450 kids who played in the game have gone on to have NFL careers. The Under Armour All-America Game also takes place in January with a roster of high school seniors hand-picked by scouts. Hosted by stadiums in Florida, the game is broadcast by ESPN, giving high school players their first national audience.

◀ Since it began in 2008, the Under Armour All-America Game has featured three future Heisman winners and 21 future NFL Pro Bowlers.

▼ Concord California's De La Salle High School has been named national champions 12 times, more than any other school. The team holds the record for the longest winning streak in sports history, going 151 games undefeated, from 1992–2004.

"NATIONAL CHAMPIONS"

There are lots of different rankings of high school players and teams put out by various organizations. Since high school teams generally don't play across state lines, and there's no national tournament system due to the difficulty of travel and unfair demands on student athletes, national rankings are determined by "selectors", not championship games. Various organizations of sports analysts have served as selectors over the years, but today the rankings are determined by experts at media groups like USA Today and CBS Sports as well as by expert computer algorithms that crunch the stats. The state of California leads the pack with the most national champions. Their top three programs are all private Catholic schools that focus on prep sports. Florida, Georgia, Texas, and Ohio are also high school football powerhouses that always have multiple teams in the Top 100.

▲ Player Sam Gordon helped found the first all-girls prep tackle football league, the GFL, in Utah in 2015. She gained national attention after her dad posted a YouTube highlight reel of her scoring 35 rushing TDs as the only girl in the Utah Utes League in 2012.

NCAA FOOTBALL

Colleges are where gridiron football first began. And with 772 colleges and universities fielding teams, the tradition is still going strong in the National Collegiate Athletic Association.

WINNINGEST NCAA TEAMS

Michigan Wolverines, 1004–353–36
Alabama Crimson Tide, 965–337–43
Ohio State Buckeyes, 964–333–53
Notre Dame Fighting Irish, 948–337–42
Texas Longhorns, 948–392–33
Oklahoma Sooners, 944–340–53
Yale Bulldogs, 936–390–55
Penn State Nittany Lions, 930–409–41
Nebraska Huskers, 917–424–40
Harvard Crimson, 901–411–50

MILESTONES

The NCAA celebrated the 150th anniversary of the first college game, between Princeton and Rutgers, in 2019. Football was championed by Ivy League schools in New England in the 1870s and had spread to the South and Midwest by the 1880s. Because of their early dominance, the Ivy League schools Yale and Princeton still top the charts for most national titles, though Yale hasn't claimed one since 1927 and Princeton since 1950. The first college football game was broadcast on radio in 1921, an early "Backyard Brawl" between historic rivals Pitt and WVU, while the first televised game was between Fordham and Waynesburg Universities and aired in 1939. The hugest crowd at a college game was 156,990 at a Tennessee home game played at a Nascar speedway in 2016. The inaugural College Football Playoff National Championship in 2015 holds the record for the most-watched NCAA game of all time, with more than 34 million viewers.

▶ University of Michigan established their football team in 1879. The 12-time national champions became the first team to pass 1,000 wins with a 31–24 away victory over Maryland on November 18, 2023.

THE SEASON

Fall semester kicks off with college football openers in late August or early September and lasts the entire term. Teams play up to 12 games during the regular season, with half of them at home and most of them against other teams in their conference. Most matchups happen on Saturday, and none are scheduled for Sunday to avoid conflicting with the NFL's busiest game day of the week. Conference championships, bowl games, and the College Football Playoff happen in December and January.

◀ Nebraska holds the record for the most consecutive sold-out home games, with 396. That means the Huskers have played every home game since November 3, 1962 in front of a capacity crown at Memorial Stadium.

DIVISIONS

Like all NCAA sports, football programs are split into three divisions based on their size, resources, and competitiveness. Division 1 (D1) schools are the most competitive and are often larger schools with the biggest budgets for athletic programs and scholarships. For football alone, the D1 schools are also divided into two subdivisions: the Football Bowl Subdivision (FBS) and the Football Championship Subdivision (FCS). FBS teams are the highest level and are eligible to play in bowl games and compete for the College Football Playoff National Championship. Because programs in the FBS bring in more money than any other college sport, they are allowed to award 85 scholarships per year, covering around 70% of their rosters.

◀ The Jacksonville State Gamecocks are one of the newest additions to the FBS. They joined in 2023 and won their first bowl—the 23rd Annual New Orleans Bowl—the same year, with a 34–31 overtime victory over the Louisiana Ragin' Cajuns.

FACT FILE

As of 2024, there are 134 teams in the FBS and 129 in the FCS. Ohio State (enrollment 66,444) has the biggest sport revenue, reaching $280 million in 2023.

CONFERENCES

Besides having divisions, the NCAA has conferences within each division that help set the schedule, as most of a team's games will be played within their own conference. The schools in the top subdivision, the FBS, are split among 10 conferences. While they have a loosely regional organization, many have expanded to scoop up the top football schools from around the country. The most competitive conferences have bigger budgets due to more revenue from broadcasting rights and sponsorship. Founded in 1896, the Big Ten is the oldest conference in the FBS and among its most powerful, along with the ACC, Big 12, and SEC. Conference re-alignments happen often as schools opt for the best possible opponents. The once-elite Pac-12, for instance, imploded in 2023 after 10 of its 12 schools jumped ship to join more lucrative conferences.

▼ The Southeastern Conference, or SEC, includes the South's biggest public football schools, like serial national champions Alabama (pictured), Georgia, and LSU. The SEC has 43 football titles in its history and is currently the most competitive conference in the NCAA.

THE NATIONAL FOOTBALL LEAGUE

From its humble beginnings in a Canton, Ohio, car dealership, the NFL has grown to become the highest-grossing pro sports league in the world. Today, the league is a beloved US institution with more than a century of gridiron history.

▶ AFL founder Lamar Hunt (right) joins the NFL president and NFL commissioner for a 1966 press conference announcing the forthcoming merger of the rival leagues.

HISTORY

The NFL was formed during a meeting of independent teams held at Hupmobile car dealership in Canton, Ohio, on September 17, 1920. The league launched that year with 14 teams from five states (Ohio, Illinois, Indiana, New York, and Michigan). Only two of those original franchises remain, now the Cardinals and the Bears. The college game was far more popular at the time, and it took four decades for the NFL to spread across the country and develop a national appeal. It faced many competitor leagues during that period, outlasting or merging with them to become the premiere pro football organization. The first serious challenge to its hold on the sport came from Lamar Hunt's "upstart" American Football League (AFL) in 1960. The modern NFL came out of its merger with the AFL in 1970, ushering in the first Super Bowl era (a name coined by Hunt).

◀ The NFL Kickoff Game always features the last Super Bowl winner facing a blockbuster opponent, usually in a grudge match. The 2017 season opener featured defending champs, the Pats, against the up-and-comers the Chiefs.

THE NFL SEASON

Football is a complex game, and winning doesn't happen magically. With the NFL season starting in September, preparation and practices actually start as early as May when teams host voluntary workouts and rookie minicamps. Official training camp kicks into gear in July, which is where players fight for roster spots. It's capped off with a small slate of preseason games in August before the season begins. As of 2021, the NFL season includes 17 games, which are played over 18 weeks, giving each team a "Bye Week" where they can recuperate. While most games are played on Sunday afternoons, the NFL began hosting one premier game on a Monday night in 1970 and have recently added more showcase games on other days, including Thursday and Saturday. After the regular season wraps up, the postseason begins in January, with three weeks of playoff games before the final and biggest game of the season, the Super Bowl.

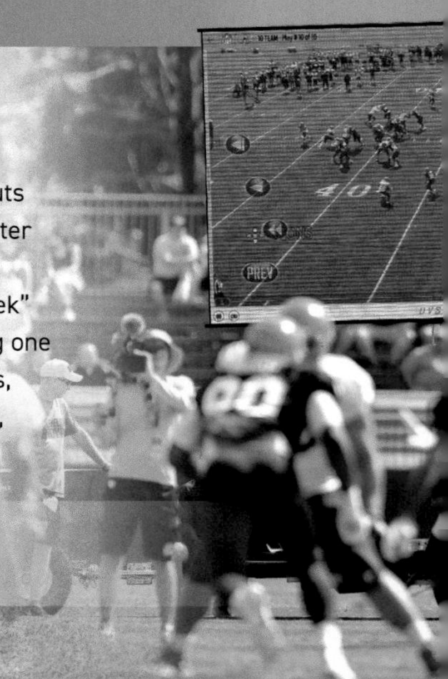

▶ Browns players run drills at training camp. NFL teams can have up to 90 players on their roster during camp, but they must cut that down to a limit of 53 by the time the season officially begins.

▲ The top exec in the NFL is the commissioner, and it has been Roger Goodell since 2006. Here, he meets with the president of the NFLPA, DeMaurice Smith, to sign a new labor agreement.

THE STRUCTURE

The current structure of the NFL has been in place since 2002, when the addition of the Houston Texans brought the league to a nice even number of teams at 32. This meant there could be an equal number of teams in each conference (16) and allowed the AFC and NFC to be split into four equal divisions (North, South, East, and West) with four teams each. The North and South divisions of each conference were new—before, there had been just East, West, and Central. The former AFL teams are in the AFC while most of the early NFL teams are in the NFC. The NFL is led by an executive committee, and changes to the structure, finances, and rules within the league must be voted on by franchises at the annual NFL Owners Meeting. The players and their interests are represented by one of the country's most powerful unions—the NFL Players Association.

▲ The NFL established a series of physical tests for prospective NFL players in the 1980s, called the NFL Combine that gives teams hard stats to compare about prospects' speed and strength.

THE DRAFT

Unlike in college football where recruits can choose between any school that makes them an offer, prospective NFL players have no control over who their first employer will be. Once a college player declares for the draft, they have to go to whichever team picks them. The annual NFL Draft was instituted in 1936 to level the playing field when it came to player recruitment, so that the top players coming out of college could be distributed fairly among the teams while keeping costs down for franchises with less buying power. The need to scope out the top talent from among thousands of college players led to elaborate scouting organizations, while franchises have learned to secretly strategize about how best to fill their team needs with players who fit their schemes. There are seven rounds of picks, and each team gets one pick per round. The order of picks is determined by your previous season—the team with the worst record picks first and the team with the strongest record goes last. Teams can also use their picks as bargaining chips to make trades for current NFL players or trade up in the draft order to try to nab the player they want.

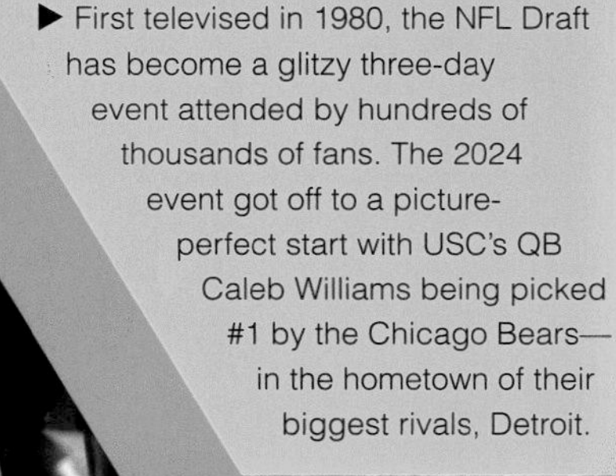

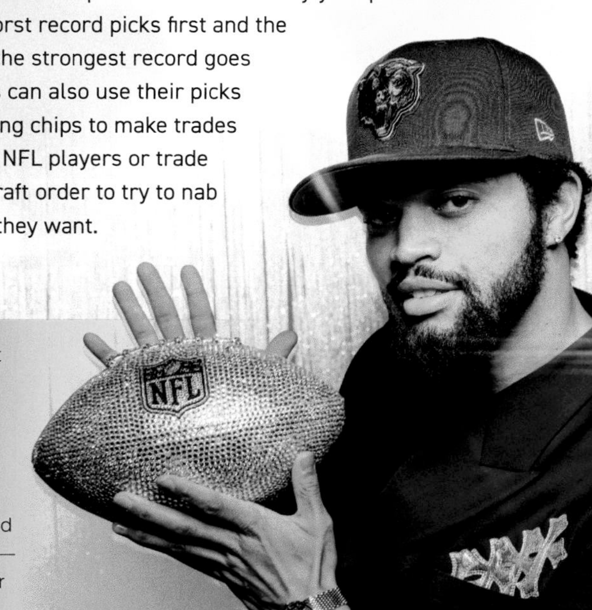

▶ First televised in 1980, the NFL Draft has become a glitzy three-day event attended by hundreds of thousands of fans. The 2024 event got off to a picture-perfect start with USC's QB Caleb Williams being picked #1 by the Chicago Bears—in the hometown of their biggest rivals, Detroit.

AFC NORTH

This division has become the toughest in the league. They've sent three teams to the playoffs three times in ten years, and all four had winning records in 2023.

▶ Three out of four of the football teams in the AFC North are linked to classic coach Paul Brown. He coached and co-founded the Browns, who are named after him. When the franchise moved to Baltimore, Cleveland decided to keep the name. When Cleveland cut ties with Brown, he moved on and founded the Bengals, where he remained president till his death in 1991. During his 25 years as a coach, he invented the face mask, pioneered modern coaching staffs, broke the color barrier in pro football by recruiting African American players, and won seven league championships.

CINCINNATI BENGALS

OHIO • FOUNDED: 1967 • STADIUM: PAYCOR STADIUM

Still owned by the son of Paul Brown, the Bengals came to be after Brown was fired from Cleveland (when a new owner took over in 1963) and looked to found another franchise in Ohio. He made it happen in Cincinnatti, naming it after a team that used to play there from 1937–1941. The Bengals were founded as an AFL extension team but merged into the NFL just two years later. The team showed promise in the 1980s, making it to the Super Bowl twice (and losing twice against the 49ers), before logging a miserable 14 losing seasons in a row in the 1990s and early 2000s. They became solid contenders under coach Marvin Lewis (2003–2018), but they've found a spark with Heisman-winning QB Joe Burrow, who helped take them all the way to Super Bowl LVI after one of the most thrilling playoff runs in history, giving fans plenty of reason to chant "Who dey?" Having triumphed in a series of close-run postseason games, they fell a field goal short of their first title.

▼ QB Joe Burrow won the Lamar Hunt Trophy during the Bengals' 2021 AFC Championship victory, a 27–24 win over the Chiefs.

▼ Baltimore's record-setting defense during the 2000 season only allowed only 156 points and 970 rushing yards the entire season.

BALTIMORE RAVENS

MARYLAND • FOUNDED: 1996 • STADIUM: M&T BANK STADIUM

The city of Baltimore lost their historic team, the Colts, to Indianapolis in 1984. When Art Modell agreed to move his franchise there for the 1996 season, there was so much excitement that their opening game was the best-attended event in Baltimore's sporting history. Fans voted in the name, which was inspired by the most famous poem ("The Raven") of early mystery and horror writer Edgar Allan Poe, who is buried there. Their mascot is still named Poe and accompanied by two real-life ravens, called Rise and Conquer. Like their fierce rivals, the Steelers, Baltimore has long had a rep for hard-hitting, dominant defensive units, which has helped them secure 15 postseason appearances, seven AFC North titles, and two Lombardi Trophies. In 2000, the Ravens D set the NFL record for fewest points allowed (165) and continued the trend to beat the Giants 34–7 in the Super Bowl. With two-time MVP Lamar Jackson at QB, they look set to be serious title contenders again.

CLEVELAND BROWNS

OHIO • FOUNDED: 1944

STADIUM: CLEVELAND BROWNS STADIUM

The Browns have had a bit of a rollercoaster history. Their first league, the All-America Football Conference went bust four seasons after the team started playing in it. The team was adopted by the NFL and won three league titles in its first six seasons. The last league championship they won was in 1964—just after the departure of their namesake and coach of 17 years, Paul Brown. They did it on the back of another Brown—Hall-of-Fame running back Jim Brown. In 1995, owner Art Modell announced he was up and moving the franchise to Baltimore, but the city successfully petitioned to keep the Browns name and history, rebooting the team with an expansion draft in 1999. They've struggled to put together a winning season since and have yet to make a Super Bowl, but their current coach Kevin Stefanski, has won the NFL Coach of the Year twice after leading the Browns to their first two playoff appearance since 2002 in 2020 and 2023, giving their loyal fans, the "Dawg Pound" a reason to celebrate.

◀ The Browns overcame a league-high 17-season playoff drought at the end of the 2020 season, beating their rivals the Steelers in a 48–37 thriller in the wild card round.

PITTSBURGH STEELERS

PENNSYLVANIA • FOUNDED: 1933

STADIUM: ACRISURE STADIUM

The oldest team in the AFC North, the Pittsburgh franchise was founded by Art Rooney in 1933 and named the Steelers after the city's main industry in 1940. It was more than four decades before Rooney hoisted his first championship trophy, following Super Bowl IX. As the steel industry began collapsing in Pittsburgh in the 1970s, the Steelers provided some comfort to the suffering region by going on one of the most impressive winning streaks in pro sports history. Under coach Chuck Noll, the Black and Gold won back-to-back Super Bowls TWICE with a team stacked with future Hall-of-Famers and a legendary D-line known as the "Steel Curtain." The franchise saw another peak in the naughts, with a promising rookie QB, "Big Ben" Roethlisberger, and a punishing "Blitzburgh" defense. In 2009, they became the first franchise to win six Lombardis, under coach Mike Tomlin, who has yet to post a losing season in his 17 years and counting with the team.

▲ The Steelers debuted the "rally towel" in a 1975 playoff game. Today, the stands are still filled with waving black-and-gold Terrible Towels, and fans have brought them everywhere from the International Space Station to Mount Everest.

AFC EAST

These four teams originally played against each other in the Eastern Division of the AFL before it merged with the NFL. Only the Bills have no Lombardis while the Pats have six.

FACT FILE

This division boasts the only two teams in NFL history to have posted perfect regular-season records, the Miami Dolphins of 1972 and the New England Patriots of 2007.

BUFFALO BILLS

NEW YORK • FOUNDED: 1959

STADIUM: HIGHMARK STADIUM

An original member of the American Football League (AFL), the Bills were founded by Ralph Wilson and won the league title twice during the decade before it merged with the NFL in 1970. They have yet to win it since, even though they are the NFL's only team to make it to the Super Bowl four years in a row (from 1990–1993, with a team led by future Hall-of-Famers QB Jim Kelly, RB Thurman Lee, and DE Bruce Smith). Sadly for the "Bills Mafia," who are famous for their rowdy, all-weather tailgating, they lost them all. The team name is a nod to the Wild West showman, Buffalo Bill, and they have a charging bison as their logo with the colors of the American flag. During the heyday of division rivals, the Patriots, the Bills had lackluster results, but, after coach Sean McDermott came in with QB Josh Allen in 2018, they've begun to return to their winning ways. In fact, the Bills have been division champs four times to start the 2020s.

▲ The Bills have finished top of the AFC East recently, with four consecutive division titles from 2020–2023.

MIAMI DOLPHINS

FLORIDA • FOUNDED: 1966 • STADIUM: HARD ROCK STADIUM

The AFL's ninth expansion team, Miami started so strong, it only took them six years from coming onto the scene as a rookie franchise to take home their first Lombardi in Super Bowl VII—after notching the new NFL's first perfect season. The 17-0 Dolphins of 1972 are still the stuff of legend, managing a feat no other team has yet to match. In 1973, they pulled off the repeat to become the first NFL team in history to win back-to-back Super Bowls in an emphatic 24-7 victory over the Vikings. The Dolphins would go on to win two more AFC titles in the 1980s and enjoy a resurgence with QB Dan Marino, who took the NFL MVP in 1984 after passing for more than 5,000 yards but lost in that season's Super Bowl. Since the retirement of Don Shula, their coach of 26 years and the winningest in NFL history, the franchise has not lived up to its legacy of success. Phin fans have seen their team make it to the playoffs in 2022 and 2023, but their postseason win drought—currently the longest in the NFL—is still going.

◀ Dolphins Hall-of-Fame QB Bob Griese became the first quarterback to start in three Super Bowls in a row, from 1971–1973.

NEW ENGLAND PATRIOTS

MASSACHUSETTS • FOUNDED: 1959
STADIUM: GILLETTE STADIUM

The Patriots' two decades of dominance to start the 21st century made them one of the most popular and valuable teams in all of pro sports. Founded as a Boston-based franchise, the Pats were one of the AFL's original eight teams and became the New England Patriots when they moved to Foxborough, Massachusetts, in 1971. The name refers to soldiers fighting for independence in the American Revolutionary War, and their now-famous logo is known as the "Flying Elvis" because of its resemblance to the dead rockstar. The Pats didn't give fans much to cheer about in the first 40 years of their franchise, but things started looking up when coach Bill Parcells helped them to their Super Bowl debut in XXXI and accelerated exponentially when coach Bill Belichick and a little-known backup QB Tom Brady helped win their first title five years later in Super Bowl XXXVI. The dynasty forged by Belichick and Brady from 2001–2018 led to a raft of records and a historic nine AFC Championship titles and six Super Bowl wins.

▼ The Belichick-Brady era in New England marked one of the most successful periods for any team in the history of pro sports. Together, they had zero losing seasons and took 17 AFC East titles.

▼ Cornerback Darrelle Revis (right), who played for the Jets from 2007–2016, is one of 20 Jets players enshrined in the Pro Football Hall of Fame.

NEW YORK JETS

NEW YORK / NEW JERSEY • FOUNDED: 1959
STADIUM: METLIFE STADIUM

Originally known as the Titans of New York, the Jets were one of the charter members of the AFL. They would go on to become the first AFL team to beat an NFL team for the Super Bowl title at the end of the 1968 season, but they haven't been to a championship game since then or even made the playoffs since 2010, when they lost a 24–19 heartbreaker to the Steelers in the AFC Championship. The core of their early title-winning side was the team's #1 draft pick in 1965, QB Joe Namath. When the press kept saying that the AFL wasn't as competitive as the NFL before Super Bowl III, Namath responded by guaranteeing a Jets victory and then delivering it. His 206 yards through the air led to a 16–7 upset of the Baltimore Colts that silenced AFL naysayers and earned him the game MVP. The Jets have only won the AFC East title twice, in 1998 and 2002, in decades that have been dominated by their fiercest rival, the Pats. They pulled off one of their most satisfying wins in franchise history under Rex Ryan in January 2011, beating New England 28–21 to knock them out of the playoffs. Today, they're looking for a fresh start with coach Robert Saleh and elite veteran QB Aaron Rodgers at the helm.

AFC SOUTH

Founded in 2002 with teams that hadn't played long in their current home cities, the AFC South is the NFL's newest division.

FACT FILE

As the youngsters of the league, it's not surprising that the AFC South have yet to become strong title contenders. These teams have the fewest Super Bowl wins of any division (2), and the Colts got both of them.

▲ The Texans finally have a franchise QB in CJ Stroud, a Heisman finalist from Ohio State who won NFL Offensive Rookie of the Year after his debut season in 2023.

HOUSTON TEXANS

TEXAS • FOUNDED: 1999

STADIUM: NRG STADIUM

The youngest team in the NFL, the Texans are the league's 32nd franchise. After the Oilers left Houston in 1997, local businessman Bob McNair was determined to bring an NFL team back to his community. He made it happen just five years later in 2002, when the Texans announced they had come to play by becoming the first expansion team in more than 40 years to win their opening game, a 19–10 victory over the Cowboys. It took 10 years of building for the team to win its first AFC South title in 2011, but they'd go on to win six in the 2010s. In 2023, the Texans returned to their winning form, becoming the first team in NFL history to take their division title with a rookie head coach and quarterback in DeMaco Ryans and C.J. Stroud—the #2 overall draft pick out of Ohio State. Today, the former Houston-based franchise, the Titans, are the Texans biggest rivals.

INDIANAPOLIS COLTS

INDIANA • FOUNDED: 1953 • STADIUM: LUCAS OIL STADIUM

The original Colts were established in Baltimore as part of the All America Football Conference that also gave rise to teams like the 49ers and Browns. After going bust in 1950, a new NFL franchise under the same name was awarded to Baltimore in 1953. The team began to flourish under coach Weeb Ewbank and QB Johnny Unitas, along with nine-time All-Pro lineman Jim Parker and six-time All-Pro receiver Raymond Berry, who teamed up to win back-to-back NFL Championships in 1958 and 1959. The 1958 title decider against the Giants was the first playoff game won in sudden-death overtime. The Colts won "The Greatest Game Ever Played" 23–17. The franchise took its first Super Bowl title (V) in Baltimore before moving to Indianapolis in 1984. Peyton Manning became the franchise QB in 1998, winning eight division titles and a Super Bowl (XLI) in his 13 seasons with the team and turning them into the most successful team in the AFC South.

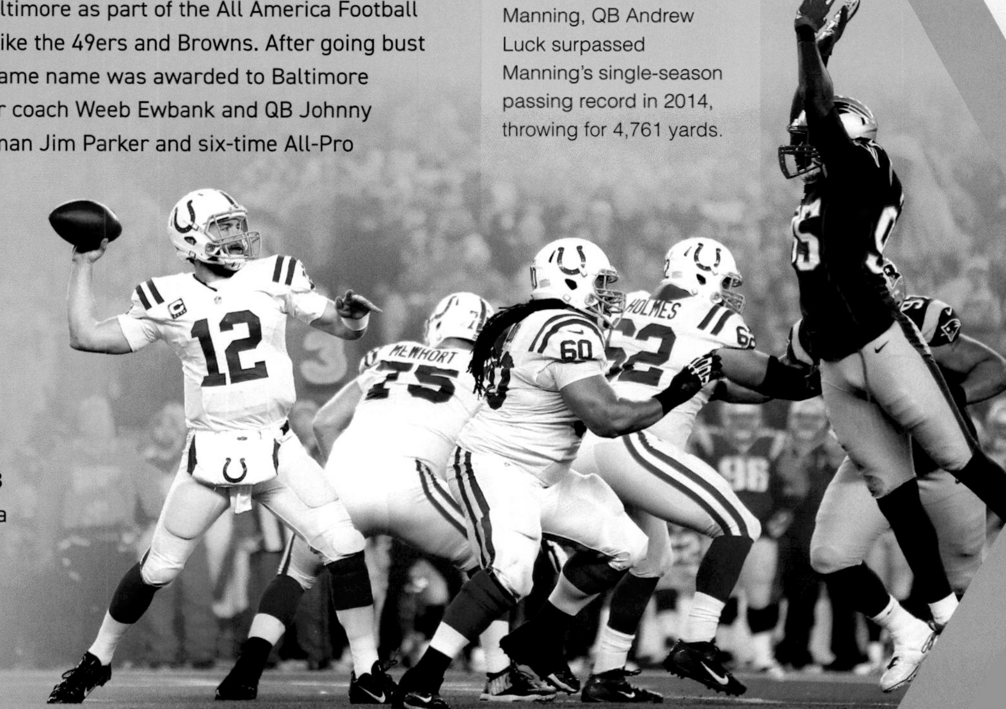

▼ Brought in to replace Colts legend Peyton Manning, QB Andrew Luck surpassed Manning's single-season passing record in 2014, throwing for 4,761 yards.

TENNESSEE TITANS

TENNESSEE • FOUNDED: 1959 • STADIUM: NISSAN STADIUM

The Titans franchise began life as the Houston Oilers. One of the eight original AFL teams that began playing in 1960, the Oilers were also the original AFL champions, winning back-to-back titles in 1960 and 1961. The founding owner, Bud Adams, was a co-founder of the AFL, and his daughter Amy Adams Strunk is the controlling owner today. The franchise moved to Nashville in 1997 and was renamed the Tennessee Titans in 1999, the same year the team took its first AFC Championship title. With coach Jeff Fisher and QB Steve McNair at the helm, they triumphed over future division rivals the Jaguars to earn their spot in Super Bowl XXXIV, which they narrowly lost to the Rams. The Titans took two AFC South titles in 2020 and 2021 under coach Mike Vrabel, with RB Derrick Henry leading the league in rushing yards two seasons in a row. With a new stadium slated to open in 2027, the Titans have become a Tennessee institution.

◀ Derrick Mason returns a kickoff 80 yards for touchdown in the Titan's 33–14 victory over the Jags, which saw them crowned 1999 AFC champs.

▲ QB Trevor Lawrence and his teammates take to the field for a home game.

JACKSONVILLE JAGUARS

FLORIDA • FOUNDED: 1995 • STADIUM: EVERBANK STADIUM

The Jags became the NFL's 30th franchise in 1993, playing their first game in 1995 against fellow expansion team, the Carolina Panthers. They lost, but it only took a year for them to record their first winning season under Tom Coughlin in his first-ever head coaching job. They finished their season strong, winning six of their last seven games, before making an incredible playoff run all the way to the 1996 AFC Championship Game. The next three seasons also gave Jags fans plenty of reasons to chant "Duuuuval!!" (Jacksonville's home county) as they went to three more playoffs in a row, including the 1999 AFC Championship Game. They've never made it to a Super Bowl and have only won two division titles since the formation of the AFC South. The latest came in 2022 under coach Doug Pederson, with their #1 draft pick Trevor Lawrence leading them to a remarkable playoff win, coming back from 27–0 down to triumph 31–30 over the Chargers. The Jags have fans reach from Florida to across the pond, where they've played one home game in London since 2013.

AFC WEST

This competitive division has seen all four teams go to the Super Bowl and two win back-to-back NFL Championships. All four of these teams were also founding franchises of the AFL in 1960. Many of them have moved around, but the rivalries stayed the same.

FACT FILE

As of 2022, all four teams in the AFC West had won exactly 15 division titles each. The Chiefs snuck into the lead in 2023 after securing their eighth division title in a row.

DENVER BRONCOS

COLORADO • FOUNDED: 1959
STADIUM: EMPOWER FIELD AT MILE HIGH STADIUM

This franchise has always called the "Mile-High City" of Denver home. They play at the highest altitude of any NFL team, and they've reached phenomenal heights in pro football, with eight AFC championships and three Super Bowls (XXXII, XXXIII, and 50) to their name. They may have won the first-ever AFL game (a 13–10 victory over the Boston Patriots played on September 9, 1960), but the Broncos weren't an immediate success. They didn't make their first playoff appearance until 1977, then lost three Super Bowls in four years in the 1980s. It took drafting John Elway, the QB who'd lead the team for 16 seasons (plus more than a decade as an exec off the field) to finally give the Broncos the extra kick they needed to hoist the Lombardi. Under coach Mike Shanahan and with the help of the RB who'd become their all-time leading rusher, Terrell Davis, Denver won two Super Bowls in a row in 1997 and 1998. Peyton Manning and a stellar D known as the "No Fly Zone" saw the Broncos top the AFC West five years running from 2011–2015 and win their third Super Bowl.

▶ Hall-of-Fame quarterback John Elway led the Broncos to two consecutive NFL titles in Super Bowl XXXII and XXXIII.

KANSAS CITY CHIEFS

MISSOURI • FOUNDED: 1959 • STADIUM: ARROWHEAD STADIUM

Owned by AFL founder Lamar Hunt and his family, this franchise was established in Dallas (as the Texans) but moved to Missouri when the Cowboys came on the scene just four years later. Fans voted to rename the team the "Chiefs," after the nickname of Kansas City's mayor at the time. "Lenny the Cool" Dawson, who led the AFL in passer rating six times, helped bring the team early success, as the Chiefs racked up three AFL Championship titles. Kansas City played in Super Bowl I and won Super Bowl IV before dropping into a postseason funk for decades. When coach Andy Reid joined the organization in 2013, the tide began to turn. The Chiefs had a strong record with QB Alex Smith, but Patrick Mahomes elevated them to dynasty status. The Chiefs' first-ever NFL MVP in 2018, Mahomes got the best out of weapons like TE Travis Kelce to make KC into playoff wizards. They've gone to four Super Bowls and won three during his tenure.

◀ The Chiefs, with Hall-of-Fame QB Len Dawson at the helm, played in the very first Super Bowl.

LAS VEGAS RAIDERS

NEVADA • FOUNDED: 1960 • STADIUM: ALLEGIANT STADIUM

The Oakland Raiders became a founding member of the AFL after the planned Minneapolis franchise defected to the NFL. In 1963, they hired the 33-year-old Al Davis, the youngest coach in NFL history and future Raiders owner who brought them their first winning season. The Black and Silver won their first AFL Championship in 1967 and continued to dominate in the newly merged NFL under coach John Madden. They developed a vicious rivalry with their frequent playoff opponent, the Steelers, who they finally beat 24–7 in the 1976 AFC Championship. Tom Flores, the NFL's first Hispanic head coach, saw them win three Super Bowls in 1976, 1980, and 1983, with talent like NFL MVP running back Marcus Allen. They haven't topped their division since 2002. The Raider Nation, sometimes called "The Black Hole," has seen their team move from Oakland to Los Angeles and back again. In 2020, they relocated to Las Vegas to become Nevada's first NFL team.

▼ The Raiders have a strong international following. A third of their fanbase lives outside of the US, including many in Mexico, where they're known as the "Malosos" (bad boys).

LOS ANGELES CHARGERS

CALIFORNIA • FOUNDED: 1959
STADIUM: SOFI STADIUM

The Chargers were founded in Los Angeles but moved to San Diego their second season in 1961. They moved back to their hometown 56 seasons later in 2017 to share a stadium with the newly relocated Rams. The franchise started strong, going to five AFL Championship Games in six years and winning the title in 1963. The Bolts also had bright spots under coach Don Coryell (1976–1986), who introduced the pass-driven "Air Coryell" offense, and Bobby Ross (1992–1996), who led the Bolts to their first and only Super Bowl appearance in 1994, a 49–26 loss to the 49ers. They have taken 10 AFC West titles since 1979, including five in the 2000s, when they had one of the league's top rushers in future Hall-of-Fame running back LaDainian Tomlinson and eight-time Pro-Bowl QB Philip Rivers. The pieces are in place for another good run, with rookie Justin Herbert rising to the occasion to become a new franchise quarterback in 2020 and the hiring of former Chargers QB Jim Harbaugh as their head coach in 2024.

◀ QB Justin Herbert passes in a 19–16 win over division rivals the Broncos. Herbert won NFL Offensive Rookie of the Year in 2020.

NFC NORTH

These four teams have played together in the same division since 1967, so the rivalries run deep. Hailing from the "Frozen North," the gritty franchises that make up this Midwestern wing of the NFC have been called the "Frostbite Division" because many of their home games have been played in the snow and the "Black and Blue Division" because their face-offs can get pretty rough.

FACT FILE

The NFC North has hosted six of the top ten coldest games in NFL history. The coldest ever was a 1967 NFC Championship game between the Cowboys and Packers, nicknamed the "Ice Bowl." The temp reached a frosty −18°F at Lambeau Field by the fourth quarter. Needless to say, the Packers had a serious homefield advantage.

CHICAGO BEARS

ILLINOIS • FOUNDED: 1919 • STADIUM: SOLDIER FIELD

One of the NFL's founding franchises, the Bears were one of the top contenders in the early league, winning eight championships pre-1970. Their four titles in the 1940s under QB Sid Luckman saw them dubbed the "Monsters of the Midway." Luckman set team passing records that have only been surpassed by Pro Bowler Jay Cutler (2009–2015). The Bears' name and orange-and-navy gear come from founder George Halas whose daughter Virginia McCaskey still owns the team today. A former Bears tight end, "Iron Mike" Ditka, was hired to coach the team in 1982, seeing them crowned league champions in 1985—the only Super Bowl they've won to date. While they've won five division titles in the 2000s, they often occupy the #3 spot behind the Vikings and Packers. The Bears-Packers rivalry dates all the way back to 1921, and Chicago's overall win total is second only to Green Bay's. The Bears take the cake, though, for the most players inducted in the Hall of Fame.

◀ The team recorded a Grammy-nominated single in 1985, "The Super Bowl Shuffle," on their path to the Big Game. Miraculously, the hit song didn't derail their championship hopes, as the Bears shuffled to the title with a commanding 46–10 victory.

DETROIT LIONS

MICHIGAN • FOUNDED: 1930 • STADIUM: FORD FIELD

Historically, Detroit has been the underdog of the NFC North, with one of the lowest overall winning percentages in league history. The team was founded in 1930 as the Portsmouth Spartans before moving from Ohio to Detroit, Michigan, in 1934 and being rebranded as the Lions to complement the city's pro baseball team, the Tigers. By 1957, the team had taken four NFL Championship titles—three of them during their heyday in the 1950s with QB Bobby Layne. Since then, the Lions have only twice posted playoff victories. In 2008, they had the dubious distinction of becoming the first team to go 0–16 during the regular season. They took a big step toward overcoming their serious postseason drought in 2023, after taking their first NFC North division title. Many beyond the Lions Nation were rooting for them to go to all the way. They fell a heart-breaking field goal short of going to the Super Bowl, but hopefully it's a sign of a bright future to come.

▶ The Lions have had their share of Hall-of-Famers, from CB Lem Barney (1967–1977) to RB Barry Sanders (1989–1998) to WR Calvin "Megatron" Johnson (2007–2015), seen here beating triple coverage by division rivals, the Vikings.

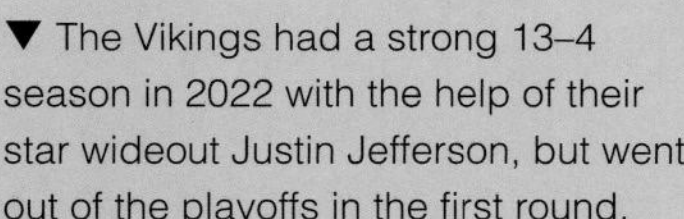

▼ The Vikings had a strong 13–4 season in 2022 with the help of their star wideout Justin Jefferson, but went out of the playoffs in the first round.

MINNESOTA VIKINGS

MINNESOTA • FOUNDED: 1961 • STADIUM: U.S. BANK STADIUM

The Minnesota Vikings are solid competitors in the league and lead the NFC North in division titles but have yet to taste championship glory. In fact, they've lost (badly) in four early Super Bowls and in six NFC Championship Games... which makes some Purple and Gold fans think they have a postseason curse. The franchise is the youngest in the NFC North, added as an expansion team in 1960. The name is a celebration of the strong Scandinavian heritage within their host state, with supporters chanting the Swedish salute "Skol!" at games. In the 1970s, a D-line lead by Alan Page—the first defensive player to be crowned League MVP—made the Vikes one of the NFL's strongest teams. In 1998, the offense shined, with the team going 15–1 and scoring a then-record 556 points before losing the NFC Championship by a field goal—the only one kicker Gary Anderson had missed all season. They've convincingly topped the division six times in the 2000s, but the playoff curse has yet to be broken.

GREEN BAY PACKERS

WISCONSIN • FOUNDED: 1919 • STADIUM: LAMBEAU FIELD

One of the oldest and most storied teams in football, the Pack also have the rare status of being the US's only major-league sports team to be run as a community-owned nonprofit. The team's 537,000 stockholders defy the NFL's latest rule that limits a team to 32 "owners." This financial structure has allowed the small-town franchise to survive and thrive even though it's technically the country's tiniest market in pro sports. Season tickets are hot commodities, with a waiting list 140,000 names long and an average wait time of 30+ years. Green Bay's iconic outdoor stadium is named after co-founder Early "Curly" Lambeau while their name comes from the original 1919 sponsors—a meat-packing company. They won their first NFL Championship in 1929, racking up 11 titles before the Super Bowl era. Their legendary coach Vince Lombardi (1959–1967) saw them come away as winners of the first two Bowls. They won two more in 1996 and 2010 under Mike Holmgren and Mike McCarthy, with superstar QBs Brett Favre and Aaron Rodgers at the helm. Playing in gold and hunter green since 1958, Green Bay has more wins on the books than any other NFL team.

FACT FILE

The NFC North only has five Super Bowl titles to its name despite three of the four teams falling in the top 10 for highest all-time win percentages. Four of the five championship titles in the division have fallen to the Green Bay Packers.

▶ Packers fans have embraced the nickname "Cheeseheads"—a nod to Wisconsin's most famous agricultural product. Many supporters sport correspondingly "cheesy" headgear, including superfan Steve Tate, who is also a proud stockholder in the team.

NFC EAST

Historically the most competitive division in the NFL, the NFC East has more NFC Championships (21) than any other division in the conference. These teams (with the exception of Dallas) all play within driving distance of one another, making each matchup a must-see chapter in the book of rivalries that continues to produce year after year. It's been dubbed the "NFC Beast" or the "NFC Least" depending on the season, but you can always count on drama and high-octane action when watching these four teams play.

FACT FILE

The NFC East is the only division in which all four teams have at least one Lombardi to their name. They also hold the division record for most Super Bowl victories (13).

DALLAS COWBOYS

TEXAS • FOUNDED: 1960 • STADIUM: AT&T STADIUM

Referred to by many as "America's Team," the Dallas Cowboys are among the most popular and successful teams in NFL history. The youngest franchise in the NFC East, they're also the division's most decorated team by some margin, with eight NFC Championships and five NFL titles to their name. Dallas was added as an expansion team in 1960 and for its first 28 years had Tom Landry as head coach. When their current owner, Jerry Jones, took over in 1989, he angered fans by firing Landry, but they soon forgave him when he ushered in a decade of utter dominance. Their glory years in the 1990s saw them win three Super Bowls and five consecutive NFC East titles. Once a true football dynasty, the Cowboys have become somewhat of a fallen giant in recent years despite promising squads helmed by QBs Tony Romo and Dak Prescott. They're always a threat to make a deep playoff run, but luck has evaded them over the last decade or so, with the team having failed to get to the NFC Championship game since 1995.

◀ QB Troy Aikman, RB Emmitt Smith, and WR Michael Irvin were called the "Triplets." All Hall-of-Famers, these offensive powerhouses were at the core of Dallas's three-title team in the 90s.

PHILADELPHIA EAGLES

PENNSYLVANIA • FOUNDED: 1933 • STADIUM: LINCOLN FINANCIAL FIELD

While their team might only have one Super Bowl win, Eagles fans are among the most passionate in the world, maxing out stadiums across the league on a weekly basis—and often letting loose with a chorus of screeches reminiscent of their namesake bird of prey. Launched as an expansion team in 1933, they got off to a rocky start, losing to the Giants 56-0. Their first decade didn't go much better, but Philly hit their stride in the late 1940s with two NFL championship titles. With their gritty work ethic and never-say-die attitude, the Eagles have pulled off some truly historic comebacks and victories over the last few decades. Their most impressive—in Super Bowl LII—marked the official downfall of the Patriots' dynasty, as backup quarterback Nick Foles guided them to their first ever Lombardi Trophy. After coach Andy Reid's departure at the end of 2011, the team went through several rollercoaster seasons before finally finding a footing with coach Nick Sirianni and QB Jalen Hurts at the helm. Today, the Birds have one of the most star-studded rosters in football, and they're likely to be among the NFC juggernauts for years to come.

▶ In 2010, after Philly had been down 24-3 against division rivals the Giants, wideout DeSean Jackson created a "miracle in the New Meadowlands" by sealing the comeback win in the dying seconds with a 65-yard punt return TD.

▲ The Giants take to the field for Super Bowl XLII where they pulled off a shock 17–14 victory against the Pats.

NEW YORK GIANTS

NEW YORK • FOUNDED: 1925

STADIUM: METLIFE STADIUM

New York was once an NFC monster, winning four Super Bowls in two impressive streaks under coaches Bill Parcels and Tom Coughlin, but the last time they took the crown was in 2011. Owned by members of the Mara family since the franchise's founding, the Giants played their first three decades at Manhattan's Polo Grounds and today share their ultramodern New Jersey stadium (often called the "Meadowlands") with the Jets. The G-men were a powerhouse of the early league, taking titles in 1927, 1934, and 1938. Their strong 1950s team featured safety Emlen Tunnell, who'd go on to be the first black player inducted into the Pro Football Hall of Fame, and their dominant 1980s roster included one of the greatest defenses of all time. Nicknamed the "Big Blue Wrecking Crew," it was led by NFL MVP linebacker Lawrence Taylor. More recently, the Giants, fronted by QB Eli Manning, notched one of the biggest upsets of all time in Super Bowl XLII against the Patriots and beat them again in another close one in XLV. Since then, they've only managed four winning seasons, but even when their team is struggling, fans have a century of huge wins, championship rings, and marquee moments to reminisce over.

WASHINGTON COMMANDERS

WASHINGTON, DC • FOUNDED: 1932 • STADIUM: COMMANDERS STADIUM

Once known as the Redskins, a racial slur offensive to Indigenous Americans, this historic team underwent a re-name and makeover starting in 2020 to become the Washington Commanders. The franchise has called the nation's capital home since 1937, when they took home their first NFL title with ground-breaking QB Sammy Baugh. That same year saw the debut of their marching band—the oldest in the league—which still plays their fight song after touchdowns. Washington had a remarkable run in the decade from 1982–1991 under head coach Joe Gibbs, advancing to four Super Bowls and winning three—with three different starting quarterbacks! Since then, the team has struggled to find a consistent foundation to build on... although they might well be in the process of turning the corner. WR Terry McLaurin and QB Jayden Daniels (who they took with the #2 overall draft pick in 2024) headline an offense packed with talent, and the defense appears to be improving steadily. With a new ownership group at the helm, fans are hoping for the winning culture to be restored to the Commanders, who've won just three divisional titles since 2012.

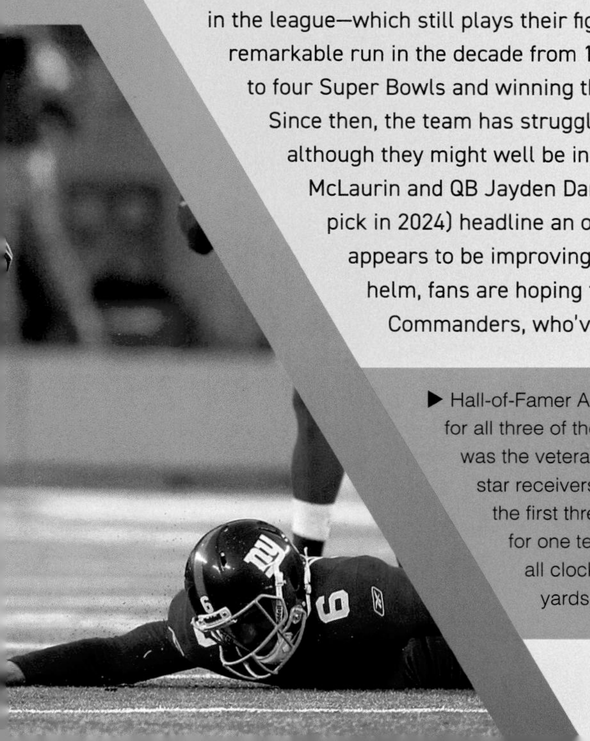

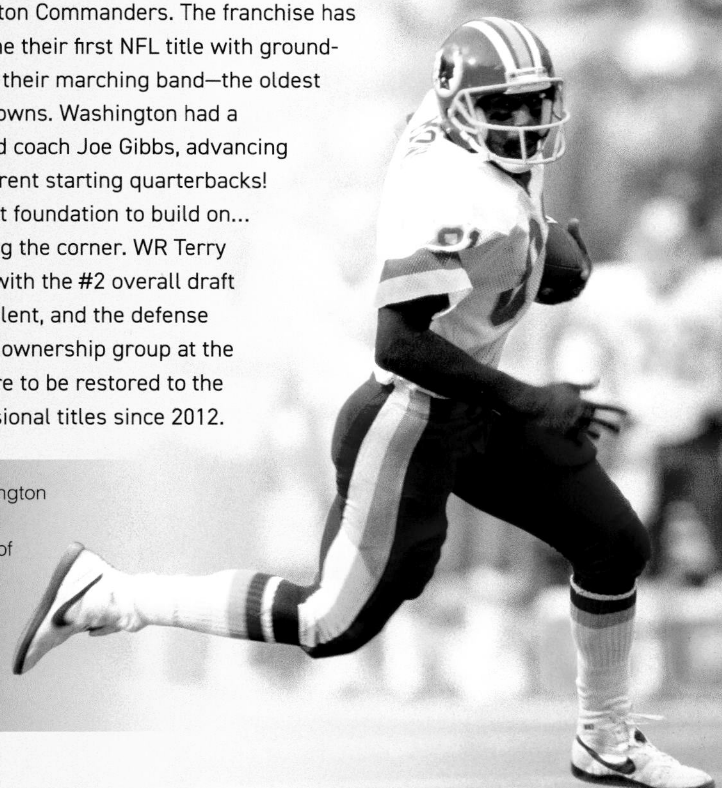

▶ Hall-of-Famer Art Monk was with Washington for all three of their Super Bowl wins and was the veteran on the "Posse," a trio of star receivers who in 1989 became the first three wideouts (playing for one team) in NFL history to all clock 1,000+ receiving yards in a single season.

NFC SOUTH

The NFC South is a young division. Its oldest team, the Falcons, was established in 1965. While it lacks the old-school NFL franchises that pepper the rest of the conference, it's a division of competitors who have all made it to a championship game since the division's founding in 2002.

FACT FILE

The Saints have had the most success in the NFC South since its founding despite having 20 losing seasons in a row to start and not winning a playoff game until their 34th season as a franchise.

ATLANTA FALCONS

GEORGIA • FOUNDED: 1965 • STADIUM: MERCEDES-BENZ STADIUM

Founded as an NFL expansion team, the Falcons played their first season in 1966. Their first three seasons all ended with rough 3–11 records, and they only had two winning seasons in their first twelve. Atlanta made their playoff debut in 1978 and won their first postseason game, defeating the Eagles 14–13 in the wild card round, and scored their first division title in 1980 with the help of quarterback Steve Bartkowski, who led the league in passing TDs that year. They've won five since, in 1998, 2004, 2010, 2012, and 2016. The Dirty Birds have also been crowned NFC Champions twice, including in a 30–27 overtime upset of the No. 1 seed, the Vikings in 1998, but have yet to win the league. They came close in 2016 with NFL MVP Matt Ryan at QB, losing Super Bowl LI in a heart-breaking fashion after allowing the Patriots to erase a 25-point deficit and score the biggest comeback win in championship history. In a bid to get back to being one of the NFC's top contenders, Atlanta recruited superstar Kirk Cousins in 2024.

◀ Nicknamed "Matty Ice," QB Matt Ryan was with the Falcons for 14 seasons and holds the franchise records for passing yards and TDs.

CAROLINA PANTHERS

NORTH CAROLINA • FOUNDED: 1993
STADIUM: BANK OF AMERICA STADIUM

The NFC's youngest team, the Panthers have won two Conference Championships but are still prowling for their first Lombardi. In 1995 the Carolinas were selected as the spot for 29th NFL franchise—the NFL's first expansion team since way back in 1976. The Panthers' credible 7–9 record that year was the most successful start for any expansion team in league history. The very next year they improved to 12–4, going all the way to the NFC Championship Game in their first postseason outing. They suffered a record 15 losses in a row in one season in 2001 before coach John Fox came in to right the ship, taking Carolina to the team's first Super Bowl appearance in 2003. They lost a 32–29 nail-biter against the Pats in one of the greatest Super Bowl battles of all time. With Ron Rivera as coach and Heisman-winner Cam Newton as QB, the Panthers made it back to the Big Game for Super Bowl 50 but lost to the Broncos. Carolina hasn't made the playoffs since 2017, but hopes are high for the future of another Heisman winner, the Panthers' #1 overall draft pick in 2023, Bryce Young.

▶ A rushing quarterback supreme, Cam Newton led the Panthers to a near-perfect 15–1 season in 2015. It earned him the NFL MVP, but his team fell just shy of the title.

NEW ORLEANS SAINTS

LOUISIANA • FOUNDED: 1966 • STADIUM: CAESARS SUPERDOME

The Saints played their first season as an NFL expansion team in 1967 and got off to a limping start, with two decades straight of losing seasons, leading to the nickname the "Ain'ts." The franchise's first successes came after the it was acquired by Tom Benson in 1985, who hired head coach Jim Mora in 1986. The following year, Mora captained New Orleans to its first winning season and their first division title in 1991. However, despite having a crew of elite linebackers known as the "Dome Patrol" in the early 1990s—the only time four LBs from the same team have made the Pro Bowl together, they didn't win their first playoff game until 2000. In 2006, the Saints came back to the Superdome after it was damaged by Hurricane Katrina with a new coach, Sean Payton, and a new QB, Drew Brees. It marked the dawn of new era as the team resurged along with its home city to win seven NFC West titles and their first Super Bowl victory in 2009, beating the favored Colts 31-17 in one of the most-watched TV events of all time.

◀ A sell-out crowd turned out in September 2006 to watch the Saints stomp division rivals the Falcons in a 23–3 victory. It was the first game played in the restored Superdome after Hurricane Katrina.

TAMPA BAY BUCCANEERS

FLORIDA • FOUNDED: 1974
STADIUM: RAYMOND JAMES STADIUM

This up-and-down franchise has the worst win percentage in the league but have won two Super Bowls. The Bucs started in the NFL with a 0–26 record, but by their fourth season in 1979 had notched their first division title and gone to their first conference championship game. When Malcom Glazer bought the team in 1995 for a then-record $192 million, he was determined to bring a title to Tampa. Coach Tony Dungy helped the franchise on its way by pioneering the hugely successful "Tampa 2" defense that would be emulated by so many other teams. With defensive giants in LB Derrick Brooks and CB Ronde Barber, coach Jon Gruden saw them across the finish line in 2002, with a 48–21 win over the Raiders in the "Pirate Bowl." When the Bucs achieved one of the greatest coups in NFL history by signing Tom Brady in 2020, they hadn't been to the playoffs since 2007. The G.O.A.T. helped take them all the way to another NFL title that year in Super Bowl LV. They won it in their home stadium, not allowing defending champs the Chiefs a single touchdown.

▶ Bucs defenders celebrate during an emphatic 32–9 victory in the 2023 wild card round over their playoff nemesises, the Eagles.

NFC WEST

Since 2016 when the Rams moved back to L.A., all four of these teams have played west of the Rockies. One of the solidest divisions in the league, every team in the NFC West has been to a Super Bowl since it was established in 2002.

FACT FILE

The most decorated team in the NFC West is the 49ers. They've won 22 division titles, eight NFC Championships, and five Super Bowls.

▲ The Cards play in their home stadium in Phoenix, Arizona. They moved there from St. Louis in 1967.

ARIZONA CARDINALS

ARIZONA • FOUNDED: 1898
STADIUM: STATE FARM STADIUM

The Cardinals are the oldest continuously active franchise in football. They're also the team with the longest championship drought in US pro sports history, having won their second and last NFL Championship title in 1947. The team traces its history back to Chicago's Morgan Athletic Club, which was renamed the Racine Street "Cardinals" after the red color of their uniforms in 1901. The Cards became one of the NFL's founding teams in 1920, eventually moving to St. Louis in 1960 where they were known as the "Football Cardinals" to distinguish them from the city's baseball team of the same name. In 1988, the franchise left Missouri without a single playoff win to go to Phoenix where it was renamed the Arizona Cardinals in 1994. They didn't pose a serious postseason threat until 2008, when they signed the Rams' MVP QB Kurt Warner, who led them to Super Bowl XLIII. Larry Fitzgerald, their 11-time Pro Bowl WR, put in an epic performance, but they lost to the Steelers 27–23 in the final seconds of the game. The "Red Sea" is still hoping fresh talent like Heisman-winner Kyler Murray and Marvin Harrison Jr. will bring them their first Lombardi.

LOS ANGELES RAMS

CALIFORNIA • FOUNDED: 1936
STADIUM: SOFI STADIUM

The Rams franchise was founded in Cleveland and won its first NFL Championship there in 1945 before moving to Los Angeles the following year. They won another NFL title there in 1951 and an NFC Conference Championship in 1979 but couldn't shake the rep of being too Hollywood for the NFL. That changed when the franchise relocated to St. Louis, Missouri, in 1995, and started winning under coach Dick Vermeil. When undrafted backup QB Kurt Warner was forced to start after an injury to Trent Green in 1999, he ended up being the lynchpin in one of the greatest offensive units of all time. With MVP Marshall Faulk rushing and Isaac Bruce leading a battery of receivers who stretched the field to enable a high-scoring aerial attack, the Rams racked up record-breaking points and yards while cruising to their first Super Bowl win in 1999. In 2015, the Rams moved their "Mob Squad" back to L.A. where Sean McVay, the youngest head coach in NFL history, propelled them to their second NFL Championship title in 2021, winning Super Bowl LVI in their brand-new home, SoFi Stadium.

▶ Between 1999–2001, the Rams offense was so explosive, it was nicknamed the "Greatest Show on Turf". The Rams led the NFL in total yards for three seasons straight and went to two Super Bowls.

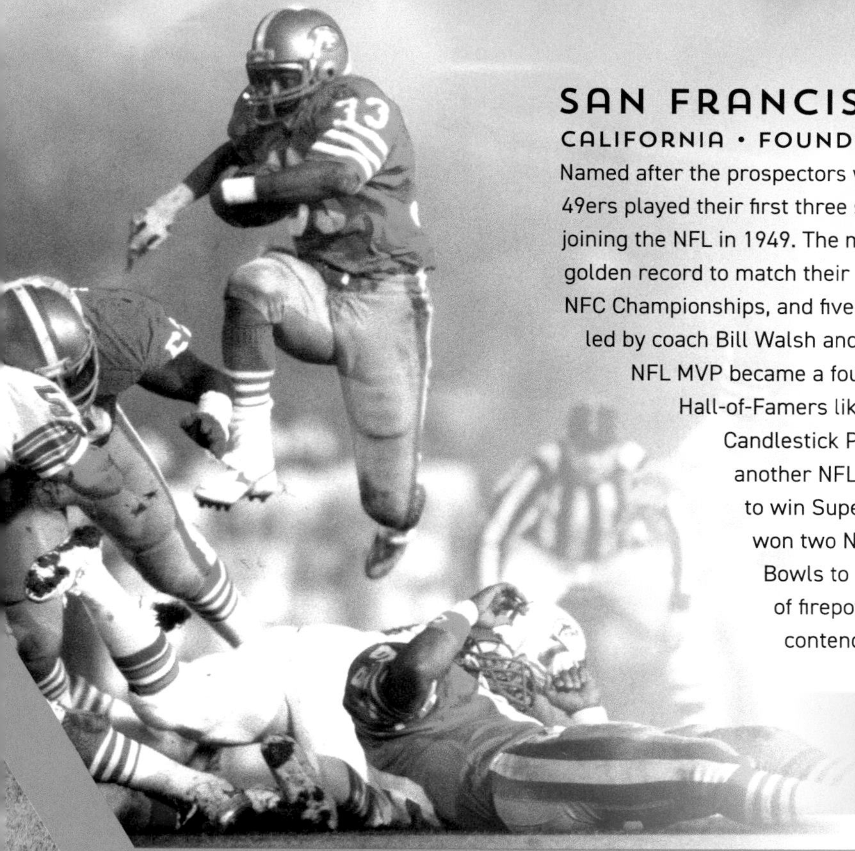

SAN FRANCISCO 49ERS

CALIFORNIA • FOUNDED: 1944 • STADIUM: LEVI'S STADIUM

Named after the prospectors who came to California during the 1849 Gold Rush, the 49ers played their first three seasons in the All-American Football Conference before joining the NFL in 1949. The most decorated team of the NFC West, the Niners have a golden record to match their namesake. To date, they've won 22 division titles, eight NFC Championships, and five Super Bowls. Their heyday was in the 1980s, with a team led by coach Bill Walsh and his first-ever draft pick, QB Joe Montana. The two-time NFL MVP became a four-time Super Bowl champion, playing alongside future Hall-of-Famers like WR Jerry Rice and safety Ronnie Lott at the legendary Candlestick Park. QB Steve Young capped their dynasty claim with another NFL title in 1994, throwing a record six touchdown passes to win Super Bowl XXIX. Under coach Kyle Shanahan, the team has won two NFC Championships (2019 and 2023), then lost two Super Bowls to the Chiefs where they had significant leads. With plenty of firepower on both sides of the ball, the 49ers are bound to be contenders for a long time to come.

◀ Fullback Roger Craig became the first player to score three TDs in one Super Bowl during the Niners victory in Super Bowl XIX, rushing for one and catching two.

SEATTLE SEAHAWKS

WASHINGTON • FOUNDED: 1974 • STADIUM: LUMEN FIELD

▼ Russell Wilson was named the 2012 Rookie of the Year in his first season under coach Pete Carroll.

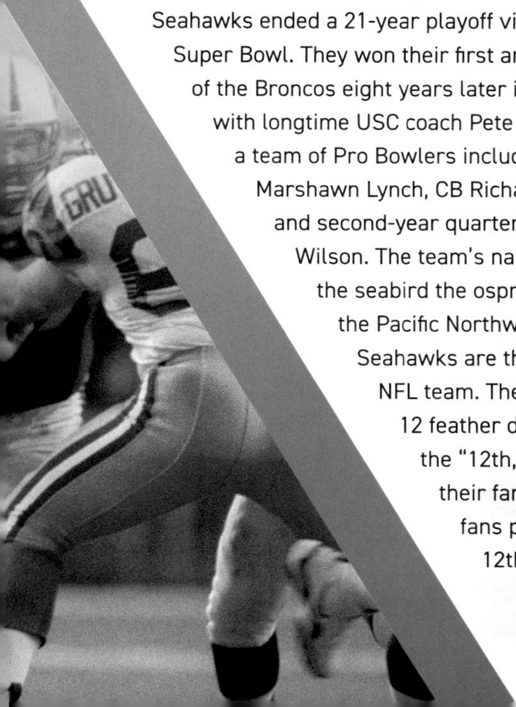

The Seahawks joined the NFL as an expansion team in 1976. Originally assigned to the NFC, they shifted to the AFC for 25 years before returning to the NFC and their current division in 2002. They're the only NFL team to have played in both Conference Championship games, but their three conference titles in 2005, 2013, and 2014 have all come since rejoining the NFC. In 2005, under coach Mike Holmgren, the Seahawks ended a 21-year playoff victory drought and went to their first Super Bowl. They won their first and only Lombardi in a 43–8 rout of the Broncos eight years later in Super Bowl XLVIII, with longtime USC coach Pete Carroll leading a team of Pro Bowlers including RB Marshawn Lynch, CB Richard Sherman, and second-year quarterback Russell Wilson. The team's name refers to the seabird the osprey, found in the Pacific Northwest, where the Seahawks are the region's only NFL team. Their uniforms sport 12 feather details representing the "12th," the nickname for their fanbase, a reference to fans playing the part of the 12th player on the field.

BEYOND THE NFL

Though the NFL is the most elite football league, there are other pro leagues in the US and internationally, for both men and women. Some of them follow similar rules to those of the NFL while others have strikingly different formats.

CANADA, EH?

Rugby football was played in Canada from the 1860s. Canadians introduced the sport to Americans and helped develop the gridiron version of the sport we know and love today—some even say they invented it! It's not surprising, then, that the US's northern neighbor has a pro gridiron football league founded in 1958 with the merger of two leagues, the IRFU and the WIFU, that date back to 1907 and 1936. Today, the Canadian Football League (CFL) has nine teams that play in two divisions, the East and West. The CFL season starts in June and runs through October with a three-week postseason in November that culminates in the Grey Cup, Canada's most-watched annual sporting event. The Grey Cup trophy was created by the Earl of Grey in 1909 and has been used for Canadian football championships since.

▶ The Toronto Argonauts play in a snowy championship game, the 105th Grey Cup. The team has 22 CFL titles—the most in the league.

SOUTH OF THE BORDER

Football is popular in Mexico and has been played there for more than century, but it hasn't had a long-running pro league like Canada. The most recent pro league there—the LFA, or Liga de Fútbol Americano Profesional—started up in 2016 with four teams in Mexico City: the Maya, Raptors, Eagles, and Condors. The young organization has battled through financial strains and the Covid-19 pandemic to grow to 11 teams in 2023. Its players are drafted from college teams in Mexico or recruited from abroad, giving players who didn't make it in the NFL a chance to play pro. The LFA has a short spring season that runs opposite to the NFL's and culminates with the Tazón México (Mexico Bowl) in May. The first two titles were won by the Maya while the last two have been won by an expansion team, the Caudillos of Chihauhau.

▲ The Gallos Negros (Black Roosters) competed in the Tazon Mexico in 2022, their first year in the LFA.

ACROSS THE POND

US troops brought football to Europe during and after WWII, and the continent's first pro team sprung up in Germany in 1976. Some NFL players have gotten their start abroad, such as QB Kurt Warner, who went from helming the Amsterdam Admirals to winning a Super Bowl as the Rams' starter. A championship, the Eurobowl, was played from 1986–2019 with teams from various pro organizations, but the latest umbrella pro league across the pond is The European League of Football (ELF). It launched in 2021 and currently has 17 teams in nine countries, with a 14-week season that runs from May through August, ending with playoffs and a Championship Game in September. The ELF has a growing fanbase (a 2023 game passed 30,000 fans) and wants to develop homegrown talent, so each team is limited to four US players.

▲ The San Antonio Brahmas beat the St. Louis Battlehawks at home in the 2024 XFL Conference Championships.

◀ The 2022 EFL Champions, the Vienna Vikings, had a perfect 12–0 regular season in 2023.

THE NFL ALTERNATIVE

There have been many "minor leagues" for football over the years that promise high-intensity action, but none of them have proven financially viable in the long term. In 2023, two struggling leagues, the XFL and USFL, merged to create the United Football League (UFL), a pro minor league designed to court NFL fans in the long off-season. The format is constantly changing, but the current one sees eight teams play a 10-game season with Conference and League Championship games in June. The UFL has picked up undrafted college players, international prospects who need more development, and NFL players released from their teams. It's an innovative incubator for players and rules—the NFL even adopted some of the UFL's kickoff rules in 2024. Maybe they'll go for the two forward passes in one play rule next!

▼ The Bay Area Panthers play at the SAP Center in San Jose, California.

INDOOR FUN

The Indoor Football League (IFL) was founded in 2009 from the merger of the United Indoor Football League and the Intense Football League and is now the US's longest-running indoor football organization. The IFL offers a high-speed, high-scoring version of the sport with a 19-week season that runs from spring through summer, when NFL fans are especially football-starved. Games have eight players per side and are played on 50-yard fields with padding around the sidelines. There's lots of crossover with gridiron football rules, but the IFL has some fun rules all its own, like players can do a rugby dropkick, and if it goes through the uprights, it counts as a four-point field goal! There are currently 16 teams competing in the IFL, and franchises have sprung up in places that don't have their own NFL team, like Iowa, South Dakota, Oklahoma, and New Mexico. Arizona has three teams—the Wranglers, Rattlers, and Sugar Skulls. More than 80 IFL players have made the jump to the NFL.

SURGE
10
WFA
BOSTON MILITIA
SUBARU

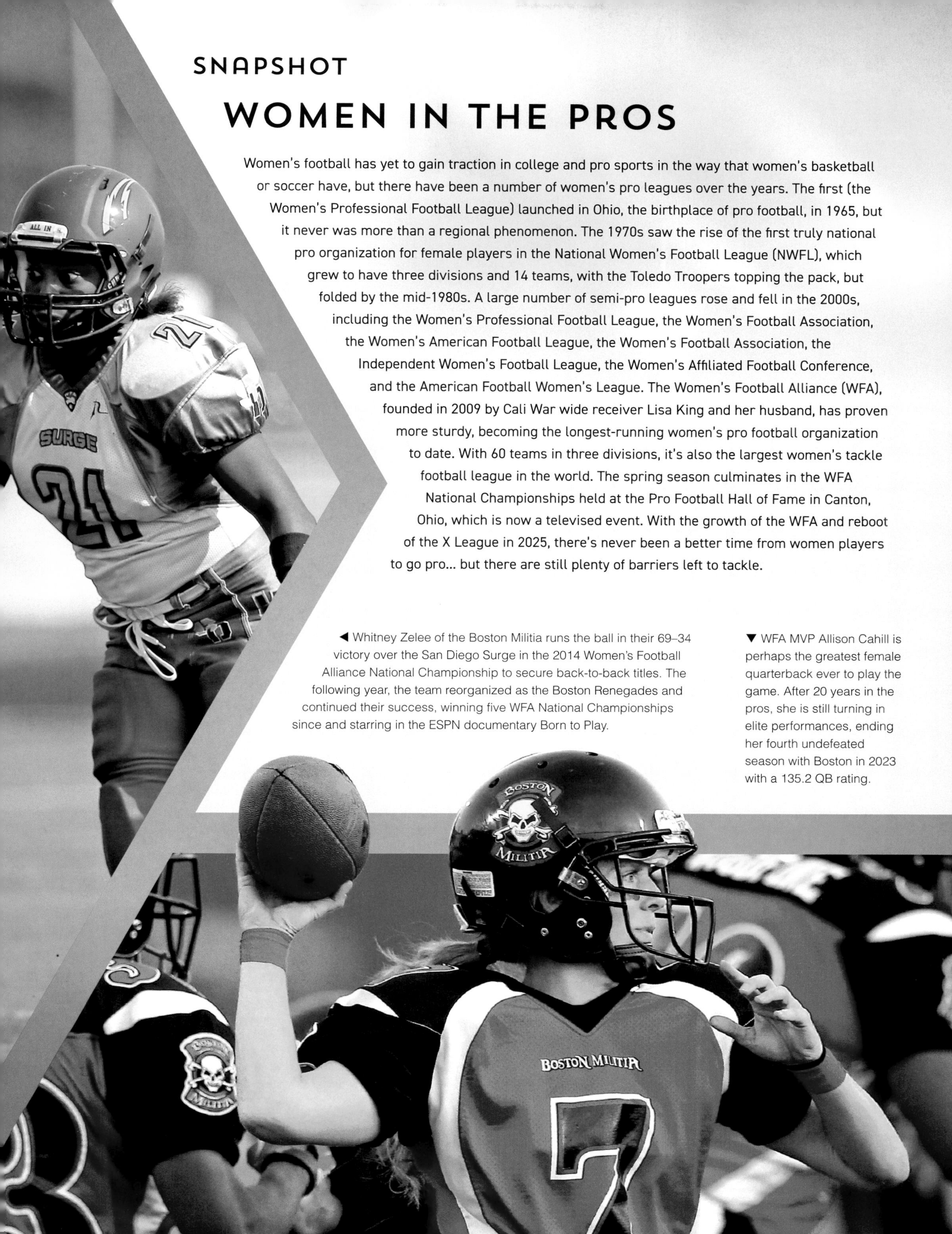

SNAPSHOT

WOMEN IN THE PROS

Women's football has yet to gain traction in college and pro sports in the way that women's basketball or soccer have, but there have been a number of women's pro leagues over the years. The first (the Women's Professional Football League) launched in Ohio, the birthplace of pro football, in 1965, but it never was more than a regional phenomenon. The 1970s saw the rise of the first truly national pro organization for female players in the National Women's Football League (NWFL), which grew to have three divisions and 14 teams, with the Toledo Troopers topping the pack, but folded by the mid-1980s. A large number of semi-pro leagues rose and fell in the 2000s, including the Women's Professional Football League, the Women's Football Association, the Women's American Football League, the Women's Football Association, the Independent Women's Football League, the Women's Affiliated Football Conference, and the American Football Women's League. The Women's Football Alliance (WFA), founded in 2009 by Cali War wide receiver Lisa King and her husband, has proven more sturdy, becoming the longest-running women's pro football organization to date. With 60 teams in three divisions, it's also the largest women's tackle football league in the world. The spring season culminates in the WFA National Championships held at the Pro Football Hall of Fame in Canton, Ohio, which is now a televised event. With the growth of the WFA and reboot of the X League in 2025, there's never been a better time from women players to go pro... but there are still plenty of barriers left to tackle.

◀ Whitney Zelee of the Boston Militia runs the ball in their 69–34 victory over the San Diego Surge in the 2014 Women's Football Alliance National Championship to secure back-to-back titles. The following year, the team reorganized as the Boston Renegades and continued their success, winning five WFA National Championships since and starring in the ESPN documentary Born to Play.

▼ WFA MVP Allison Cahill is perhaps the greatest female quarterback ever to play the game. After 20 years in the pros, she is still turning in elite performances, ending her fourth undefeated season with Boston in 2023 with a 135.2 QB rating.

PLAYER PAYDAYS

Pro football players are elite athletes with a risky, demanding job. It's no secret that they're very well compensated for doing it. Even very specialized players like the long snapper on special teams can earn more than $1 million a year while the top earners make more than 60 times that.

SALARY CAPS

All NFL teams have the same salary cap that they cannot exceed each year. For the year of 2024, it was $255.4 million per team. This rule is intended to keep the league competitive and avoid wealthier franchises "buying" championships because they can afford to snap up all the top players. This means that signing and retaining a hugely talented squad can involve a lot of negotiation. Teams that don't have any "cap space" are often forced to trade their most expensive players.

▶ Teams can pick one player to put a "franchise tag" on each year. The tag means that the player is essential to the team and allows the team to retain them a year beyond the expiration of their contract for a hefty set fee. Bengals star WR Tee Higgins was franchise-tagged in 2024 while Cincy hopes to work out a longer-term contract with him.

PRO CONTRACTS AND SALARIES

Most players who enter the NFL for the first time do so by declaring for the draft (see p.77). The round and position you get picked in play a big part in the rookie salary you'll get, but the wage scale for new roster signings is much lower than that for proven veterans. Rookies are usually given four-year contracts, and first-round picks can make more than $12 million over that time while last-round picks get less than $4 million. These rules help keep teams under the salary cap while allowing them to gamble on untested recruits. After players fulfill their rookie contract, they're free to sign another with whoever gives them the best deal. Top players may field multiple offers, which will include a salary, bonuses, and incentives spread over a set number of years. Franchises protect themselves from investments that aren't worthwhile by only guaranteeing a portion of the money agreed to in the contract. A player won't get their full payday unless they're meeting high performance standards.

◀ Famous players get an extra payday through endorsement deals where they agree to represent a company. Cowboys popular QB Dak Prescott has topped up his salary with more than $50 million in endorsement earnings.

A NEW DEAL FOR NCAA PLAYERS

Though top football universities earn millions from their teams in ticket sales, broadcasting, and endorsement deals, the NCAA has always had a ban on paying its players. Instead, top recruits are tempted with scholarship packages and "non-monetary compensation." In the early days of football, playing for money was looked down upon. Recently, athletes have begun to push back against the idea that their programs should earn so much money out of their performances while they earn none. Many are calling out the rules as unfair or even unlawful, and the NCAA is being forced to listen. As of 2021, student athletes won the right to earn money from their own name, image, and likeness. Now, they're pushing for their share of revenue.

▶ Former college players have been challenging NCAA rules around not paying athletes or allowing them to earn money in court. Former West Virginia RB Shawne Alston took his case all the way to the Supreme Court and won a landmark ruling in 2021 that allowed college players to earn money from endorsements.

◀ Former Duke DT Dewayne Carter (now of the Bills) is one NCAA athlete fronting a lawsuit intended to pave the way for "pay-for-play" in college sports.

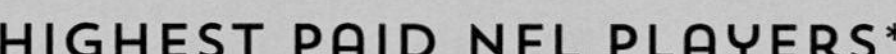

HIGHEST PAID NFL PLAYERS*

*According to average yearly pay in 2024

Quarterback
Joe Burrow, Bengals—$62.9 million

Receiver
Justin Jefferson—$35 million

Running Back
Christian McCaffrey, 49ers—$17.2 million

Offensive Lineman
Penei Sewell, Lions—$30 million

Defensive Lineman
Nick Bosa, 49ers—$34.7 million

Linebacker
Roquan Smith, Ravens—$20 million

Defensive Back
Jaire Alexander, Packers—$21.8 million

Kicker
Justin Tucker, Ravens—$6.2 million

Punter
Michael Dickson, Seahawks—$3.9 million

▲ The Lions took OT Penei Sewell with the seventh overall pick in the 2021 Draft. In 2024, they made him the highest-paid lineman, with a four-year $112 million contract extension, including a massive $85 million guaranteed.

MONEY AND SPONSORSHIP

FACT FILE
Of the top 100 most-watched TV events in 2023, 93 of them were NFL games.

Today, the NFL is the richest sports league in the world with an annual revenue of around $20 billion, and seven out of the top 10 most valuable sports teams in the world are NFL franchises. But how do they make all their money? It's definitely not just from ticket sales...

▲ NBC, CBS, ABC, ESPN, and Fox are longtime broadcasters of NFL games. In 2022, Amazon Prime Video became the newest player in the NFL media market, taking over the rights to Thursday Night Football.

THE BIGGEST PIECE OF THE PIE

NFL games regularly return some of the highest ratings for viewership each year, so the league can demand top dollar for TV rights. Selling the permissions to broadcast games is the number one source of income for NFL teams, with national media deals accounting for 67 percent of all their football-related income. In the league's latest media contract, signed in 2021, the NFL upped its rates by 80 percent, agreeing to a $113 billion deal over 11 years with six networks. Teams also make millions from local media deals as well as from licensing and merchandising—that is, selling a bunch of stuff with the official NFL and team logos and letting other people pay to make products with the official NFL seal.

SPONSORSHIP

The NFL and its teams seek corporate partners to bolster their revenue. Companies buy into the NFL because it gives them visibility and associates them with a beloved national brand. They pay to display the NFL logo on their products and ads or to display their logos and ads in stadiums. In 2023, sponsorship income topped $2 billion for the first time—that's 50% more than the US's next largest pro sports organizations, the MLB and NBA. The most coveted sponsorship, the naming rights for stadiums, can cost $30 million a year.

◀ Often, sponsorships involve endorsements. Telecomms giant Verizon is a multimillion-dollar sponsor of the NFL, which also means they are designated as the "official 5G network of the NFL."

HOME GAMES

With tickets going for an average of more than $150 and stadiums seating 60–80 thousand fans, ticket sales do give a team a healthy bump. As we all know, concession prices are also sky-high, which adds to a home team's profits, along with renting out their stadium for other events, such as concerts. Still, with only eight or nine home games a year, the home crowd alone is not enough to keep a team afloat.

◀ Mascot Viktor the Viking leads fans in the team's "Skol!" chant during a home game at US Bank Stadium.

MOST VALUABLE NFL TEAMS

Dallas Cowboys, $9 billion
New England Patriots, $7 billion
Los Angeles Rams, $6.9 billion
New York Giants, $6.8 billion
Chicago Bears, $6.3 billion

▶ When an NFL Films editor dubbed Dallas "America's Team" in 1978, it was a marketing win for the Cowboys.

"AMERICA'S TEAM"

Jerry Jones purchased the Dallas Cowboys for $150 million in 1989. It's now worth 60 times that and, according to Forbes, is the most valuable sports club on Earth—pretty amazing seeing as their last Super Bowl appearance was in January 1996! How have the 'Boys produced a fanbase so broad and so loyal that all of their games since 2002 have been played in front of sell-out crowds? It's probably because of the mystique they still have from their strong start in the league. They had 20 straight winning seasons from 1966–1985 and won three of four Super Bowls from 1992–1995. Many attribute the consistent strength of the team to the franchise pioneering modern scouting strategies to find the best players.

STADIUMS

At the heart of any home game is the stadium. Team identities are shaped by their stadiums. Historic or brand new, each one has its own character, designed to give their players the home-field advantage.

TIME AND MONEY

Building new stadiums is extremely expensive and time-consuming. The construction alone can take four years with costs running into the billions. While NFL owners will put up and borrow a portion of the money to construct a new venue, they often rely on public funding to foot part of the bill. For instance, more than half of the Titan's new $2.1 billion stadium in Nashville will be paid for with tax-payer money. The NFL argues that cities get a return on their investment because stadiums can boost the local economy and ensure that owners aren't tempted to move their franchise elsewhere.

CLASSIC TO MODERN

The first stadiums were bowl-shaped outdoor venues with grass fields. When the Astrodome became the new home of the Houston Oilers in 1968, it opened up a new realm of possibilites. It was the first indoor NFL stadium covered with a dome roof and the first with artificial turf. Megascreens only began appearing in the 1990s, with the JumboTron in the Bucs' Tampa Stadium.

FACT FILE

First built in 1924, the Chicago Bears' Soldier Field is the oldest stadium still in use by an NFL team, though the team only began playing there in 1971. Located on the south side of the city, it is also the league's smallest stadium, with a capacity of just 62,500.

▲ The ultramodern SoFi Stadium is the most expensive ever built, costing an eye-watering $5.5 billion. The home of the Rams and Chargers features the largest videoboard of any pro sports venue, a 70,000 square-foot "infinity screen" that hangs 122 feet above the field.

TODAY'S NFL STADIUM

The newest NFL stadiums, such as Mercedes-Benz Stadium in Atlanta, GA, and SoFi Stadium in Inglewood, CA, combine stunning futuristic architecture with the latest technology to make fan's gameday experience better than ever. They have retractable roofs that unfold like birds' wings when the sun is shining, creating versatile indoor-outdoor venues. They have multiple lounges and luxury suites, and the tiers of seats have been built up with less of a slope so that the top tiers are closer to field than ever before. Videoboards have become bigger and sharper than ever, allowing spectators to see the expressions on playmakers' faces while following all the game stats. Recent stadiums also have a new focus on sustainability, with solar panels, rainwater-storage systems for water conservation, and recyclable or compostable containers for food and drinks.

FAMOUS STADIUMS

Each stadium is unique, reflecting the franchise that calls it home and the city where it's built. Here are some of the most famous and infamous fields from around the league.

THE BIGGEST

METLIFE STADIUM

Home to both the New York Giants and the New York Jets, MetLife Stadium has the biggest capacity of any NFL stadium, with seating for 82,500 fans. The design of the enormous open-air stadium in East Rutherford, NJ, was inspired by the New York City skyscrapers, with aluminium panels on the outside that glow blue for the Giants and green for the Jets. In 2014, it became the first cold-weather venue to host the Super Bowl with a crowd that exceeded its capacity by 29 fans!

▶ The MetLife Stadium is nicknamed the "New Meadlowlands" after the Giants' previous stadium.

FACT FILE

The Superdome in New Orleans boasts the biggest fixed dome structure in the world. The enormous curved roof is 680 feet across and 9.7 acres in area.

THE HIGHEST

EMPOWER FIELD AT MILE HIGH

The home of the Denver Broncos has the highest elevation of any stadium in the league. True to its name, Mile High is 5,280 feet above sea level. The altitude can be a factor in games, especially for the visiting team who aren't used to playing that high up, where the oxygen levels are lower than normal. You'll often see players wearing oxygen masks on the sidelines there between plays.

▲ The new Mile High opened in 2001. Playing a mile up, the Broncos arguably have the strongest home-field advantage in the NFL.

THE LOUDEST

ARROWHEAD STADIUM

The Kansas City Chiefs have called the Arrowhead Stadium home since 1972. They've always known that it was a hostile place for visiting teams, but in 2014, they decided to make their loudest-stadium-in-the-league status official. In a game against the Pats, the home crowd set the Guinness World Record for stadium noise—142.2 decibels. That's louder than a jet taking off!

▶ The videoboards encourage fans to make the noise they're famous for. GEHA Field at Arrowhead Stadium is open-air with natural bermudagrass turf.

THE COLDEST

LAMBEAU FIELD

The iconic home of the Packers, Lambeau Field opened its doors in 1957. It has been renovated to hold 81,441 people since then, but the franchise has not changed its commitment to playing outdoor football in one of the US's coldest climates. Playoff games there are almost always below freezing temperature, with a record of -13°F (-48°F with wind chill)—perfect for freezing out opponents!

▼ Lambeau gets snowfall to match the cold. Things can get pretty slippery in blizzard conditions, and refs have to keep brushing the hashmarks off.

FANS

Football would be nothing without its fans. If there are 11 players on the field for each side, the crowd is often called the "twelfth player" because they have such a strong impact on games and teams. For many fans, football isn't just a casual interest, it's a life passion.

SHOW OF SPIRIT

Fans show their passion and bring energy into the stadium by dressing up for their teams. For many, that means going well beyond wearing an official jersey or cap. Some come with facepaint in team colors, some in full costume. Sometimes groups of fans conspire to write messages across their bodies, with one letter on each person's stomach. Many carry signs and sport tattoos that let everyone know their allegiances.

▶ Starting in 1982, Rams fan Lance Goldberg randomly started wearing a carved-out watermelon on top of his head to games. He wanted to encourage other fans to be loud and wacky, and to make themselves known in the stadium. His gesture has inspired a movement of "Watermelonheads" among Rams superfans.

MAKING NOISE

Fans are there to cheer their team on, and they often do it with more than shouting and clapping. Many teams have their own fight songs. Washington fans sing "Hail to the Commanders" accompanied by their marching band while Baltimore crowds like to belt out the White Stripes' "Seven Nation Army" to praise and pump up their team.

▶ A Bears fan leads the crowd in their signature chant: "Bear Down!"

◀ Fan traditions often have unexpected backstories. The Cleveland Browns had a generic helmet logo for most of their franchise history, but a defender began pumping up their defense by calling them the "Dawgs" in 1982, and in 1985, the team began dubbing their fans, the "Dawg Pound." After polling fans about which kind of dog they thought best represented their team, the Browns adopted a bullmastiff as their official logo in 2023.

▲ Young Swifties turned Chiefs fans attend the Super Bowl LVIII victory parade in Kansas City.

CELEBRITY INFLUENCERS

Famous fans can often make new fans. During the 2023 season, one of the most famous people on the planet, pop diva Taylor Swift, began showing up at Kansas City Chiefs games. She was there to support her boyfriend, arguably the greatest tight end of all time, #87 Travis Kelce, but her mere presence significantly boosted viewership and social media engagement, especially with younger and female audiences. Even though cutaways to Tay only accounted for seconds of game coverage, Swifties from among her enormous fanbase began tuning in to watch her watching football. Many ended up being drawn into the drama of the NFL in the process, as KC beat the odds to become back-to-back champions. There are no hard figures to quantify her impact, but some marketing agencies think the "Taylor Swift Effect" upped the brand value of the NFL and the Chiefs by hundreds of millions.

FANS ON THEIR WORST BEHAVIOR

Rivalries raise the stakes of games, and the competition can be fun, but sometimes fans take that a step too far. Unfortunately, brawls have broken out between fans from opposing teams in many NFL stadiums. With the reach of today's social media, videos of these incidents have gone viral, magnifying the aggression of a few fans. The NFL is trying to crack down on bad and illegal behavior by being tougher about alcohol (for instance, not admitting visibly drunk fans) and banning fans who break the rules from all NFL stadiums, something that could be a costly mistake for a season ticketholder.

▼ Face and body paint are common ways for fans to show support. The first row of the student section at college football games almost always features superfans in all-over body paint, such as these Clemson Tigers fans.

GAME DAY

The crowds. The theatrics. The edge-of-your-seat excitement. There's nothing quite like game day! From outside to inside the stadium, here's some of what fans can expect when they rock up to watch their team.

▲ Denver fans tailgate out of the back of a pickup before a Broncos game.

TAILGATING

Before the game, football fans assemble in the parking lot outside the stadium to eat, drink, and be merry as they mix with fellow diehards. The tradition began by having pre-game parties out of the backs of trucks. The door at the back of a pickup is called a tailgate, and it can be dropped down to form the perfect parking-lot picnic table. As "tailgating" has become more popular, the setups have become way more elaborate, with tents, tables, chairs, bbqs, football-themed party games, and lots of team-specific décor.

▼ Fans tailgate in a parking lot outside the University of Miami's stadium before a game.

SAFETY

NFL stadiums are built with crowd safety in mind. They use multiple, monitored entrances and exits with gates to control the flow of foot traffic and check attendees for safety issues, such as carrying weapons or being visibly intoxicated. Security staff are posted throughout the stadium during games to address any unsafe behavior and assist in the case of an emergency evacuation. They wear bright neon uniforms so that they are clearly visible to the crowd. All public areas are monitored by security cameras that catch any illegal activity.

◀ A security guard searches fans with a metal detector as they enter the stadium through a designated gate.

▲ Fireworks go off over Mercedes-Benz Stadium during Super Bowl LIII.

SHOWBUSINESS

If there's one thing the NFL is great at, it's spectacle. They know how to make a game into an unforgettable event, with everything from fireworks to flame-throwers. Teams pump up their fans by making grand entrances, bringing in celebs to lead the crowd in the national anthem, and playing signature music over massive speakers while cheerleaders and mascots perform impressive and funny routines.

► Jacksonville gets set to take to the field for a home game through a massive jaguar mouth, flanked by their cheerleaders and mascot.

FACT FILE

Of the 32 NFL franchises, 24 have cheerleaders. The Baltimore Colts became the first team to have its own squad in 1954. Only the NY Giants and Cleveland Browns have never had them.

CONCESSIONS

All stadiums have gameday staples, like pretzels, soda, and hot dogs, but they also showcase local favorites. For instance, the Eagles' Lincoln Financial Field has multiple vendors of Philly cheesesteaks (pictured), their home city's signature sandwich, while the Saints' Superdome celebrates Louisiana classics, like alligator jambalaya, beignets, and po' boys.

▶ Penn State fans cheer on the home team as they come onto the field for an 2021 game against conference rivals Indiana. Penn State is known for their "white out" games, with supporters sporting all-white ensembles, but in this case, they went for the "stripe out." The home of Penn State's Nittany Lions, Beaver Stadium, is the second largest venue in the college game with a capacity of 106,572. Attendees were told to come wearing one or the other of the home team's two colors according to which section of the stands they were seated in. "Striping the stadium" has taken off in recent years around football as an annual tradition for home games. It's a pretty spectacular way to show support—not to mention, intimidating to the visitors!

SNAPSHOT

THE GROWTH OF THE COLLEGE GAME

The first college football game, held in New Jersey in 1869, had a scant 100 spectators, but it's popularity grew quickly and has always rivalled the pros when it comes to gameday attendance. Today, the biggest stadiums can hold more than 100,000 fans, and college football has become big business for universities, generating more than $3 billion for the top 65 programs each year. Top-tier schools rake in an average of over $150 per head for tickets—the same as or higher than for an NFL game. Still, most schools try to maintain the rowdy collegiate atmosphere by designating dedicated student sections with free or significantly discounted admissions. Penn State has one of the largest, reserving 21,000 seats for students—although usually none of them are sitting down. Student fans are generally the loudest supporters. They stay standing for the entire game and cheer on their classmates. Halftime shows often spotlight the home team's marching band, playing traditional fight songs as they step out impressive formations on the field.

THE PENNSYLVANIA STATE UNIVERSITY

NFL REGULAR SEASON

The weekend after Labor Day, the NFL kicks off a new season. The league's 32 teams play in 272 games over 18 weeks to see who will top their division.

SCHEDULE

Like most things in the NFL Calendar, the upcoming season's schedule release has become a major event, with fans tuning in to see who their team with be playing. Released every May, the NFL intentionally designs the schedule to create the maximum drama and set up showcase games between elite teams and fierce rivals that will attract the most viewers. The current regular season has 17 games, so the AFC and NFC teams alternate each year between having eight or nine home games. Each team gets one week off at some point, called a "bye week," that they can use to rest, recuperate, and reset. The core of a franchise's schedule is their division. They will also play once against all four teams in two other divisions, one from the NFC and one from the AFC. This leaves three matchups that are pretty much up to NFL execs to pick. Otherwise, the schedule rotates, so each team is guaranteed to play against the other 31 at least one time every four years.

▲ The NFL execs in charge of the schedule try to predict which teams will be the most exciting each year when they decide who will get the primetime slots. In 2024, the 49ers and Jets had the most primetime games on the schedule. Both have big markets, and the Niners were the Super Bowl runner-ups while the Jets had a lot of buzz because they signed superstar QB Aaron Rodgers.

PRIMETIME

Most NFL regular season games are played on Sunday afternoons during two slots—either 1pm or 4:05/4:25pm—which means several simultaneous games are competing for viewers. There are also a series of showcase matchups each week in time slots that don't overlap with other games. The most coveted spots are for Sunday and Monday Night Football, broadcast on the NBC and ESPN networks respectively, but the NFL also added a Thursday Night game on the streaming service Amazon Prime. Teams are not guaranteed to play in any of these primetime slots. The schedulers favor franchises that have the biggest followings and were the most competitive the previous season.

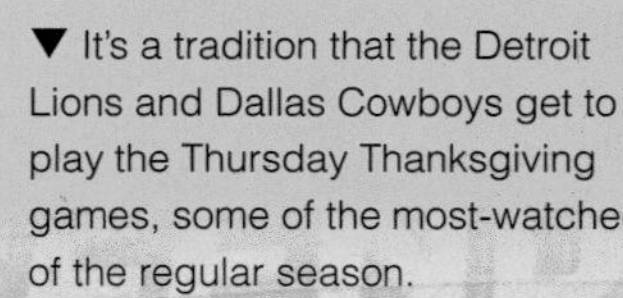

▼ It's a tradition that the Detroit Lions and Dallas Cowboys get to play the Thursday Thanksgiving games, some of the most-watched of the regular season.

FACT FILE

The Pittsburgh Steelers have the best regular-season record since the AFL-NFL merger in 1970, with a record of 514-325-4 and a winning percentage of 61%.

STANDINGS

Each team's record of wins, losses, and ties are kept track of in a table arranged by conference and division. Teams are ranked 1–4, then, according to their standing within their division rather than their overall ranking in the league as a whole. This is because the main object of every team during the regular season is to win their division since all eight division champions are guaranteed a spot in the playoffs. Most standings will also contain lots of other information that provides context for their overall record, such as the points they've scored and allowed, their home versus away records, their records within their conference and division, and the streak that they've been on in recent games.

DIVISIONAL GAMES

NFL teams square off against each of the other three teams in their division twice a season, once on the road and once at home. These six games play a big part in the division title race, which often comes down to the wire. Week 18, the last of the season, is known unofficially as "Rivalry Week" and is reserved for divisional matchups to capitalize on the drama of tight title races. And when you take on the same opposition over and over again, year after year, for the chance to make the postseason, the rivalries can get intense.

◀ The Philadelphia Eagles and Dallas Cowboys of the NFC East have one of the bitterest division rivalries in the NFL.

HOME GAMES

Around half of a team's games are played at "home." Competing in your own familiar stadium in front of your own fans without the need to travel has traditionally been seen as an advantage for NFL teams. Standings compare home and away records because teams are more likely to win at home, but some teams seem to thrive at home more than others. For instance, the Seahawks regularly outscore their opponents at home by several points more than they do on the road, while Baltimore almost always wins more at home. Win or lose, home games are a team's bread and butter, and their chance to showcase what their stadium and city has to offer.

▼ The Ravens have one of the best overall home records in the league. Their biggest home victory came in a 48–3 stomping of the Lions in 2009.

NFL PLAYOFFS

When weather is at its coldest in January, that's when the competition really begins to heat up in the NFL. After the regular season finishes, 14 teams get the chance to duke it out for the championship title in the postseason.

THE BRACKET

To qualify for the postseason, a team must either win their division or have one of the best records in their conference. Most often, the "playoff picture" isn't fully known until the final day of the regular season. Seven teams from each conference make the cut, and they are "seeded" to determine the schedule. The division winners are seeds Nos. 1–4, with the top seed going to the team with the best record in the conference. The remaining seeds go to the other teams with the best records in the conference, in order of their winning percentages. If two teams have the same record, other factors can come into play to break the tie, such as the outcome of their head-to-head matchups and their records within their divisions. Playoff games take place over three weeks immediately following the regular season. The higher the seed, the greater your advantage in terms of where you play and who you play against. The No. 1 seeds on each side even get to sit out the first round before getting to host the divisional round on their home turf.

▲ Playoff spots and division title races can come down to the wire. In the last game of the 2010 season, the Seahawks beat division rivals the Rams to put them out of the playoffs and secure their own spot with a losing 7–9 season.

THE WILD CARD ROUND

A "wild card" team was added to the NFL playoffs in 1970, and, while the format has changed a lot since then, wild card teams have been a part of the postseason ever since. In the current format, in place since 2020, each conference has three wild card slots, seeded Nos. 5–7. These spots are still competitive—if a wild card team is coming from a strong division, there's a good chance that they might even have a better record than one or more of the division winners. There are six wild card games in the first round of the playoffs, with the top seeds hosting the lower ones. These fun matchups add to the postseason drama, allowing teams that failed to win their division a chance to take the league title.

◀ Cornerback Lester Hayes ran back a fumble recovery for a TD as the Raiders beat the Oilers 27–7 in the 1980 AFC Wild Card Game. The Raiders became the first wild card team to win the Super Bowl that year.

FACT FILE

A wild card team has gone on to win the Super Bowl seven times. A No. 1 seed has won 52% of the time since seeding began in 1975.

CONFERENCE CHAMPIONSHIPS

Teams only play against other teams in their conference in the playoffs so that the Super Bowl will be a showdown between the best each conference has to offer. The third and last round of the playoffs is for the AFC and NFC title games. AFC teams compete for the Lamar Hunt Trophy, named after the founder of the AFL, and NFC teams compete for the George Halas Trophy, named in honor of one of the founders of the NFL.

▼ The Niners show off the George Halas Trophy after winning the 2023 NFC Championship Game against the Lions.

▲ The Browns lost to the Broncos three times in the AFC Championship Game from 1986–1989. The first is considered to be one of the greatest games of all time. It was a 23–20 thriller that Denver, led by Hall-of-Fame QB John Elway, won in the closing seconds with a series of plays so stunning that is has been dubbed "The Drive."

FACT FILE

The Patriots have the most AFC titles (11) while the Cowboys and 49ers are tied for the most NFC titles with eight each.

THE BIG GAME

The NFL Championship is known for spectacular drama—on and off the field. It's regularly America's most-watched sporting event and LVIII was the most-watched telecast in history, so it's earned its name: the Super Bowl.

HISTORY

Played on a Sunday evening two weeks after the Conference Championships, the Super Bowl is the NFL's biggest showpiece and advertisement for the league. The NFL introduced playoffs with a championship in 1933, but the Super Bowl didn't come along until its merger with the AFL. As part of the 1966 deal, they agreed that the champion of the AFL would play the champion of the NFL each year to crown the champion of champions. When the merger became official in 1970, it shifted to a competition between the top team in each conference, as the AFL was folded into the AFC. It has been called the "Super Bowl" since 1969, a name that, as legend would have it, was inspired by AFL founder Lamar Hunt seeing his kids play with a Super Ball. Winners are crowned "World Champions," which is strange for an entirely US-based competition, but it has become a genuinely global event with huge entertainment value. Even the ads, tailored specially to the event, are talking points since brands pay upward of $7 million per 30-second spot to run them.

SUPER BOWL RECORDS

Most Appearances
The Patriots, 11

Most Wins
The Steelers and Patriots, 6

Most Losses
The Broncos and Patriots, 5

Biggest Victory
Super Bowl XXIV (Jan. 28, 1990)
49ers (55–10) Broncos

Highest-Scoring
Super Bowl XXIX (Jan. 29, 1995)
49ers (49–26) Chargers

Most-Watched
Super Bowl LVIII (Feb. 11, 2024)
Chiefs (25–22) 49ers
202.4 million viewers

THE SILVERWARE

The team that wins the Big Game get their very own Lombardi Trophy to put on their shelf. Crafted by Tiffany & Co., it stands 22 inches high and is made of sterling silver. The design has not changed since its debut in 1966. The MVP award is called the Pete Rozelle Trophy after a former NFL commissioner. The game MVP is chosen by a panel of sports analysts and fan voting, weighted 80/20.

VENUES

Cities once competed to host the Super Bowl by submitting bids, but the NFL has stopped making it a contest. Since 2018, the league picks which stadium they want to host and invites them to make a deal (years in advance of the actual event). Prospective hosts have to meet a lot of criteria, like seating for 70,000+ and good weather conditions, along with plenty of attractions and accomodations for visiting media, teams, and fans. New Orleans' Superdome has hosted the most Super Bowls (7).

▶ The first Super Bowl was played in the Coliseum, a classic Los Angeles stadium.

THE GREATEST SHOW ON EARTH

It wouldn't be the Super Bowl without a bit of spectacle. Teams take to the field with fireworks and smoke machines, listen to the national anthem sung by a chart-topping singer, and retire to their locker rooms while the audience is entertained by a no-holds-barred 15-minute halftime show. With so many guaranteed viewers, celebrities line up to headline it—and many viewers are more interested in these greatest-hit concerts than in the game itself! Halftime shows have taken many forms over the years, from classic rock singalongs with the likes of The Rolling Stones to full-blown pop extravaganzas—think: Katy Perry rocking up on an animatronic tiger and shooting across the stadium like a firework. According to the critics (yes, they review these performances every year), nothing can beat Prince leading a singalong to "Purple Rain" in the pouring rain at Super Bowl XLI.

▶ Beyoncé and Bruno Mars showed up to help Coldplay light up the Super Bowl 50 halftime show at the 49ers' Levi's Stadium.

CELEBRATIONS

Super Bowl celebrations start from the final blow of the whistle, with team staff and their families allowed to join the players on the field as confetti rains down. The Lombardi was once handed over to teams in their locker room, but, since 1996, the trophy ceremony has become part of the TV broadcast of the event. A podium is moved onto the field, and the winning team's owner steps up to receive the coveted silverware. The coach, game MVP, and other top players are also given their chance to lift the trophy and do interviews for the crowd. After the game, winning teams are greeted with victory parades in their home cities. Players usually travel in open-top buses as thousands of fans swarm the streets and gather at a rally to celebrate together. In Tampa Bay, the Bucs celebrated with boat parade down the Hillsborough River following Super Bowl LV while a million people have crowded to the streets of Kansas City to catch a glimpse of their three recent Lombardis.

▲ The Rams crowd onto and around a podium for the trophy ceremony to celebrate their victory in Super Bowl LVI.

▼ Super Bowl champs get specially designed, jewel-encrusted rings to commemorate their victory. Big-win bling!

▶ Kansas City hosts a victory parade for the Chiefs following their win in Super Bowl LIV.

THE SUPER BOWL: 1960s AND 1970s

THE SUPER BOWL: 1960s AND 1970s

Year*	Host	Result
1966 / I	Los Angeles, CA	Green Bay (35–10) Kansas City
1967 / II	Miami, FL	Green Bay (33–14) Oakland
1968 / III	Miami, FL	New York Jets (16–7) Baltimore
1969 / IV	New Orleans, LA	Kansas City (23–7) Minnesota
1970 / V	Miami, FL	Baltimore (16–13) Dallas
1971 / VI	New Orleans, LA	Dallas (24–3) Miami
1972 / VII	Los Angeles, CA	Miami (14–7) Minnesota
1973 / VIII	Houston, TX	Miami (24–7) Minnesota
1974 / IX	New Orleans, LA	Pittsburgh (16–6) Minnesota
1975 / X	Miami, FL	Pittsburgh (21–17) Dallas
1976 / XI	Pasadena, CA	Oakland (32–14) Minnesota
1977 / XII	New Orleans, LA	Dallas (27–10) Denver
1978 / XIII	Miami, FL	Pittsburgh (35–31) Dallas
1979 / XIV	Pasadena, CA	Pittsburgh (31–19) Los Angeles Rams

*The year indicates the season, not the date played.

FACT FILE

The first four Super Bowls took place before the NFL and AFL merged, pitting the champions of both pro leagues against one another. The pressure to show up the other league was intense, but they turned out to be worthy rivals, with each side winning two.

WINNING COACH TO TROPHY NAMESAKE

Hollywood stars came out in droves to L.A.'s Coliseum stadium and 65 million viewers tuned in for the first Super Bowl—but the game wasn't much of a blockbuster, especially in the second half. The Packers, with Hall-of-Fame QB Bart Starr at the helm, went on a 21–0 scoring run against the Chiefs to become the undisputed champions. The Pack put in a similarly dominant performance the following year against the Raiders to take their fifth national title under coach Vince Lombardi. When the game-changing leader and strategist died of cancer a few years later in 1970, the sterling-silver "World Professional Football Championship Trophy" was immediately re-named in his honor. The "Lombardi" does sound a bit catchier.

▲ Coach Lombardi is carried off the field by his players after their victory in Super Bowl I.

▲ Hall-of-Fame QB Fran Tarkenton scrambles away from the Oakland defense in Super Bowl XI. The Raiders set 21 Super Bowl records against the Vikings to be crowned champions of the 1976 season.

THE VIKINGS CURSE

Minnesota went to the Big Game five times in eight years between the 1969 season and the 1976 season. They managed to lose the championship every single time...badly. Their run of routs started with Super Bowl IV, where the Chiefs almost completely shut down the Vikes' offense to pull off a historic 23–7 upset. Before the game, a Vikings hot air balloon had actually smashed into the stands and caught on fire, foreshadowing how the franchise would continue to crash and burn in title games. In fact, the Vikings have been one of the league's winningest teams during the regular season, but they have yet to taste victory in the Super Bowl. Some fans link this "curse" to the controversial founding of the team, with the owners going back on a deal they had with the AFL to join the NFL instead. Minnesota's original AFL bid and players ended up moving to Oakland and becoming the Raiders franchise—the team that would go on to rack up a record 429 yards of offense against the Vikings to win Super Bowl XI.

▶ The 1972 Dolphins team reunited 40 years later at the White House, giving President Barack Obama a jersey to commemorate their perfect 17–0 record.

FACT FILE

The 1972 Dolphins are the only team in the Super Bowl era to have a perfect season, winning every single regular season and postseason game, including a very well-deserved victory after a defensive battle in Super Bowl VII.

▼ WR Lynn Swann beats the Dallas defenders in Super Bowl XIII. He was one of nine players on the 1978 Steelers team who have since been enshrined in Canton. The others include QB Terry Bradshaw, Center Mike Webster, RB Franco Harris, WR John Stallworth, DT Joe Greene, DB Mel Blount, LB Jack Ham, and LB Jack Lambert.

THE BATTLE OF CHAMPIONS

In the 1970s, the Cowboys and Steelers were both stacked with future Hall-of-Famers, including their Hall-of-Fame coaches Tom Landry and Chuck Noll. When they faced off for the second time in the Super Bowl following the 1978 season, both franchises had already won the Big Game—twice. The matchup between two dominant sides was dubbed the "Battle of Champions" in the lead-up to the game, and it 100% lived up to that billing. The fourth quarter saw four touchdowns as the 35–31 game went right down to the wire. But, after giving up two last-minute TD passes to Dallas QB Roger Staubach, the Steelers recovered the Cowboys' onside kick to prevent a comeback victory and earn the title Champion of Champions. Pittsburgh would go on to pull off a repeat against the Rams the following year, securing their fourth league championship in six years.

THE SUPER BOWL: 1980s AND 1990s

THE SUPER BOWL: 1980s AND 1990s

Year*	Host	Result
1980 / XV	New Orleans, LA	Oakland (27–10) Philadelphia
1981 / XVI	Pontiac, MI	San Francisco (26–21) Cincinnati
1982 / XVII	Pasadena, CA	Washington (27–17) Miami
1983 / XVIII	Tampa, FL	Los Angeles Raiders (38–9) Washington
1984 / XIX	Palo Alto, CA	San Francisco (38–16) Miami
1985 / XX	New Orleans, LA	Chicago (46–10) New England
1986 / XXI	Pasadena, CA	New York Giants (39–20) Denver
1987 / XXII	San Diego, CA	Washington (42–10) Denver
1988 / XXIII	Miami, FL	San Francisco (20–16) Cincinnati
1989 / XXIV	New Orleans, LA	San Francisco (55–10) Denver
1990 / XXV	Tampa, FL	New York Giants (20–19) Buffalo
1991 / XXVI	Minneapolis, MN	Washington (37–24) Buffalo
1992 / XXVII	Pasadena, CA	Dallas (52–17) Buffalo
1993 / XXVIII	Atlanta, GA	Dallas (30–13) Buffalo
1994 / XXIX	Miami, FL	San Francisco (49–26) San Diego
1995 / XXX	Tempe, AZ	Dallas (27–17) Pittsburgh
1996 / XXXI	New Orleans, LA	Green Bay (35–21) New England
1997 / XXXII	San Diego, CA	Denver (31–24) Green Bay
1998 / XXXIII	Miami, FL	Denver (34–19) Atlanta
1999 / XXXIV	Atlanta, GA	St. Louis (23–16) Tennessee

*The year indicates the season, not the date played.

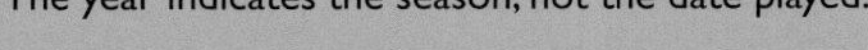

FACT FILE

The Bears defensive end Richard Dent was named MVP of Super Bowl XX, during which the 1985 Bears' league-topping D put in a record-breaking performance against New England, including seven sacks, two forced fumbles, and a pick six that brought the score line to 37-3.

WIDE RIGHT

Super Bowl XXV was Buffalo's first trip to the Big Game. They got off to a flying start against the Giants, with the Bill's superstar end Bruce Smith—who had just been dubbed the NFL's Defensive Player of the Year—leading the defensive battle. He tackled the Giants' QB in the end zone for a safety and the lead. By the fourth quarter, the Bills were down in the finely poised competition, 19–20. With just eight seconds left on the clock, Scott Norwood lined up to take the game-winning 47-yard field goal, but he missed—wide right. That phrase has haunted Bills fans since, who lost that championship by a point, then saw their team also lose the next three in a row by wide margins. In the playoffs at the end of the 2023 season, Bills fans had an unfortunate flashback to that moment, with kicker Tyler Bass missing a last-minute game-tying FG against the Chiefs, the eventual champions. It went "wide right." The franchise still has yet to take home a Lombardi.

WEST COAST REPRESENT

When Hall-of-Fame coach Bill Walsh took over the 49ers in 1979, he took them from a losing franchise to the top of the league. With superstar Joe Montana as his QB, he developed the revolutionary "West Coast" offense—a style founded on quick, short, pinpoint passes—that allowed San Francisco to reign for nearly two decades. Under Walsh, the Niners won their first three Super Bowls and then two more under his former defensive coordinator, George Seifert. Their first title, at the end of the 1981 season, was a nail-biter. Played against the Bengals, it was the debut Super Bowl appearance for both teams. San Francisco took a commanding 20–0 lead in the first half only to see it evaporate in the second. Their D stood firm, making an interception and goal-line stand to finish the job. They also won a rematch with Cincy in Super Bowl XXIII, scoring their only two TDs in the fourth quarter to pull off a 20–16 comeback victory.

◀ In Super Bowl XXIII, WR Jerry Rice had a record 215 receiving yards, and in Super Bowl XXIV, he had a record three receiving TDs.

THREE IN FOUR

Triumphing over the Steelers 27–17 in Super Bowl XXX, the Cowboys became the first franchise in history to win three championships in four years on the back of a spectacular offense led by future Hall of Famers QB Troy Aikman, RB Emmitt Smith, and WR Michael Irvin. The Cowboys were appearing in a record eighth Super Bowl, but they had faced Pittsburgh in two previous title games and lost. Sure enough, the Steelers were threatening a second-half comeback when Dallas's cornerback Larry Brown (a 12th-round pick who'd surprised everyone by winning the starting job his rookie season) refused to let them win. He made two crucial interceptions to halt Steelers' drives and returned them for a total of 77 yards to set up two game-clinching TDs.

▲ Jerry Jones, owner and manager of the Cowboys since 1989, presents his third Lombardi to his players following Super Bowl XXX. Jones's franchise has not won a Super Bowl since.

◀ Scott Norwood's title-winning kick looked like it was going in before fading "wide right" as the Bills lost a heartbreaker.

FACT FILE

Super Bowl XXXI was the only time a special teams player has been named game MVP. Green Bay's Desmond Howard had 244 return yards, including a 99-yard kickoff return for a TD in the Pack's 14-point win over the Pats.

THE SUPER BOWL: 2000s

THE SUPER BOWL: 2000s

Year*	Host	Result
2000 / XXXV	Tampa, FL	Baltimore (34–7) New York Giants
2001 / XXXVI	New Orleans	New England (20–17) St. Louis
2002 / XXXVII	San Diego, CA	Tampa Bay (48–21) Oakland
2003 / XXXVIII	Houston, TX	New England (32–29) Carolina
2004 / XXXIX	Jacksonville, FL	New England (24–21) Philadelphia
2005 / XL	Detroit, MI	Pittsburgh (27–10) Seattle
2006 / XLI	Miami, FL	Indianapolis (29–17) Chicago
2007 / XLII	Phoenix, AZ	NY Giants (17–14) New England
2008 / XLIII	Tampa, FL	Pittsburgh (27–23) Arizona
2009 / XLIV	Miami, FL	New Orleans (31–17) Indianapolis

*The year indicates the season, not the date played.

▼ The NFC's St. Louis Rams went to two Super Bowls in three years. League MVP Kurt Warner (13) became the first undrafted QB to win a Super Bowl in 1999 but lost a heartbreaker to the Pats in 2001.

FACT FILE

The AFC triumphed in seven of 10 Super Bowls in this decade, with only a handful of AFC powerhouses dominating. In fact, from 1995–2018, just five teams accounted for 22 of 24 AFC appearances in the championship.

▲ In 2006–07, Manning helped end the Colts' 37-year championship drought—appropriately enough, during the first Super Bowl to be played in the pouring rain.

PEYTON'S FIRST TITLE

Quarterback Peyton Manning had already been named league MVP twice by 2006, but his lackluster postseason record had raised serious question marks about whether he was championship material. Leading his team to a record comeback in the AFC Championship Game against arch rivals the Patriots went a long way toward silencing doubters. Super Bowl XLI, which pit them against the Chicago Bears, was the Colts' first since the team moved from Baltimore to Indianapolis in 1984 and the first time that two teams with African American head coaches—Tony Dungy and Lovie Smith—had faced each other in the Big Game. The first quarter didn't get off to an auspicious start for the franchise QB, with Devin Hester returning the opening kickoff for a TD and Peyton throwing an interception on his first drive. But the Colts remained patient, as Peyton went 25/38 for 247 yards to take home the game MVP and a 29–17 win for Indianapolis.

THE "SIX PACK"

After taking championship titles in 2005 and 2008, the Pittsburgh Steelers became the very first team to win six Super Bowls. The history-making moment was playfully commemorated with memes showing a six pack of Lombardi Trophies. The milestone win was also one of the all-time greatest Super Bowls, watched by a record 98.7 million viewers. The Steelers were up 17–7 at half-time after an incredible 100-yard interception return for a TD by veteran LB James Harrison, who faked a blitz to pick off a pass at the goal line. Arizona scored 16 unanswered points in the fourth to take the lead, including a 64-yard TD reception by star Larry Fitzgerald. Pushed back to their own 12-yard line with 2:30 on the clock, QB Ben Roethlisberger found his go-to WR Santonio Holmes three times for 73 yards. Holmes made the dramatic, championship-winning catch in the back corner of the end zone, keeping just his tippy toes inbounds before falling backward in a play that broke the hearts of Arizona fans, who are still waiting for the franchise's first Super Bowl victory.

◀ Quarterback Ben Roethlisberger hoists the Lombardi Trophy next to coach Mike Tomlin after the Steelers' victory in Super Bowl XLIII.

THE DYNASTY BEGINS

The New England Patriots won a staggering three Super Bowls in four years between 2001 and 2004—all close-run competitions where the Pats found ways to eke out impressive wins. This dominant postseason form in the early 2000s marked the dawn of the Brady-Belichick partnership between the Pats' QB and head coach that would ultimately lead to 17 division titles, 13 AFC championship appearances, nine Super Bowl appearances, and six titles. The Dynasty all began with Tom Brady accidentally getting the starting job in his second season at New England after the team's #1, Drew Bledsoe, suffered an injury. Brady ended up leading the team all the way to the Super Bowl that year, where they beat the Rams with a last-second Adam Vinatieri field goal. Super Bowl XXXVIII was won the same way. Brady's 354 passing yards and record 32 completions earned him his second championship MVP. At the end of the 2004 season, New England pulled off the repeat, holding off the Philadelphia Eagles to again win by a narrow three-point margin.

▶ Super Bowl XXXIX MVP Deion Branch catches a record 11th pass, leaping over Eagles' CB Sheldon Brown.

LEGENDARY COMEBACK

The first 16–0 season in history made the Pats favorites for yet another title in 2007, but the Giants pulled off a shock 17–14 upset in a defensive battle that was decided by one of the greatest game-winning drives of all time. New York had the ball at their own 17, down by four, with 2:39 on the clock. They faced a 4th & 1 and 3rd & long but managed to keep the drive going for the 83 necessary yards. Wideout David Tyree had the most memorable play of the 12, beating out star safety Rodney Harrison to haul in a catch that he somehow secured by pinning the ball against his helmet for a massive 32-yard gain. In the end, wide receiver Plaxico Burress pulled in a 13-yard TD reception on a slant-and-go with 35 seconds to play to put the kibosh on New England's perfect 19–0 season and win Super Bowl XLII.

◀ Giants' wide receiver David Tyree makes his famous 32-yard "Helmet Catch" to keep New York's championship hopes alive in the final minutes of Super Bowl XLII.

THE SUPER BOWL: 2010s

THE SUPER BOWL: 2010s

Year*	Host	Result
2010 / XLV	Arlington, TX	Green Bay (31–25) Pittsburgh
2011 / XLVI	Indianapolis, IL	New York Giants (21–17) New England
2012 / XLVII	New Orleans, LA	Baltimore (34–31) San Francisco
2013 / XLVIII	East Rutherford, NJ	Seattle (43–8) Denver
2014 / XLIX	Glendale, AZ	New England (28–24) Seattle
2015 / 50	Santa Clara, CA	Denver (24–10) Carolina
2016 / LI	Houston, TX	New England (34–28) Atlanta
2017 / LII	Minneapolis, MN	Philadelphia (41–33) New England
2018 / LIII	Atlanta, GA	New England (13–3) Los Angeles Rams
2019 / LIV	Miami, FL	Kansas City (31–20) San Francisco

*The year indicates the season, not the date played.

▶ Foles (9) goes unmarked in the confusion, allowing the QB to haul in a touchdown pass from his TE Burton (36).

LEGION OF BOOM

When the Seahawks met up with the Broncos in Super Bowl XLVIII, both teams had 13-3 records. Denver were actually slight favorites, but what the bookies didn't seem to factor in was Seattle's outstanding, tenacious defense. One of the greatest defenses of all time, they topped the league that year across the board, with fewest yards and points allowed, and the most takeaways. Their X-factor was a rowdy secondary nicknamed the "Legion of Boom," a play on the DC Comics league of supervillains, the Legion of Doom. The Hawks embarrassed the oddsmakers with a huge blowout in one of the most lopsided championships ever played. After scoring a safety just 12 seconds into the game, Seattle shut Denver out in the first half, intercepting QB Peyton Manning twice, one of which was returned for a 69-yard pick six. The dominant defensive performance landed the Seahawks their first NFL title with a 43-8 rout.

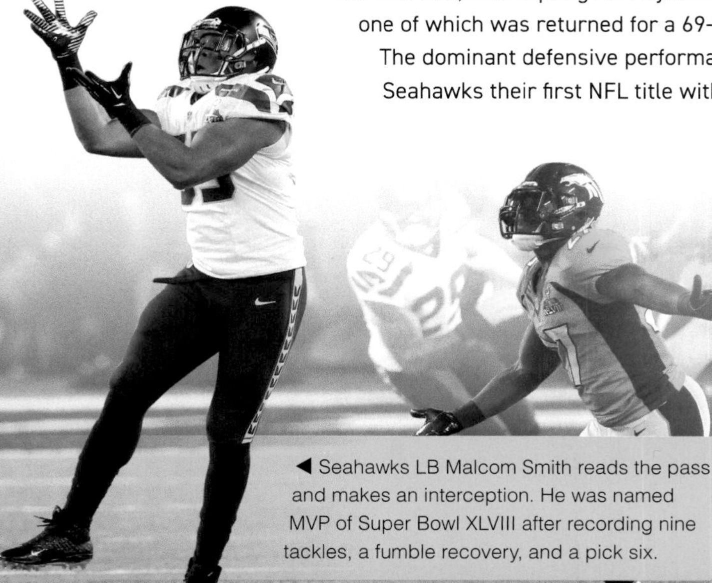

◀ Seahawks LB Malcom Smith reads the pass and makes an interception. He was named MVP of Super Bowl XLVIII after recording nine tackles, a fumble recovery, and a pick six.

▲ The Philly Special has become so iconic, that diagrams of the play feature on merchandise and the Eagles put up a nine-foot-tall bronze statue of Foles and Pederson discussing the play-call in front of their stadium.

◀ RB James White muscles his way into the end zone to score the first winning overtime TD in Super Bowl history.

FACT FILE

Super Bowl LIII has the dubious distinction of being the lowest-scoring Super Bowl in NFL history. The Rams and Pats both had high-powered offenses but went into halftime tied 0–0 and into the fourth quarter tied 3–3. The game ended 13–3 in favor of the Pats.

PEAK NEW ENGLAND

The Pats went to half of the Super Bowls in the 2010s and won three of them, bringing the franchise's (and Tom Brady's) Lombardi Trophy total to six. The most memorable of these wins saw the Pats come back from 25 points down at the start of the third quarter to beat Atlanta 34–28 in Super Bowl LI. It was in fact the largest comeback in Super Bowl history. Brady took to the air to make up the deficit, throwing for 466 yards as the Pats scored 19 unanswered points in the fourth quarter to take the Super Bowl into overtime for the first time ever. Running back James White also had a standout performance, single-handedly scoring 20 points, including the game-winning TD. The incredible game set 30 Super Bowl records. One of the strangest is them being the first winning team to never have had the lead during the whole game—never count the Pats out!

THE PHILLY SPECIAL

Super Bowl LII gave us what might be the most iconic trick play of all time in the "Philly Special." The Eagles chose the biggest stage to make one of the gutsiest calls in football history—and it paid off. At the end of the second quarter, the Eagles held a narrow three-point lead against the Pats and had driven their way down to near the goal line. Instead of playing it safe with a field goal, they decided to go for the TD on fourth down, with QB Nick Foles asking coach Doug Pederson if they could run the "Philly Philly." Foles, who had played backup for most of the season, moved up to the tight-end spot to seemingly call an audible, but the ball was snapped into the hands of running back Corey Clement, who quickly pitched it to moving tight end Trey Burton. While this was happening, Foles snuck into the end zone to catch one of the most magical TDs in NFL history, a move that helped secure the teams' first-ever Super Bowl win. The Eagles' bold play-calling in this game made an impact on the league, significantly boosting the number of fourth-down conversion attempts in following seasons.

FACT FILE

Super Bowl LII was an incredible offensive showcase with 1,151 yards of total offense—the most in Super Bowl history. Philly won in spite of not forcing the Pats to punt once, and the chief trickster Foles was named MVP.

THE SUPER BOWL: 2020s

THE SUPER BOWL: 2020s

Year*	Host	Result
2020 / LV	Tampa, FL	Tampa Bay (31–9) Kansas City
2021 / LVI	Inglewood, CA	Los Angeles Rams (23–20) Cincinnati
2022 / LVII	Glendale, AZ	Kansas City (38–35) Philadelphia
2023 / LVIII	Las Vegas, NV	Kansas City (25–22) San Francisco

*The year indicates the season, not the date played.

BRADY DOES IT AGAIN

After his victory with the Patriots in Super Bowl LIII, Tom Brady announced that he would be leaving New England and entering free agency for the first time in his 20-year career. The 42-year-old superstar was up for grabs, and he landed in Tampa Bay in 2019. People were wondering if he was over the hill or if he would lose his magic after leaving behind his longtime partnership with coach Bill Belichick. The very next year, Brady proved he could bring his championship-winning ways with him, leading the Bucs in a 31–9 stomping of the Chiefs in Super Bowl LV and notching the GOAT's astonishing seventh Lombardi Trophy—more than any single franchise has won in all of NFL history! He lured one of his favorite targets out of retirement to help him do it, with TE Rob Gronkowski catching two touchdowns that gave Tampa a controlling lead. Meanwhile, the Bucs' D refused to give KC a break, picking off a Patrick Mahomes pass in the end zone and limiting their normally explosive offense to three field goals.

▶ Clark Hunt celebrates his third Super Bowl win as Chiefs CEO with the franchise founded by his father.

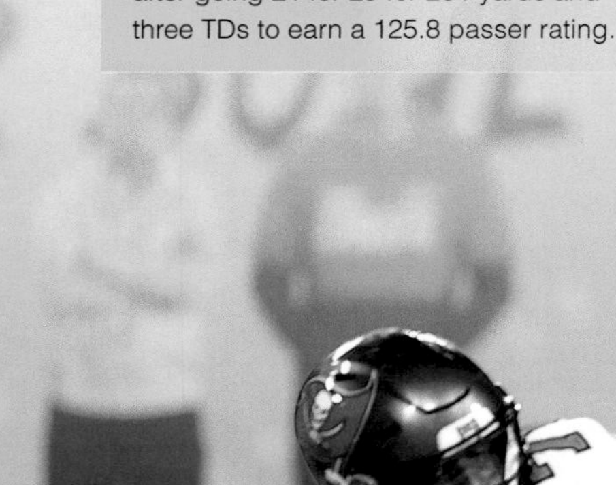

▶ Brady won his fifth Super Bowl MVP after going 21 for 29 for 201 yards and three TDs to earn a 125.8 passer rating.

NO. 4 NO MORE

The Rams and Bengals were both the No. 4 seeds in their conferences heading into the playoffs but came up big in the postseason to face off in the Big Game. Cincy seemed like the team of destiny. After decades of lackluster performances, they had posted a 10–7 record to make it into the postseason, then held on and came back to win nail-biters in each of their three playoff games, including an OT win in the AFC Championship against the Chiefs after being down 21–3. In the end, they fell just short of their first title after a tight game that saw three lead changes and never more than a few points between the two sides. The Rams put together an impressive game-winning drive in the fourth quarter, going 15 plays for 79 yards and converting on a fourth down in their own territory before halting the Bengal's last drive and championship dreams on downs.

◀ The game MVP, wideout Cooper Kupp, scores the game-winning TD in Super Bowl LVI, giving the Rams their second NFL title and their first since moving to L.A.

◀ All-Pro CB Trent McDuffie aced it in Super Bowl LVIII, allowing only two receptions for nine yards, saving a TD, getting three deflections and tackles, and pressuring Purdy into multiple key incompletions.

THE REPEAT

KC went to four Super Bowls and won three in five years, marking the dawn of a new dynasty. They won back-to-back Super Bowls in LVII and LVIII, both in close-fought, high-drama games with record viewership. Both times, the Chiefs' offense was quiet the first half before springing to life in the second. In Super Bowl LVIII, their defense kept them in the game, leaving San Francisco 3 for 12 on third-down conversions. In the second half, Mahomes came up big while the defense held firm. TE Travis Kelce, who had been held to a single yard in the first half, also went into overdrive to record three vital receptions for 90 yards. On the 22-yard reception that set up their game-tying FG, the 34-year-old mega-competitor was clocked by NextGen stats running faster than he had in seven years (19.68 mph). The champs weren't the favorites, but they triumphed again anyway, cementing the 2020s as the Era of the Chiefs.

THE NCAA POSTSEASON

With so many teams and such short seasons, it has been difficult for the NCAA to figure out how to determine a bonafide "national champion." Instead of having a centralized tournament, the college postseason began as a series of regional games called "bowls" that invited top-tier teams with strong records to face off for national audiences.

▶ This illustration accompanied a front-page newspaper headline: "Michigan's Team Routs the Cardinals." And they did, beating the home side Stanford 49–0 in the first Rose Bowl. Today, the Big Ten powerhouse Michigan holds the record for the most Rose Bowl appearances at 21!

ESTABLISHED IN 1902

The first bowl game was played in 1902, as part of the Tournament of the Roses, an event in Pasadena, California, that featured a New Year's parade of floats decorated with flowers with prizes for the most impressive displays. Today known as the Rose Bowl, it has been played every year since 1916—that's more than a century! Originally, it was a showcase for two top teams from the East and West. Since 1947, it has become a showdown between the champions of the Pac-12 and the Big Ten conferences. Today, it's part of the College Football Playoff tournament that crowns a national champion.

FACT FILE

The term "bowl" comes from Pasadena's Rose Bowl Stadium, which was completed in 1922. Its name and round design were inspired by one of the very first gridiron football stadiums, the Yale Bowl.

▲ Bowls are usually played on neutral grounds in locations that don't get too wintry since all postseason games are scheduled for December and January.

▲ Ohio State beat top-ranked Alabama 42–35 in the 2015 Sugar Bowl to advance to the very first College Football Playoff Championship Game where they were crowned the first "undisputed champions."

COLLEGE FOOTBALL PLAYOFF CHAMPIONSHIPS

Year	Result
2015	Ohio State (42–20) Oregon
2016	Alabama (45–40) Clemson
2017	Clemson (35–31) Alabama
2018	Alabama (26–23) Georgia
2019	Clemson (44–16) Alabama
2020	LSU (42–25) Clemson
2021	Alabama (52–24) Ohio State
2022	Georgia (33–18) Alabama
2023	Georgia (65–7) TCU
2024	Michigan (34–13) Washington

BOWLS AND THE NCAA NATIONAL CHAMPIONSHIP

For many years, the annual "national champion" in college football was determined by votes among sports journalists, coaches, and others, not by a postseason victory in a bowl. Performance at bowl games did factor into the voting, but the rankings were subjective since top contenders for the title often did not meet head-to-head during the season. In 1992, the NCAA began designating one of the bowls as the national championship game and inviting the two top-ranked teams to play in it. The BCS National Championship became a standalone game in 2006, not hosted by any bowl, but, as of 2014, the NCAA restored the connection between the championship and the bowls by initiating a postseason tournament for the first time, with the two semifinal games hosted by bowls. As of 2024, there will be 12 seeded teams competing in the College Football Playoff, with the quarterfinal and semifinal rounds hosted by bowls.

THE NEW YEAR'S SIX

Generally, the bowls with the most history are the most prestigious and competitive—and carry the highest financial rewards for the teams involved. Besides the Rose Bowl, there are five other major bowls that all teams want an invitation to. They include the Sugar Bowl (est. 1935), Orange Bowl (est. 1935), the Cotton Bowl (est. 1937), the Peach Bowl (est. 1968), and the Fiesta Bowl (est. 1971). As of the 2024 season, these bowls will host the quarterfinals and semifinals for the College Football Playoff leading up to the NCAA College Football Playoff Championship Game.

▶ WR Michael Thomas makes a memorable 13-yard TD on a flea flicker trick play in a 2015 Sugar Bowl win that booked Ohio State's spot in the national championship.

FACT FILE

Alabama appeared in six of the first 10 College Football Playoff Championship Games, and teams from Bama's conference, the SEC, won six of them.

BEST BOWL GAMES

Bowls have a long history, so there are plenty of historic showdowns in the mix. Here are a few of the most memorable matchups in college football.

TEAMS WITH THE MOST BOWL APPEARANCES

Alabama Crimson Tide—77
Georgia Bulldogs—62
Texas Longhorns—59
Oklahoma Sooners—57
Tennessee Volunteers—56

THE 1979 COTTON BOWL AND SUGAR BOWL

1979 was a great year for bowls, with two legendary games. The 1979 Cotton Bowl was dubbed the "Chicken Soup Game" because there had been an ice storm in the host city of Dallas, and Notre Dame's QB Joe Montana had to be taken off and treated for hypothermia with blankets, IV fluids, and soup during the first half. He returned to find his team losing 34–12 against Houston. "Cool Joe" led the Fighting Irish to three TDs in the last eight minutes of the game to eke out a legendary 35–34 victory. Things were cozier in Louisiana's Superdome, where the #1 and #2 ranked teams, Penn State and Alabama, met up in the 45th Annual Sugar Bowl. The Nittany Lions suffered their first defeat of the season in a bruising 14–7 defensive showdown for the ages. The climax came in the 4th quarter when Penn State was down by seven. They had 1st & goal from the 8-yard line but Bama's strong D made them turn the ball—and trophy—over on downs.

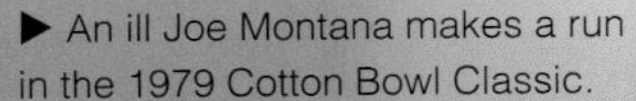

▶ An ill Joe Montana makes a run in the 1979 Cotton Bowl Classic.

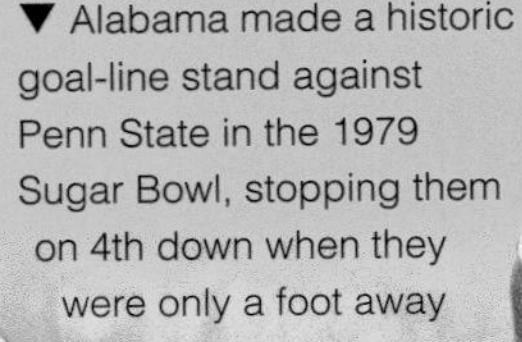

▼ Alabama made a historic goal-line stand against Penn State in the 1979 Sugar Bowl, stopping them on 4th down when they were only a foot away from the end zone.

▲ Aiona Key celebrates with fans following Boise State's shock win over Oklahoma.

THE 2007 FIESTA BOWL

This insane game comes in at #1 on a lot of best-ever bowl lists. Not only did Boise State win the game over a heavily favored Oklahoma team, they did so by pulling off THREE do-or-die trick plays! The first—a masterful "hook and ladder" on a 4th & 18, where a receiver caught the ball, reeled in the defenders, then made a lateral pass to another receiver running in the opposite direction—got them the tie with seven seconds left on the clock. Oklahoma scored first in overtime, and Boise had one possession to match them. They scored on fourth down, with a wideout making the TD pass, then boldly went for the win with a two-point conversion. They got it by faking a pass to three receivers on the right before sneaking a handoff to a running back on the left. The cherry on top was game-winner, RB Ian Johnson, proposing to his cheerleader girlfriend on national TV. (She said yes, and they're still together, aww.)

◀ The Orange Bowl trophy is very literal.

THE 1984 ORANGE BOWL

Nebraska went into the 1984 Orange Bowl unbeaten and ranked #1 in the country, but 10–1 Miami (who started the season unranked) came to play. They ended up beating the Huskers by a single point, but it was enough to secure the Hurricanes their first national title. The deciding play happened with less than a minute left on the clock. On the previous play, Nebraska had coverted a 4th & 8 into a 24-yard touchdown. Instead of going for the tie, coach Tom Osborne went for the win, watching his team's hopes for their third national title evaporate as Miami's Kenny Calhoun swatted down the pass on their two-point conversion attempt to secure a 31–30 victory for the Hurricanes in their home city.

THE 2018 ROSE BOWL AND CFP NATIONAL CHAMPIONSHIP

Since the launch of the College Football Playoff in 2015, only two games have gone into overtime—and they both happened in 2018. Georgia squared off against Oklahoma in the Rose Bowl, which was that year's Semifinal for the National Championship. The game ended up going into double overtime as the Bulldogs blocked a 27-yard field goal and ran in a 27-yard TD to win 54–48! With a total of 102 points, it takes the cake for the highest-scoring bowl game of all time. Two weeks later, Georgia went on to lose the CFP National Championship Game to SEC rival Alabama in another OT thriller. Georgia went up by 13 in the first half, but Bama came back in the second to tie the game 20–20. The Crimson Tide's backup QB, freshman Tua Tagovailoa was sacked for a loss of 16 on 1st down. Faced with a daunting 2nd & 26, he threw a perfect 41-yard touchdown pass to see him team crowned National Champions for the 17th time.

FACT FILE

Four bowl games have ended in a 0–0 draw, but they all took place before 1960. The biggest blowout took place in the 2023 Orange Bowl where Georgia scored nine straight TDs to beat FSU 63–3 after the Seminoles lost their star starting QB Jordan Travis.

▼ Georgia takes the field for the 2018 Rose Bowl.

▶ Alabama's DeVonta Smith scores the game-winning TD in the 2018 CFP National Championship.

IFAF CHAMPIONSHIPS

The International Federation of American Football (IFAF) was established in 1998 to oversee international amateur competitions and development in the sport. Today, they have 75 member federations across six continents. The IFAF invite the top-ranked national teams in both tackle and flag football to participate in world championship tournaments every two to four years, and they recently oversaw a successful bid to get flag football included as an Olympic sport.

WOMEN'S TACKLE CHAMPIONSHIPS

This tournament has only been held four times, but it's safe to say that the US women are the undisputed queens of gridiron football—for now. In the first IFAF Women's World Championship held in 2010 in Sweden, the US not only won the final 66–0, they never even allowed another team to score a single point against them the entire tournament. The US went on to convincingly take the title in the next three championships in 2013, 2017, and 2022, too.

▶ Team USA's Jeanette Gray breaks away in the 2013 championship game against Canada.

◀ The US men's team celebrate after pulling off a narrow three-point victory over hosts Japan in the 2007 IFAF World Championship title game. It was the US's first time participating in the tournament.

MEN'S TACKLE CHAMPIONSHIPS

The IFAF members network includes amateur men's national teams from 71 countries. Every four years, the IFAF invites the top eight teams to face off against one another to crown a world champion. As of 2025, there will be 12 teams invited to participate. As in the women's game, the US men have dominated at every IFAF World Championship that they've appeared in, but hopefully as the popularity of gridiron football grows, the competition will grow more fierce, too.

IFAF WORLD CHAMPIONSHIP

Year	Host	Result
1999	Italy	Japan (6–0) Mexico
2003	Germany	Japan (34–14) Mexico
2007	Japan	US (23–20) Japan
2011	Austria	US (50–7) Canada
2015	US	US (59–12) Japan

FLAG COMPETITIONS

The IFAF has been sponsoring international flag football tournaments every two years since 2002. They've taken place in host countries on four different continents with nations hailing from five continents. With up to 42 teams taking part and a variety of winning teams, the flag world championships have proven to be more competitive than the IFAF global gridiron tournaments.

▲ Ashlea Klam, a 19-year-old player on the US Women's National Flag Football Team, displays the gold she won in the 2023 IFAF Americas Championship, a regional tournament leading up to the 2024 world championship. The US women took their first golds in the last two IFAF Flag Football World Championships held in 2018 in Panama and 2021 in Israel.

WOMEN'S MEDAL TABLE, 2002–2023

Rank	Country	Medals
1	Mexico	3 Gold, 1 Silver, 1 Bronze
2	US	2 Gold, 3 Silver
3	Canada	2 Gold, 1 Silver, 1 Bronze
4	France	1 Gold, 1 Silver, 2 Bronze
5	Panama	1 Gold, 1 Silver
6	Sweden	1 Gold, 1 Bronze
7	Austria	1 Silver, 3 Bronze
8	Finland	1 Silver, 1 Bronze
9	Japan	1 Silver

MEN'S MEDAL TABLE, 2002–2023

Rank	Country	Medals
1	US	5 Gold, 1 Silver
2	Austria	3 Gold, 1 Silver
3	France	1 Gold, 3 Bronze
4	Canada	1 Gold
5	Denmark	4 Silver, 2 Bronze
6	Mexico	2 Silver, 1 Bronze
7	Germany	2 Silver
8	Italy	2 Bronze
9	Panama	1 Bronze
10	Thailand	1 Bronze

▼ The IFAF also regularly hold regional tournaments in the lead-up to their world championship. Here, Austria's men's team celebrate beating Finland to take the 2023 IFAF European Championship title.

KC

◀ Chiefs QB Patrick Mahomes celebrates his back-to-back NFL Championship titles and third Super Bowl MVP at Disneyland in 2024.

SNAPSHOT

"I'M GOING TO DISNEYLAND!"

It has become a tradition for Super Bowl MVPs to deliver this line during post-game interviews. It all started in 1987, when Giants quarterback Phil Simms was named MVP after eking out a one-point victory in Super Bowl XXI over the Broncos. As he walked off the field, a reporter asked him what he was going to do next. He replied, "I'm going to go to Disney World!" As it turns out, this was a paid promotion used to advertise the classic theme parks, but the tagline has stuck. And the tagline is also truthful. Disney does in fact invite Super Bowl MVPs and their families to Disneyland or Disney World and throws them a victory parade in the Magic Kingdom. It's happened almost every year since Simms, with a few interesting twists. When Tom Brady won his fourth Super Bowl MVP, he gifted his Disney World celebration to RB James White, who, to be fair, had put in an MVP-worthy performance, scoring three TDs in the title game.

NCAA FOOTBALL

The top tier of college teams in the US are in the Division I FBS (Football Bowl Subdivision). As of 2024, it included 134 teams divided into 10 conferences, but which teams play in which conference can change from year to year. FBS schools are eligible to play in bowl games by invitation and to compete for the national championship title in the College Football Playoff.

2024 NCAA DI FBS TEAMS

AMERICAN ATHLETIC CONFERENCE
Army Black Knights
Charlotte 49ers
East Carolina Pirates
Florida Atlantic Owls
Memphis Tigers
Navy Midshipmen
North Texas Mean Green
Rice Owls
South Florida Bulls
Temple Owls
Tulane Green Wave
Tulsa Golden Hurricane
UAB Blazers
UTSA Roadrunners

ACC
Boston College Eagles
California Golden Bears
Clemson Tigers
Duke Blue Devils
Florida State Seminoles
Georgia Tech Yellowjackets
Louisville Cardinals
Miami (FL) Hurricanes
NC State Wolfpack
North Carolina Tar Heels
Pittsburgh Panthers
SMU Mustangs
Stanford Cardinal
Syracuse Orange
Virginia Cavaliers
Virginia Tech Hokies
Wake Forest Demon Deacons

BIG 12
Arizona Wildcats
Arizona State Sun Devils
Baylor Bears
BYU Cougars
Cincinnati Bearcats
Colorado Buffaloes
Houston Cougars
Iowa State Cyclones
Kansas Jayhawks
Kansas State Wildcats
Oklahoma State Cowboys
TCU Horned Frogs
Texas Tech Red Raiders
UCF Knights
Utah Utes
West Virginia Mountaineers

BIG TEN
Illinois Fighting Illini
Indiana Hoosiers
Iowa Hawkeyes
Maryland Terrapins
Michigan Wolverines
Michigan State Spartans
Minnesota Golden Gophers
Nebraska Cornhuskers
Northwestern Wildcats
Ohio State Buckeyes
Oregon Ducks
Penn State Nittany Lions
Purdue Boilermakers
Rutgers Scarlet Knights
Washington Huskies
Wisconsin Badgers
UCLA Bruins
USC Trojans

CONFERENCE USA
FIU Panthers
Jacksonville State Gamecocks
Kennesaw State Owls
Liberty Flames
Louisiana Tech Bulldogs
Middle Tennessee Blue Raiders
New Mexico State Aggies
Sam Houston Bearkats
UTEP Miners
Western Kentucky Hilltoppers

FBS INDEPENDENTS
Massachusetts Minutemen
Notre Dame Fighting Irish
UConn Huskies

MID-AMERICAN
Akron Zips
Ball State Cardinals
Bowling Green Falcons
Buffalo Bulls
Central Michigan Chippewas
Eastern Michigan Eagles
Kent State Golden Flashes
Miami (OH) Redhawks
Northern Illinois Huskies
Ohio Bobcats
Toledo Rockets
Western Michigan Broncos

MOUNTAIN WEST
Air Force Falcons
Boise State Broncos
Colorado State Rams
Fresno State Bulldogs
Hawai'i Rainbow Warriors
Nevada Wolf Pack
New Mexico Lobos
San Diego State Aztecs
San Josè State Spartans
UNLV Rebels
Utah State Aggies
Wyoming Cowboys

PAC-12

Oregon State Beavers
Washington State Cougars

SEC

Alabama Crimson Tide
Arkansas Razorbacks
Auburn Tigers
Florida Gators
Georgia Bulldogs
Kentucky Wildcats
LSU Tigers
Mississippi State Bulldogs
Missouri Tigers
Oklahoma Sooners
Ole Miss Rebels
South Carolina Gamecocks
Tennessee Volunteers
Texas A&M Aggies
Texas Longhorns
Vanderbilt Commodores

SUN BELT (EAST)

Appalachian State Mountaineers
Coastal Carolina Chanticleers
Georgia Southern Eagles
Georgia State Panthers
James Madison Dukes
Marshall Thundering Herd
Old Dominion Monarchs

SUN BELT (WEST)

Arkansas State Red Wolves
Louisiana Ragin' Cajuns
Louisiana-Monroe Warhawks
South Alabama Jaguars
Southern Miss Golden Eagles
Texas State Bobcats
Troy Trojans

NCAA FOOTBALL CHAMPIONS BY YEAR

1869 Princeton, Rutgers
1870 Princeton
1871 None selected
1872 Princeton
1873 Princeton
1874 Princeton
1875 Harvard
1876 Yale
1877 Yale
1878 Princeton
1879 Princeton
1880 Princeton, Yale
1881 Yale
1882 Yale
1883 Yale
1884 Yale
1885 Princeton
1886 Yale
1887 Yale
1888 Yale
1889 Princeton
1890 Harvard
1891 Yale
1892 Yale
1893 Princeton
1894 Yale
1895 Pennsylvania
1896 Lafayette, Princeton
1897 Pennsylvania
1898 Harvard
1899 Harvard
1900 Yale
1901 Michigan
1902 Michigan
1903 Michigan, Princeton
1904 Michigan, Pennsylvania
1905 Chicago
1906 Princeton
1907 Yale
1908 LSU, Pennsylvania
1909 Yale
1910 Harvard, Pittsburgh
1911 Penn State, Princeton
1912 Harvard, Penn State
1913 Harvard
1914 Army
1915 Cornell
1916 Pittsburgh
1917 Georgia Tech
1918 Michigan, Pittsburgh
1919 Harvard, Illinois, Notre Dame, Texas A&M
1920 California
1921 California, Cornell
1922 California, Cornell, Princeton
1923 Illinois, Michigan
1924 Notre Dame
1925 Alabama
1926 Alabama, Stanford
1927 Illinois, Yale
1928 Georgia Tech
1929 Notre Dame
1930 Alabama, Notre Dame
1931 Southern California
1932 Southern California
1933 Michigan
1934 Minnesota
1935 Minnesota
1936 Minnesota
1937 Pittsburgh
1938 Texas Christian
1939 Texas A&M
1940 Minnesota
1941 Minnesota
1942 Ohio State
1943 Notre Dame
1944 Army
1945 Army
1946 Notre Dame
1947 Notre Dame
1948 Michigan
1949 Notre Dame
1950 Oklahoma
1951 Tennessee
1952 Michigan State
1953 Maryland
1954 UCLA, Ohio State
1955 Oklahoma
1956 Oklahoma
1957 Ohio State, Auburn
1958 LSU, Iowa
1959 Syracuse
1960 Minnesota, Mississippi
1961 Alabama, Ohio State
1962 Southern California
1963 Texas
1964 Alabama, Arkansas, Notre Dame
1965 Michigan State, Alabama
1966 Notre Dame, Michigan State
1967 Southern California
1968 Ohio State
1969 Texas
1970 Nebraska, Texas, Ohio State
1971 Nebraska
1972 Southern California
1973 Notre Dame, Alabama
1974 Southern California, Oklahoma
1975 Oklahoma
1976 Pittsburgh
1977 Notre Dame
1978 Alabama, Southern California
1979 Alabama
1980 Georgia
1981 Clemson
1982 Penn State
1983 Miami (FL)
1984 Brigham Young
1985 Oklahoma
1986 Penn State
1987 Miami (FL)
1988 Notre Dame
1989 Miami (FL)
1990 Colorado, Georgia Tech
1991 Washington, Miami (FL)
1992 Alabama
1993 Florida St.
1994 Nebraska
1995 Nebraska
1996 Florida
1997 Michigan, Nebraska
1998 Tennessee
1999 Florida State
2000 Oklahoma
2001 Miami (FL)
2002 Ohio State
2003 LSU, Southern California
2004 Southern California
2005 Texas
2006 Florida
2007 LSU
2008 Florida
2009 Alabama
2010 Auburn
2011 Alabama
2012 Alabama
2013 Florida State
2014 Ohio State
2015 Alabama
2016 Clemson
2017 Alabama
2018 Clemson
2019 LSU
2020 Alabama
2021 Georgia
2022 Georgia
2023 Michigan

HEISMAN TROPHY WINNERS BY YEAR

Named after the director of athletic club that established the award in 1935, the Heisman Trophy is awarded annually to the student who is considered to be the very best player in college football that season. The winner is determined by balloting 870 sports media representatives from around the country as well as all previous Heisman winners. The public is also granted one vote. Each voting member of the Heisman Trust ranks their top three players, which then determines the winner and other finalists. While a quarterback is most likely to win in recent years, running backs have historically been the biggest winners. USC is the school that has had the most Heisman Trophy winners with eight awardees since 1965.

1935 Jay Berwanger, HB, Chicago
1936 Larry Kelley, End, Yale
1937 Clinton Frank, HB, Yale
1938 Davey O'Brien, QB, TCU
1939 Nile Kinnick, QB/HB, Iowa
1940 Tom Harmon, HB, Michigan
1941 Bruce Smith, HB, Minnesota
1942 Frank Sinkwich, HB, Georgia
1943 Angelo Bertelli, QB, Notre Dame
1944 Les Horvath, QB/HB, Ohio State
1945 Felix "Doc" Blanchard, FB, Army
1946 Glenn Davis, HB, Army
1947 John Lujack, QB, Notre Dame
1948 Doak Walker, HB, SMU
1949 Leon Hart, End, Notre Dame
1950 Vic Janowicz, HB/P, Ohio State
1951 Dick Kazmaier, HB, Princeton
1952 Billy Vessels, HB, Oklahoma
1953 John Lattner, HB, Notre Dame
1954 Alan Ameche, FB, Wisconsin
1955 Howard Cassady, HB, Ohio State
1956 Paul Hornung, QB, Notre Dame
1957 John David Crow, HB, Texas A&M
1958 Pete Dawkins, HB, Army
1959 Billy Cannon, HB, LSU
1960 Joe Bellino, HB, Navy
1961 Ernie Davis, HB/LB/FB, Syracuse
1962 Terry Baker, QB, Oregon State
1963 Roger Staubach, QB, Navy
1964 John Huarte, QB, Notre Dame
1965 Mike Garrett, HB, USC
1966 Steve Spurrier, QB, Florida
1967 Gary Beban, QB, UCLA
1968 O.J. Simpson, HB, USC
1969 Steve Owens, FB, Oklahoma
1970 Jim Plunkett, QB, Stanford
1971 Pat Sullivan, QB, Auburn
1972 Johnny Rogers, WR/RB, Nebraska
1973 John Capelletti, RB, Penn State
1974 Archie Griffin, RB, Ohio State
1975 Archie Griffin, RB, Ohio State
1976 Tony Dorsett, RB, Pittsburgh
1977 Earl Campbell, RB, Texas
1978 Billy Sims, RB, Oklahoma
1979 Charles White, RB, USC
1980 George Rogers, RB, South Carolina
1981 Marcus Allen, RB, USC
1982 Herschel Walker, RB, Georgia
1983 Mike Rozier, RB, Nebraska
1984 Doug Flutie, QB, Boston College
1985 Bo Jackson, RB, Auburn
1986 Vinny Testaverde, QB, Miami
1987 Tim Brown, WR, Notre Dame
1988 Barry Sanders, RB, Oklahoma State
1989 Andre Ware, QB, Houston
1990 Ty Detmer, QB, BYU
1991 Desmond Howard, WR/PR, Michigan
1992 Gino Torretta, QB, Miami (FL)
1993 Charlie Ward, QB, Florida State
1994 Rashaan Salaam, RB, Colorado
1995 Eddie George, RB, Ohio State
1996 Danny Wuerffel, QB, Florida
1997 Charles Woodson, CB, Michigan
1998 Ricky Williams, RB, Texas
1999 Ron Dayne, RB, Wisconsin
2000 Chris Weinke, QB, Florida State
2001 Eric Crouch, QB/WR, Nebraska
2002 Carson Palmer, QB, USC
2003 Jason White, QB, Oklahoma
2004 Matt Leinart, QB, USC
2005 Reggie Bush, RB, USC
2006 Troy Smith, QB, Ohio State
2007 Tim Tebow, QB, Florida
2008 Sam Bradford, QB, Oklahoma
2009 Mark Ingram II, RB, Alabama
2010 Cam Newton, QB, Auburn
2011 Robert Griffin III, QB, Baylor
2012 Johnny Manziel, QB, Texas A&M
2013 Jameis Winston, QB, Florida State
2014 Marcus Mariota, QB, Oregon
2015 Derrick Henry, RB, Alabama
2016 Lamar Jackson, QB, Louisville
2017 Baker Mayfield, QB, Oklahoma
2018 Kyler Murray, QB, Oklahoma
2019 Joe Burrow, QB, LSU
2020 Devota Smith, WR, Alabama
2021 Bryce Young, QB, Alabama
2022 Caleb Williams, QB, USC
2023 Jayden Daniels, QB, LSU

NFL FOOTBALL

NFL CHAMPIONS BEFORE THE SUPER BOWL ERA

1920 Akron Pros
1921 Chicago Staleys
1922 Canton Bulldogs
1923 Canton Bulldogs
1924 Cleveland Bulldogs
1925 Chicago Cardinals
1926 Frankford Yellow Jackets
1927 New York Giants
1928 Providence Steam Roller
1929 Green Bay Packers
1930 Green Bay Packers
1931 Green Bay Packers
1932 Chicago Bears
1933 Chicago Bears
1934 New York Giants
1935 Detroit Lions
1936 Green Bay Packers
1937 Washington Redskins
1938 New York Giants
1939 Green Bay Packers
1940 Chicago Bears
1941 Chicago Bears
1942 Washington Redskins
1943 Chicago Bears
1944 Green Bay Packers
1945 Cleveland Rams
1946 Chicago Bears
1947 Chicago Cardinals
1948 Philadelphia Eagles
1949 Philadelphia Eagles
1950 Cleveland Browns
1951 Los Angeles Rams
1952 Detroit Lions
1953 Detroit Lions
1954 Cleveland Browns
1955 Cleveland Browns
1956 New York Giants
1957 Detroit Lions
1958 Baltimore Colts
1959 Baltimore Colts
1960 Houston Oilers (AFL), Philadelphia Eagles (NFL)
1961 Houston Oilers (AFL), Green Bay Packers (NFL)
1962 Dallas Texans (AFL), Green Bay Packers (NFL)
1963 San Diego Chargers (AFL), Green Bay Packers (NFL)
1964 Buffalo Bills (AFL), Cleveland Browns (NFL)
1965 Buffalo Bills (AFL), Green Bay Packers (NFL)

AP NFL MVPS BY YEAR

The "most valuable player" in the NFL for each season is awarded by the Associated Press (AP) by a committee of 50 sports journalists. Before 2022, each committee member got to vote for one person, and the person with the most votes won. Now, they submit their top five players in the league, ranked in order, and the person with the most points wins.

1936 Joe F. Carter, FB, Detroit Lions)
1937 Ed Danowski, QB, New York Giants)
1938 Bob Monnett, HB, Green Bay Packers
1939 Parker Hall, QB, Cleveland Rams
1940 Ace Parker, QB, Brooklyn Dodgers
1941 Joe Foss, DB, New York Giants
1942 Don Hutson, End, Green Bay Packers

1943 Sid Luckman, QB, Chicago Bears
1944 Frank Sinkwich, HB, Detroit Lions
1945 Charley Trippi, HB, Chicago Cardinals
1946 Bill Dudley, HB, Pittsburgh Steelers
1947 Sammy Baugh, QB, Washington Redskins
1948 Pat Harder, FB, Chicago Cardinals
1949 Charley Conerly, QB, New York Giants
1950 Otto Graham, QB, Cleveland Browns
1951 Norm Van Brocklin, QB, Los Angeles Rams
1952 Joe Perry, FB, San Francisco 49ers
1953 Otto Graham, QB, Cleveland Browns
1954 Joe Perry, FB, San Francisco 49ers
1955 Otto Graham, QB, Cleveland Browns
1956 Frank Gifford, HB, New York Giants
1957 Jim Brown, RB, Cleveland Browns
1958 Jim Brown, RB, Cleveland Browns
1959 Johnny Unitas, QB, Baltimore Colts
1960 Norm Van Brocklin, QB, Philadelphia Eagles
1961 Paul Hornung, HB, Green Bay Packers
1962 Jim Taylor, FB, Green Bay Packers
1963 Y.A. Tittle, QB, New York Giants
1964 Johnny Unitas, QB, Baltimore Colts
1965 Jim Brown, RB, Cleveland Browns
1966 Bart Starr, QB, Green Bay Packers
1967 Johnny Unitas, QB, Baltimore Colts
1968 Earl Morrall, QB, Baltimore Colts
1969 Roman Gabriel, QB, Los Angeles Rams
1970 John Brodie, QB, San Francisco 49ers
1971 Alan Page, DT, Minnesota Vikings
1972 Larry Brown, RB, Washington Redskins
1973 O.J. Simpson, RB, Buffalo Bills
1974 Ken Stabler, QB, Oakland Raiders
1975 Fran Tarkenton, QB, Minnesota Vikings
1976 Bert Jones, QB, Baltimore Colts
1977 Walter Payton, RB, Chicago Bears
1978 Terry Bradshaw, QB, Pittsburgh Steelers
1979 Earl Campbell, RB, Houston Oilers
1980 Brian Sipe, QB, Cleveland Browns
1981 Ken Anderson, QB, Cincinnati Bengals
1982 Mark Moseley, kicker, Washington Redskins
1983 Joe Theismann, QB, Washington Redskins
1984 Dan Marino, QB, Miami Dolphins
1985 Marcus Allen, RB, Los Angeles Raiders
1986 Lawrence Taylor, LB, New York Giants
1987 John Elway, QB, Denver Broncos
1988 Boomer Esiason, QB, Cincinnati Bengals
1989 Joe Montana, QB, San Francisco 49ers
1990 Joe Montana, QB, San Francisco 49ers
1991 Thurman Thomas, RB, Buffalo Bills
1992 Steve Young, QB, San Francisco 49ers
1993 Emmitt Smith, RB, Dallas Cowboys
1994 Steve Young, QB, San Fransisco 49ers
1995 Brett Favre, QB, Green Bay Packers
1996 Brett Favre, QB, Green Bay Packers
1997 Brett Favre, QB, Green Bay Packers
1997 Barry Sanders, RB, Detroit Lions
1998 Terrell Davis, RB, Denver Broncos
1999 Kurt Warner, QB, St. Louis Rams
2000 Marshall Faulk, RB, St. Louis Rams
2001 Kurt Warner, QB, St. Louis Rams
2002 Rich Gannon, QB, Oakland Raiders
2003 Steve McNair, QB, Tennessee Titans
2003 Peyton Manning, QB, Indianapolis Colts
2004 Peyton Manning, QB, Indianapolis Colts
2005 Shaun Alexander, RB, Seattle Seahawks
2006 LaDainian Tomlinson, RB, San Diego Chargers
2007 Tom Brady, QB, New England Patriots
2008 Peyton Manning, QB, Indianapolis Colts
2009 Peyton Manning, QB, Indianapolis Colts
2010 Tom Brady, QB, New England Patriots
2011 Aaron Rodgers, QB, Green Bay Packers
2012 Adrian Peterson, RB, Minnesota Vikings
2013 Peyton Manning, QB, Denver Broncos
2014 Aaron Rodgers, QB, Green Bay Packers
2015 Cam Newton, QB, Carolina Panthers
2016 Matt Ryan, QB, Atlanta Falcons
2017 Tom Brady, QB, New England Patriots
2018 Patrick Mahomes, QB, Kansas City Chiefs
2019 Lamar Jackson, QB, Baltimore Ravens
2020 Aaron Rodgers, QB, Green Bay Packers
2021 Aaron Rodgers, QB, Green Bay Packers
2022 Patrick Mahomes, QB, Kansas City Chiefs
2023 Lamar Jackson, QB, Baltimore Ravens

ONLINE RESOURCES

NFL.com
The official website of the National Football League, with news, analysis, game-day coverage, video highlights, stats, and scores.

nflflag.com
NFL Flag is the official international flag football program of the NFL—it's the biggest youth flag football organization in the US.

profootballhallof.com
A source to learn about the history of the pro game and it most legendary figures, including players, coaches, and more.

NCAA.org
The official website for the National Collegiate Athletic Association, with information and stats about all college football teams, players, and tournaments.

americanfootball.sport
The official website of the International Federation of American Football (IFAF), with guides to all forms of the sport, from tackle to beach flag.

cfbhall.com
The official website for the College Football Hall of Fame, with profiles of all its inductees since it was established to honor historic NCAA players and coaches in 1951.

GLOSSARY

AFC The American Football Conference, a group of 16 teams representing half of the NFL franchises. Most teams in the AFC were originally part of the American Football League (see AFL).

AFL The American Football League, a competitor to the NFL that was founded in 1959. The AFL negotiated a merger with the NFL in 1966 and became a part of it in 1970.

All-Pro Each year, sports analysts designate a first-team and second-team All-Pro, which identify the first and second best player in each position for that season. The Associated Press have become the official selectors for this annual recognition.

Backfield The area behind the offensive line where the "backs" line up, including the quarterback, halfback, and fullback.

Bowl Postseason game in the highest level of college football. The name comes from early stadiums, which were called "bowls."

Center The player who sits in the middle of the offensive line and is responsible for snapping the ball to start a play.

CFL The Canadian Football League, the top pro league for gridiron football in Canada.

College Football Playoff (CFP) The most recent system in the NCAA for determining a national champion in the top subdivision of college football. The top-ranked teams compete against one another in a tournament, with the playoff rounds hosted by historic Bowls before the CFP National Championship Game.

Cornerback (CB) A defender in the secondary who lines up in the defensive backfield opposite wide receivers and is responsible for defending passing plays. There are typically two on the field at a time.

Down The period of time in which a play is carried out, from the snap to the ball being ruled down. Teams on offense have a maximum of four "downs" to get 10 yards. If they don't reach the 10-yard mark, the ball is turned over to the other team on downs.

EFL The European Football League, Europe's premiere pro league for gridiron football.

End zone The rectangular area on either end of a football field where a player must get into with possession of the ball in order to score a touchdown.

Defense The players charged with stopping the other team from scoring.

Defensive back (DB) Any defender lining up in the defensive backfield.

Defensive backfield The area behind the defensive line where the secondary line up.

Defensive end (DE) Often called an "end," these defenders line up at each end of the defensive line and are responsible for trying to pressure the offensive backfield and stop running plays.

Defensive tackle (DT) Defensive lineman who usually line up against the guards on the offensive and try to get past them to pressure the offensive backfield and stop running plays.

Encroachment When a defender jumps over the line of scrimmage before the snap, resulting in a 5-yard penalty.

Extra point (PAT) The "try" after a touchdown, worth one point. To tack on the extra point, the kicker must kick the ball through the uprights from a play starting on the 15-yard line.

False start When a player moves before the ball is snapped to start a play, resulting in a 5-yard penalty.

FBS The Football Bowl Subdivision, the top subdivision in NCAA college football, with Division I schools eligible to play in postseason bowl games.

FCS The Football Championship Subdivision, the second-from-top subdivision in NCAA college football after the FBS. Both FBS and FCS teams are at Division I schools.

Field Goal (FG) A scoring play worth three points where the placekicker kicks the ball from the field of play and over the crossbar between the uprights of the goalposts.

Flag football A non-contact version of gridiron football where a ball-carrier is downed when a defender removes a flag from the ball-carrier's belt.

Forward progress At the end of a play, the ball is spotted at the point of the ball-carrier's furthest progress. So, even if they are pushed back by a tackle, they will be granted the yards they gained on the play.

Fullback (FB) A ball-carrier on running plays who is usually bigger and stronger than a halfback and takes on blocking responsibilities when not rushing.

Fumble When a ball-carrier loses possession of the ball during a play, for instance by dropping it.

Game clock The clock that keeps track of each 15-minute quarter in a 60-minute game.

Goal line The line marks out the front of the end zone. A ball-carrier must be over the goal line with possession of the ball to score a touchdown.

Goalposts The bright-yellow metal structure in the middle-back of the end zone. It includes a post, crossbar, and uprights.

Grey Cup, The The trophy and annual national championship game for the Canadian Football League (CFL).

Halfback (HB) A running back, usually the primary rusher on the offense who tends to be smaller and faster than a fullback.

Hashmarks Lines on a football field that serve as yard markers along the length of the field and also indicate where a ball should be placed along the width of the field to start the next play.

Holder The player who catches the long snap, then sets up and holds the football to be kicked by the placekicker for extra-point and field-goal attempts.

Huddle When players gather in a tight circle behind the line of scrimmage before each play to hear the call and get instructions. When offenses want to speed things up, they often shift to a "no-huddle offense."

IFAF The International Federation of American Football, a global governing body for country-based football associations and international contact and non-contact football competitions.

Interception When a defensive player catches a ball intended for a receiver, forcing a turnover.

Kickoff A long kick that puts the ball into play at the beginning of each half and after each scoring play. Currently, the kick is taken from a tee on the 35-yard line. The receiving team will try to catch and run back the kickoff to start their offensive drive.

Lateral A pass that goes parallel or behind the line of scrimmage. A team can do as many lateral passes as they want on a play.

Line of scrimmage The invisible line running from sideline to sideline through the front tip of the ball where it is placed to start a new play. The offense and defense line up on either side of the line and cannot cross it prior to the ball being snapped. Its location is determined by where the ball was downed on the previous play.

Linebacker (LB) Defenders who line up a few yards behind the defensive line. They're often the primary tacklers on defense.

Long Snapper The player who replaces the center for special teams plays, snapping the ball long for placekicks and punts.

MVP An acronym that stands for "most valuable player." It is used to designate the best overall player during a particular game or season. Many organizations associated with pro football designate an MVP each year. The NFL uses the Associated Press for its official honor. The Super Bowl, Pro Bowl, and various NCAA bowl and championship games also have MVPs.

NCAA The National Collegiate Athletic Association. The governing body for US college sports, the NCAA was originally founded to regulate football as it became increasingly dangerous on campuses. Today, it represents 1099 schools in three divisions competing in 24 sports.

NFC The National Football Conference, a group of 16 teams representing half of the NFL franchises. Most teams in the NFC were part of the NFL before its merger with the American Football League (see AFL).

NFL The National Football League, the premiere pro league for gridiron football.

Nose Guard The defensive lineman who lines up opposite the center on a 3-4 defense where there are only three players on the defensive line.

Offense The players with possession of the ball who are charged with trying to score points for their team.

Offensive Guard (G) The offensive lineman who line up on either side of the center and block for the offensive backfield.

Offensive Tackle (T) The offensive linemen who sit at on the ends of the offensive line on the outside of the guards and block for the offensive backfield.

Officials The team of seven who ensure the rules are enforced during a football game. They include the head referee, umpire, back judge, down judge, field judge, line judge, and side judge.

Offsides When a player lines up in the neutral zone, resulting in a 5-yard penalty.

Pass interference When a defender obstructs or makes contact with a receiver more than one yard from the line of scrimmage, preventing them from making a catch.

Penalty When one or more players violates the rules of the game, they will be given a penalty by the officials.

Placekick A kick where the football is held upright in place on the field.

Placekicker A special teams player who kicks the ball for field-goal and extra-point attempts. They may also handle kickoffs.

Play clock The 40-second timer that shows how much time a team has between plays.

Pocket The area of safety the the offensive line creates for their quarterback by forming a ring of blockers to stop pass rushers from pressuring or sacking the quarterback.

Possession The team or player in "possession" has control of the ball.

Pro Bowl An annual NFL all-star competition that began in 1951. From 1970, it pitted the top players in the NFC and AFC against one another in a showcase tackle football game. Since 2023, it has become the "Pro Bowl Games" and features skills contests and an exhibition flag football match instead of another full-contact game. Players are selected for the Pro Bowl by voting that is split evenly between coaches, players, and fans, so it can be a bit of a popularity contest.

Punter A special teams player who drop-kicks the ball as high and far as possible on fourth down to position the other team's offense as far away as possible from their end zone to start their offensive drive.

Quarterback (QB) The primary passer and play-caller on a team, the quarterback leads the offense. They signal for the ball to be snapped, hand off the ball on running plays, and throw it on passing plays.

Returner The special teams player who attempts to catch punts and kickoffs and run the ball closer to the opponent's end zone.

Running back (RB) An offensive player who lines up in the backfield and carries the ball on running plays.

Safety (position) A player in the defensive backfield who lines up 10–15 yards behind the line of scrimmage to help the other defenders shut down a play. They are typically the last line of defense against deep passes or runs.

Safety (scoring play) A defensive scoring play worth two points in which the team on offense is ruled down by contact in their own end zone, fumbles the ball out of the back of their own end zone, or commits a foul in their own end zone.

Slot receiver A receiver who lines up in the "slot" a few yards behind the offensive line.

Snap When the center or long snapper launches the ball from the ground in front of them back between their legs to the quarterback, punter, or holder to start a play.

Strong side The side of the field where the tight end lines up. It's strong because there's an extra player on that side. The other side is called the "weak side."

Super Bowl The annual NFL Championship Game, a matchup between the AFC and NFC Champions for that season.

Tackle The action that results in the end of a play when a defensive player forces the ball-carrier to the ground or out of bounds.

Tight end (TE) A receiver who lines up outside the tackle on one side of the offensive line and serves as an extra blocker when they are not receiving the ball.

Touchdown (TD) A scoring play worth six points in which a player passes their opponents' goal line and into their end zone while maintaining possession of the ball or catches a pass in the end zone.

Turnover When the defense gains possession of the ball for their team following a fumble, interception, or turnover on downs.

Two-point conversion A riskier form of "try" after a touchdown. The offense has one play to get the ball into the end zone from the 2-yard line in the NFL or the 3-yard line in the NCAA. If they succeed, they get two points.

Uprights The two tall metal arms on the goalposts. Balls must pass between them for a team to score an extra point or field goal.

WFA The Women's Football Association, the top pro league in the US for women's gridiron football.

INDEX

Page numbers in bold refer to main entries.

ACKNOWLEDGMENTS

The publisher would like to thank the following for permission to reproduce their material. Top = *t*, bottom = *b*, center = *c*, left = *l*, right = *r*

PRELIMS AND CHAPTER 1
Page 1 Cliff Welch / Action Plus Sports / Alamy Stock Photo; 1 background EFKS / Shutterstock; 2 Patrick Smith / Getty Images; 2 background EFKS / Shutterstock; 4c Bryan Bennett / Getty Images; 4bl Evan Vucci / Associated Press / Alamy Stock Photo; 5t Ed Zurga / Getty Images; 5b Alex Davidson / Getty Images; 6l Henry Browne / World Rugby via Getty Images; 6r Bettmann / Getty Images; 6b Bettmann / Getty Images; 7t FLHC DB90 / Alamy Stock Photo; 7b Abaca Press / Alamy Stock Photo; 8t Associated Press / Alamy Stock Photo; 8b Cooper Neill / Getty Images; 9t Tom Cammett / Diamond Images via Getty Images; 9c Cal Sport Media / Alamy Stock Photo; 9b Robin Alam /Icon Sportswire / Associated Press / Alamy Stock Photo; 10t Jessica McGowan / Getty Images; 10c Jacob Kupferman / Getty Images; 10b Panoramic Images / Alamy Stock Photo; 11t Michael Zagaris / San Francisco 49ers / Getty Images; 11b UPI / Alamy Stock Photo; 12–13 Rebecca Blackwell / Associated Press / Alamy Stock Photo

CHAPTER 2
14b Scott W. Grau / Icon Sportswire via Getty Images; 15t James Gilbert / Getty Images; 16tr Nando Vidal / Alamy Stock Photo; 16bl Elsa / Getty Images; 17t Peter Aiken / Associated Press / Alamy Stock Photo; 17bl Leslie Plaza Johnson / Icon Sportswire / Corbis / Icon Sportswire via Getty Images; 17r Ryan Kang / Getty Images; 18 ZargonDesign / Getty Images; 19tl Jason O. Watson (Sports) / Alamy Stock Photo; 19tr Jamie Schwaberow / Getty Images; 19br Justin Fine/Icon Sportswire / Associated Press / Alamy Stock Photo; 20tr Scott W. Grau / Icon Sportswire via Getty Images; 20cl Brian Bahr / Getty Images; 21bl Justin K. Aller / Getty Images; 21br Rich Gabrielson / Icon Sportswire via Getty Image; 22tr John Jones / Icon Sportswire via Getty Images; 22bl Elaine Thompson / Associated Press / Alamy Stock Photo; 23tl David Purdy / Getty Images; 23bl Jeffrey Brown / Icon Sportswire via Getty Images; 24tr Jayne Kamin-Oncea / Getty Images; 24cl Nick Cammett / Getty Images; 24b Brett Carlsen / Getty Images; 25t Jordan Murphy / Sports Illustrated via Getty Images; 25cr John E. Moore III / Getty Images; 25br MediaNews Group / Boston Herald via Getty Images; 26br Michael Zagaris / San Francisco 49ers / Getty Images; 26bl Cooper Neill / Getty Images; 27t Adam Hunger / Getty Images; 27c Steve Dykes / Getty Images; 27br Bob Levey / Getty Images; 28l Cal Sport Media / Alamy Stock Photo; 29t Sam Craft / Associated Press / Alamy Stock Photo; 29cl Gary McCullough / Associated Press / Alamy Stock Photo; 29br UPI / Alamy Stock Photo; 30tr Bryan M. Bennett / Getty Images; 30cl Julio Aguilar / Getty Images; 30br Steph Chambers / Getty Images; 31cl Justin Edmonds / Getty Images; 31br Kevin Sabitus / Getty Images; 32–33t Brian Bahr / Getty Images; 33b Zuma Press, Inc. / Alamy Stock Photo

CHAPTER 3
34tr Charlie Riedel / Associated Press / Alamy Stock Photo; 34cl Bettmann / Getty Images; 34br Brian Bahr / Allsport / Getty Images; 35t George Gojkovich / Getty Images; 35br Maddie Meyer / Getty Images; 36tr Andy Lyons / Getty Images; 36bl Darron Cummings / Associated Press / Alamy Stock Photo; 36br Associated Press / Alamy Stock Photo; 37tr Cliff Welch / Icon Sportswire via Getty Images; 37cl Andy Lyons / Allsport / Getty Images; 37br Cal Sport Media / Sipa US / Alamy Stock Photo; 38tr Associated Press / Alamy Stock Photo; 38cl Bettman / Corbis/ Getty Images; 38br George Rose / Getty Images; 39cl Doug Benc / Getty Images; 39br Hannah Foslien / Getty Images; 40t Mike Ehrmann / Getty Images; 40c Ian Halperin / UPI / Alamy Stock Photo; 40b Harry How / Getty Images; 41tr Chris Graythen / Getty Images; 41 background Brendan Moran / Sportsfile via Getty Images; 41cl Michael Owens / Getty Images; 41br Brian Bahr / Allsport / Getty Images; 42tr Rich Kane Photography / Alamy Stock Photo; 42bl John Cordes / Icon Sportswire / Corbis / Icon Sportswire via Getty Images; 42br Focus on Sport / Getty Images; 43tr Bettmann / Getty Images; 43cl Icon Sportswire / Getty Images; 43br Peter G. Aiken / Getty Images; 44tr Associated Press / Alamy Stock Photo; 44cl Focus on Sport / Getty Images; 44br Kevin Sabitus / Getty Images; 45tr George Gojkovich / Getty Images; 45cl Scott Taetsch / Getty Images; 45br Wade Payne / Associated Press / Alamy Stock Photo; 46tr Vic Stein / Getty Images; 46cl Cal Sport Media / Alamy Stock Photo; 46br Peter Aiken / Getty Images; 47tr Focus On Sport / Getty Images; 47cl Michael Wade / Icon Sportswire via Getty Images; 47br David Madison / Getty Images; 48cl John Iacono / Sports Illustrated via Getty Images; 48br Mitchell Layton / Getty Images; 49 tr Sean M. Haffey / Getty Images; 49cl Neil Leifer / Sports Illustrated via Getty Images; 49br Al Messerschmidt / Getty Images; 50tr Bettmann / Getty Images; 50cr Winslow Townson / Associated Press / Alamy Stock Photo; 50bl Jamie Squire / Getty Images; 51tl Rich Kane Photography / Alamy Stock Photo; 51 background Brendan Moran / Sportsfile via Getty Images; 51cr Mike Ehrmann / Getty Images; 51bl Nick Cammett / Getty Images; 52tr Tony Tomsic / Getty Images; 52cl Jim McIsaac / Getty Images; 52br Mickey Pfleger / Sports Illustrated via Getty Images; 53t Brendan Moran / Sportsfile via Getty Images; 53tr New York Daily News Archive via Getty Images; 53cl Gregory Shamus / Getty Images; 53br John Amis / Associated Press / Alamy Stock Photo; 54tr Wesley Hitt / Getty Images; 54bl Cliff Welch / Associated Press / Alamy Stock Photo; 54br Bobby Ellis / Getty Images; 55tl Focus on Sport / Getty Images; 55cl Focus on Sport / Getty Images; 55br Jonathan Daniel / ALLSPORT / Getty Images; 56 Rich Graessle / Icon Sportswire via Getty Images; 57br Jason Miller / Getty Images

CHAPTER 4
58c Robert Beck / Sports Illustrated via Getty Images; 58bl Robert Beck / Sports Illustrated via Getty Images; 58br Scott Taetsch / Getty Images; 59t Matthew Pearce / Icon Sportswire via Getty Images; 60tr Bill Frakes / Sports Illustrated via Getty Images; 60cr Simon Bruty / Sports Illustrated via Getty Images; 60bl Michael Zagaris / San Francisco 49ers / Getty Images; 61 background Brendan Moran / Sportsfile via Getty Images; 61tr Cooper Neill / Getty Images; 61cr Jack Dempsey / Associated Press / Alamy Stock Photo; 61bl Joshua Sarner / Icon Sportswire via Getty Images; 62tr Jeff Dean / Associated Press / Alamy Stock Photo; 63tr Cliff Welch / Icon Sportswire via Getty Images; 63br Rob Carr / Getty Images; 64c Peter Read Miller / Sports Illustrated via Getty Images; 64bl Rick Stewart / Getty Images; 65tr Vic Milton / Getty Images; 65cl Ezra Shaw / Getty Images; 65cr Jeff Chiu / Associated Press / Alamy Stock Photo; 65bl Allen Kee / Getty Images; 66tr Christian Petersen / Getty Images; 66bl Katelyn Mulcahy / Getty Images; 66br Chris Graythen / Getty Images; 67tr Bettmann / Getty Images; 67cl Gene Puskar / Associated Press / Alamy Stock Photo; 67br Jared Wickerham / Getty Images; 68tr Focus On Sport / Getty Images; 68cr Jamie Squire / Getty Images; 68bl Bettmann / Getty Images; 69tl Zuma Press, Inc. / Alamy Stock Photo; 69tr Joe Sargent / Getty Images; 69bl Doug Benc / Getty Images; 69br Andy Lyons / Getty Images; 70 Mark Brown / Getty Images; 71 Mark Brown / Getty Images

CHAPTER 5
72tr John W. McDonough / Sports Illustrated via Getty Images; 72bl Lynn Johnson / Sports Illustrated via Getty Images; 73tl Mark LoMoglio / Icon Sportswire / Corbis / Icon Sportswire via Getty Images; 73bl Michael Macor / The San Francisco Chronicle via Getty Images; 73br Rick Bowmer / Associated Press / Alamy Stock Photo; 74cr G Fiume / Getty Images; 74bl Steven Branscombe / Getty Images; 75tl Jonathan Bachman/ Getty Images; 75b Todd Kirkland / Getty Images; 76tr Bettmann / Getty Images; 76cl Adam Glanzman / Getty Images; 76br Frank Jansky / Icon Sportswire via Getty Images; 77tl Jason Miller/ Getty Images; 77cl Justin Casterline / Getty Images; 77br Todd Rosenberg / Getty Images; 78tr Bettmann / Getty Images; 78cr Scott Winters / Icon Sportswire via Getty Images; 78bl Michael J. Minardi / Getty Images; 79tl Joe Sargent / Getty Images; 79cr Heinz Kluetmeier / Sports Illustrated via Getty Images; 79b Justin K. Aller / Getty Images; 80tr Sarah Stier / Getty Images; 80bl Neil Leifer / Sports Illustrated via Getty Images; 81tr Maddie Meyer / Getty Images; 81bl Billie Weiss / Getty Images; 82tl Michael Owens / Getty Images; 82br Jared Wickerham / Getty Images; 83tl Allen Kee / Getty Images; 83cl Justin Ford / Getty Images; 83b Perry Knotts / Getty Images; 84cr Timothy A. Clary / AFP via Getty Images; 84bl James Flores / Getty Images; 85cl Focus On Sport via Getty Images; 85cr Jamie Schwaberow / Getty Images; 85bl John McCoy / Getty Images; 86tl Paul Natkin / Getty Images; 86br Gregory Shamus / Getty Images; 87tl Jeff Dean / Getty Images; 87br Jeff Bukowski / Shutterstock; 88cl Al Bellow / Getty Images; 88br Al Bellow / Getty Images; 89tl Tom Hauck / Getty Images; 89br Ron Vesely / Getty Images; 90tl Tom Hauck / Getty Images; 90br Streeter Lecka / Getty Images; 91tl Kevin C. Cox / Getty Images; 91c Skip Bolen / WireImage / Getty Images; 91br Perry Knotts / Getty Images; 92cl Chris Coduto / Getty Images; 92br John Biever / Sports Illustrated via Getty Images; 93tl Focus On Sport / Getty Images; 93br Streeter Lecka / Getty Images; 94cr Andre Ringuette / Getty Images; 94br Guillermo Gutiérrez / NurPhoto via Getty Images; 95tr Rick Ulreich / Icon Sportswire via Getty Images; 95cl Thomas Pichler / SEPA.Media / Getty Images; 95bl Zuma Press / Alamy Stock Photo; 96 Jonathan Daniel / Getty Images; 97b Jonathan Daniel / Getty Images

CHAPTER 6
98cr Brian Rothmuller / Icon Sportswire via Getty Images; 98bl Frazer Harrison / Getty Images; 99cl Erik Verduzco / Associated Press / Alamy Stock Photo; 99cr J. Meric / Getty Images; 99bl Rey Del Rio / Getty Images; 100cr Ric Tapia / Getty Images; 100bl Jeff Speer / Icon Sportswire via Getty Images; 101t Bailey Hillesheim / Icon Sportswire via Getty Image; 101br Greg Nelson / Sports Illustrated via Getty Images; 102bl Print Collector / Hulton Archive / Getty Images; 102b marchello74 / Shutterstock; 103t Katelyn Mulcahy / Getty Images; 103bl Diane Modafferi / Alamy Stock Photo; 104cr Matthew Ashton / AMA / Getty Images; 104bl Kirby Lee / Alamy Stock Photo; 105t Jim West / Alamy Stock Photo; 105cr Scott Winters / Icon Sportswire via Getty Images; 105b Heinz Kluetmeier/ Sports Illustrated via Getty Images; 106tr Stephen Dunn / Getty Images; 106cr Robin Alam / Icon Sportswire via Getty Images; 106br Tony Dejak / Associated Press / Alamy Stock Photo; 107tl Eric Thomas / Getty Images; 107b Dannie Walls / Associated Press / Alamy Stock Photo; 108tr David Zalubowski / Associated Press / Alamy Stock Photo; 108c Doug Murray / Icon SMI / Corbis / Icon Sportswire via Getty Image; 108bl Tom Pennington / Getty Images; 109tl Logan Riely / Getty Images; 109c Stephen Pond / Getty Images; 109bl Ricky Carioti / The Washington Post via Getty Images; 110–111 Scott Taetsch / Getty Images

CHAPTER 7
112tr Benjamin Solomon / Getty Images; 112bl Leon Halip / Getty Images; 113tl Corey Perrine / Getty Images; 113br Larry French / Getty Images; 114br Jim Bryant / UPI / Alamy Stock Photo; 115tl Michael Zagaris / Getty Images; 115cr John Biever / Sports Illustrated via Getty Images; 115bl Michael Zagaris / San Francisco 49ers / Getty Images; 116b dpa picture alliance archive / Alamy Stock Photo; 116bl Don Juan Moore / Getty Images; 116br Neil Leifer / Sports Illustrated via Getty Images; 117tl Ezra Shaw / Getty Images; 117tr Ezra Shaw / Getty Images; 117c Ronald Martinez / Getty Images; 117cr Patrick Semansky / Associated Press / Alamy Stock Photo; 117br Tammy Ljungblad / Kansas City Star / Tribune News Service via Getty Images; 118cr Focus On Sport / Getty Images; 118b Ryan Kang / Getty Images; 119tl Focus On Sport / Getty Images; 119cr Jacquelyn Martin / Associated Press / Alamy Stock Photo; 119bl Nate Fine / Getty Images; 120cr Lennox McLendon / Associated Press / Alamy Stock Photo; 120br Phil Sandlin / Associated Press / Alamy Stock Photo; 121tl Paul Popper / Popperfoto via Getty Images; 121cr Focus On Sport / Getty Images; 121br Focus On Sport / Getty Images; 122tr Focus On Sport / Getty Images; 122bl Jeff Haynes / AFP via Getty Images; 123tl Chris Graythen / Getty Images; 123cr Jeff Gross / Getty Images; 123bl John W. McDonough / Sports Illustrated via Getty Images; 124t Al Pereira / Getty Images; 124bl Stephen Dunn / Getty Images; 124br Matt Slocum / Associated Press / Alamy Stock Photo; 125bl Doug Benc /Associated Press / Alamy Stock Photo; 126bl Mike Ehrmann / Getty Images; 127tl Andy Lyons / Getty Images; 127cl Steph Chambers / Getty Images; 127br Tim Nwachukwu / Getty Images; 128b David McNew / Getty Images; 129t Jamie Schwaberow / NCAA Photos via Getty Images; 129br Tyler Kaufman / Icon Sportswire / Corbis / Icon Sportswire via Getty Images; 130cl Bettmann / Getty Images; 130cr Jonathan Ferrey / Getty Images; 130bl James Drake / Sports Illustrated via Getty Images; 131tl Doug Murray / Icon Sportswire via Getty Images; 131bl Jon Soohoo / UPI / Alamy Stock Photo; 131br Mike Ehrmann / Getty Images; 132tr Aliisa Piirla / AFP via Getty Images; 132bl The Asahi Shimbun / Getty Images; 133tl Rebecca Blackwell / Associated Press / Alamy Stock Photo; 133b Tobias Steinmaurer / APA / AFP via Getty Images; 134–135 Handout / Getty Images

Background images: EFKS/ Getty Images; Brendan Moran/ Getty Images; Lawrey / Getty Images